Praise for *Action Inquiry*

"Buckle up your seatbelt and enjoy the ride. Torbert is an original and his ideas about life, learning and leadership will rattle your brain and stir your soul."

—Charles Derber, author of
Corporation Nation, People Before Profit, and
Regime Change Begins at Home

"In *Action Inquiry,* Bill Torbert and his colleagues take on a question as old as Socrates: how to translate human understanding into right action. They argue that we must develop the capacity not only to anticipate consequences, but also to reevaluate our goals and to challenge our deepest assumptions in response to changing contexts and diverse perspectives. Their model of self-critical learning offers a much-needed alternative to views that mistake self-assertion for agency and brute force for power."

—Morris Kaplan, author of *Sexual Justice:*
Democratic Citizenship and the Politics of Desire
and Professor of Philosophy, SUNY-Purchase

"We all suffer from a lack of understanding of how to work and live together. *Action Inquiry* offers the kind of questions and practical ideas we need in order to search for effective truth in our own work and in our life with each other."

—Jacob Needleman, author of *Money and*
the Meaning of Life and *Time and the Soul*

"In this path breaking book, Torbert and his team report back from the leadership frontier that each of us faces. Through lively cases, they illustrate how the demand action inquiry makes on you grows your capacity for leadership. Torbert's work is unique. No one else combines such erudition with such evidence and such a sense of immediate applicability."

—Jay Ogilvy, Partner, The Monitor Group
of Companies; co-founder, Global Business
Network; and coauthor of *China's Futures*

ACTION INQUIRY

ACTION INQUIRY

The Secret of Timely and Transforming Leadership

BILL TORBERT

with Susanne Cook-Greuter, Dalmar Fisher, Erica Foldy,
Alain Gauthier, Jackie Keeley, David Rooke, Sara Ross,
Catherine Royce, Jenny Rudolph, Steve Taylor, and Mariana Tran

Berrett–Koehler Publishers, Inc.
a BK Business book

Berrett-Koehler Publishers, Inc.
1333 Broadway, Suite 1000
Oakland, CA 94612-1921
Tel: (510) 817-2277 Fax: (510) 817-2278   www.bkconnection.com

Ordering Information
Quantity sales. Special discounts are available on quantity purchases by corporations, associations, and others. For details, contact the "Special Sales Department" at the Berrett-Koehler address above.
Individual sales. Berrett-Koehler publications are available through most bookstores. They can also be ordered directly from Berrett-Koehler: Tel: (800) 929-2929; Fax: (802) 864-7626; www.bkconnection.com
Orders for college textbook/course adoption use. Please contact Berrett-Koehler: Tel: (800) 929-2929; Fax: (802) 864-7626.

Distributed to the US trade and internationally by Penguin Random House Publisher Services.

Berrett-Koehler and the BK logo are registered trademarks of Berrett-Koehler Publishers, Inc.

Printed in the United States of America

Berrett-Koehler books are printed on long-lasting acid-free paper. When it is available, we choose paper that has been manufactured by environmentally responsible processes. These may include using trees grown in sustainable forests, incorporating recycled paper, minimizing chlorine in bleaching, or recycling the energy produced at the paper mill.

Library of Congress Cataloging-in-Publication Data
Torbert, William R. 1944–
    Action inquiry : the secret of timely and transforming leadership / Bill Torbert & associates.
        p. cm.
    Includes bibliographical references and index.
    ISBN 1–57675–264–X
    1. Leadership   2. Organizational learning.   3. Active learning.   4. Experiential learning.   5. Communication in organizations.   6. Organizational change.   I. Title
    HD57.7.T675   2003
    658.4′092—dc22   2003063777

First Edition
22 21 20 19 18   15 14 13 12 11 10
Copyedited by Bernice Pettinato, Beehive Production Services. Proofread by Annie Belt. Designed by Bookcomp/Nighthawk Design. Composition and production services by Westchester Book Group.

This book is dedicated to

William Sloane Coffin

who has embodied the alchemy
of timely and transforming leadership
in so many spiritual and political roles . . .
not least, in my eyes, as my first mentor.

With love,

Bill Torbert

Contents

Acknowledgments

We wish to thank the evening and international MBA students at Boston College (BC), the executive participants in BC's Leadership for Change program, and the participants in our Harthill workshops—all of whom have so enthusiastically tested out the ideas in this book in their everyday work lives. As you will discover, many of their accounts of their experiments have been included, with their permission (and under fictional names), in the following pages as illustrations and as encouragements to engage in the process of action inquiry in your own daily activities.

We would also like to thank the various companies and their senior managements in Europe and America whose transformational stories appear in the pages that follow. They, too, have been willing to take many a real-time risk in applying the ideas presented here to their own executive development and to restructuring their entire companies.

Among our scholarly and consulting colleagues, during this past decade as this book has developed we are particularly grateful for the ongoing support and conversation about issues of learning, development, and consulting that we have enjoyed with Karen Ayas, Hilary Bradbury, Judy Clair, Charlie Derber, Pacey Foster, Paul Gray, Christine Harris, Janice Jackson, Bill Joiner, Rick Karash, Benyamin Lichtenstein, Judi Marshall, Richard Nielsen, Bob Putnam, Joe Raelin, Peter and Ben Reason, Otto Scharmer, Peter Senge, Eve Spangler, and Sandra Waddock.

Most of these colleagues and many others to whom we are also grateful have helped us learn how to re-create climates of public reflective inquiry in voluntary action inquiry study groups of all kinds—from the Society for Organizational Learning S4 Group, to the BC Leadership for Change Heart & Soul team that meets over dinner each month, to the three BC Organization Transformation PhD action study groups, to the Center for Action Research in Professional Practice at the University of

Bath and the three-day Harthill Executive Workshops in England that different ones of us participate in. As you will learn in this book, such ongoing, voluntary communities of inquiry are key to a continuing, humbling, and transforming engagement with action inquiry.

A number of research assistants over the past dozen years helped us with studies that contributed to this book. We are grateful to Barbara Davidson, Jennifer Leigh, Melissa McDaniel, Paul Skilton, and Rosemary Tin. Last but by no means least, Kelly Crowther has played a central, indispensable, and ever-cheerful role in preparing the final manuscript for publication.

Throughout all or parts of the past quarter century, the Carroll School of Management at Boston College has been the home organization for our senior author and four of the associates, and what a flourishing home it has been for our creative work and action inquiry. We are deeply grateful to Jean Bartunek, Jack Neuhauser, Jean Passavant, Nancy Sarnya, Safi Safizadeh, Priscilla Sliney, and all the others involved for their day-to-day leadership acts that contribute to the ongoing reconstruction of this home for inquiry.

Finally, the constellations of our families and our closest friends are our primary communities of inquiry and the ones for which we are most grateful of all.

The Promise and the Power
of Action Inquiry

Do you practice action inquiry? Most people understand what "action" and "inquiry" mean when used in sentences by themselves. Put together, as "action inquiry," new and potent ways to develop performance and learning emerge. Do you put action and inquiry together in your life?

Action inquiry is a way of simultaneously conducting action and inquiry as a disciplined leadership practice that increases the wider effectiveness of our actions. Such action helps individuals, teams, organizations, and still larger institutions become more capable of self-transformation and thus more creative, more aware, more just, and more sustainable. In principle, no matter how much or little positional power you have, anyone in any family or organization can become more effectively and transformingly powerful by practicing action inquiry.

Action inquiry is a lifelong process of transformational learning that individuals, teams, and whole organizations can undertake if they wish to become:

- Increasingly capable of making future visions come true
- Increasingly alert to the dangers and opportunities of the present moment
- Increasingly capable of performing in effective and transformational ways

Action inquiry becomes a moment-to-moment way of living whereby we attune ourselves through inquiry to acting in an increasingly timely and wise fashion for the overall development of the families, teams, and organizations in which we participate.

Surprisingly, action inquiry is a virtually unknown process, perhaps because learning how to practice it from moment-to-moment is no easy trick. For action inquiry is not a set of prescriptions for behavior that, when followed, invariably manipulate situations as we initially wish and yield the success we dreamed of. Action inquiry is not a process that can be followed in an imitative, mechanical way, learning a few ideas and imagining that parroting them back to others occasionally means we are doing action inquiry. Action inquiry is a way of learning anew, in the vividness of each moment, how best to act now. The source of both its difficulty and potential is that action inquiry requires making ourselves, not just others, vulnerable to inquiry and to transformation.

Why We Authors Try to Expand
Our Practice of Action Inquiry

Why do people want to learn action inquiry? Let's hear a few specific responses to this question from some of the associate authors of this book. One writes:

> I was introduced to action inquiry during my first year as director of a university science laboratory. This was not only my first managerial position, but also my first job. I was responsible for managing undergraduate laboratories for more than 300 enrolled students each semester. My teaching team consisted of inexperienced graduate students and part-time faculty who were either teaching only for the extra income, or just needed to leave their house to keep their and their family's sanity. Although I only had limited access to information and little power (not being a tenured faculty member), I had many administrative responsibilities that required my getting support from the department chair and faculty. A perfect scenario for failure!
>
> Action inquiry helped me analyze my situation and question many of my beginning assumptions. It helped me see people's different perspectives and utilize this knowledge to develop creative approaches that incorporated those differences. I gained access to my leadership qualities and developed them through practice. After three years, I had developed with others a new curriculum for the laboratories and had negotiated more than $200,000 for new equipment. Even more important, I was able to

bring all the teaching assistants together in working toward our common goal of providing a quality education for our students. The department recognized my contribution by promoting me to a teaching faculty position during my second year.

Another associate writes:

It happens that I began my study and practice of action inquiry shortly after I got married. In the simplest terms, I have to say action inquiry saved my marriage. Even though my skills were still very limited, the ability to look at my own actions and see how I was part of the problem and my occasional ability to practice emotional jiujitsu made the difference between allowing our relationship to grow from the problems we had and letting those problems tear our relationship apart.

One of our most senior associates writes, with characteristic humility:

I am a member of an action inquiry study group. My fellow members are helping me to intervene more often in the group. One result of this is I am feeling increasingly good about myself. Another is that in day-to-day conversations I am struggling, often with success, to combine my assertions with inquiry, inquiry into the other person's experience, inquiry into what my feelings are and where they are coming from, and inquiry into how to express these things. I'm improving and this excites me because it implies that learning really is lifelong.

One of the associates who is a mother tells this story about a bedtime moment:

The youngest, a whirling dervish of a character, dances around the bedroom while I attempt to read to her older sister who loves a good yarn and rightly feels that her time should allow for quiet absorption into the story. Moments later my eldest is biting her nails, an activity I find particularly annoying when I am reading to her. I get cross with her and we end up in a small fight with her sobbing with frustration and indignation.

I am able to see what has happened—my exasperation with the youngest dancing around has been taken out, unfairly, on the eldest. I apologize and also explain what I see has happened. My eldest is able to move on quickly to be cuddled and consoled . . . she is not always in the

habit of doing so since injustice cuts deep for her. The youngest has overheard and quietens her exuberance, allowing some space for the story
reading. They both sleep easily and would not have done so had this situation escalated.

Still another associate writes, as if about the previous scene:

The ability to notice with immediacy what is going on in me has been, I
would honestly say, the most important ingredient in the progress of my
personal development. Over the years, this capacity has grown exponen-
tially. Fifteen years ago, it could take me weeks to figure out what had
been going on inside me during a troubling encounter. Now, I am aware as
I experience moments unfolding. Besides enabling me to revel in the dis-
coveries and sheer experience of what "is," it equips me to be proactively
more appropriate and effective in any social situation. It sounds as though
it must take a lot of time and energy to be paying attention to so much all
the time, but that's not the case at all. At its simplest, action inquiry is just
a natural part of conscious living.

How hard is it to learn "conscious living"? How hard is it to interweave action and inquiry in each moment? Conscious living requires
that we carefully attend from the inside-out to the experiences we have,
hoping to learn from them and modify our actions and even our way of
thinking as a result. But to live consciously requires us to overturn some
orthodoxies. Let's remember that both modern university-based empirical science (so-called pure research conducted from the ivory tower of
academia) and modern organizational and political practice (Machiavel-
lian "*real politik*" practiced in the messy real world) have historically
separated inquiry from action.

How Action Inquiry Differs from Our Modern Views of Political Action and Scientific Inquiry

Modern political/organizational practice and modern scientific inquiry
work primarily from the outside-in, whereas action inquiry works primarily from the inside-out. Modern politics presumes that power is the

ability to make another do as we wish from the outside-in (indeed, most of us think of this as the very definition of power). Likewise, modern scientific theory and method presumes that what happens is caused from the outside-in—that the hammer head hitting the nail is what causes the nail, whether it wants to or not, to enter the wood. (Indeed, this sounds like plain common sense, doesn't it?) Modern science also presumes that we can best learn what causes what by having external investigators (objective, disinterested, professional scientists) study people from the outside-in.

We see the results played out in the news every day. Corporate or international actions based on unilateral power and devoid of inquiry result in corporate scandals and wars that, in retrospect, appear unjust. And inquiry devoid of action robs us of opportunities that occur unexpectedly and require a timely response, or else they disappear. Yet separating inquiry from action is today the norm both in the university and in the nonacademic world. The reason you may not have heard of or intentionally tried to practice action inquiry is that it is a new kind of scientific inquiry and a new kind of political/organizational action that has been exercised before only rarely, for moments.[1]

By contrast, action inquiry works primarily from the inside-out (although it recognizes the presence and influence of outside-in perspectives as well). Action inquiry begins because we (any one of us, or any family, or organization) experience some sort of gap between what we wish to do and what we are able to do. The awareness of this gap can lead to the development of a clear intent to accomplish something beyond our own current capacity. In such a case, the very intent to act includes two elements: (1) the intent to do the inquiry necessary to learn how to do this new thing and (2) the inquiry necessary to learn whether we really have accomplished it. So, action inquiry begins with inner ex-

---

1. In this regard, we refer our more research-oriented colleagues to the Appendix. There we discuss some ancient roots of action inquiry and several other strands of the exploration toward an action inquiry that integrates subjective, intersubjective, and objective inquiry. We also review the objective measures and studies that underlie our discussion of action inquiry throughout the body of the book. We have left such scholarly discussions for the Appendix because the body of this book is addressed to all of us citizens as beginners in the personal and organizational practices of action inquiry—whether we are men or women, junior or senior, managers or researchers.

periences of gaps and intents. Intending to build a bookshelf leads to the strategy of nailing boards together. You choose a hammer as a tactical instrument and your capacity for assessment determines whether your arm has swung so that the hammer has hit the nail at the right angle to cause the nail to enter the wood. Yes, the hammer hitting the nail is the most immediate and visible cause of the nail entering the wood, but the hammer cannot even move, let alone cause anything constructive, on its own.

If our intent is clear and strong, we will wish to learn the truth as soon as possible about whether our strategies, tactics (e.g., our use of the hammer), and outcomes are accomplishing the intent or not. If our intent has not been accomplished, the sooner we learn this, the sooner we may correct the course of action in order to move closer to our intent. From this point of view, a method that can correct error in the midst of ongoing action is qualitatively more useful to us, more beneficial for others, and more powerful in a scientific sense than methods that *alternate* action and inquiry. Action inquiry *interweaves* research and practice in the present.

Indeed, action inquiry asks each of us to recognize how every action we take is, in fact, also an inquiry. The reverse is also true: every inquiry we make is also, simultaneously, an action that influences the response given. In this sense, all action and all inquiry is action inquiry. (For example, we don't know what response we'll get, even when we remind one of our children of a family rule in a tone that we hope brooks no dissent. The subsequent response of our child is in part a commentary on the efficacy of our action, as well as representing an inquiry about what we are going to do next.)

But, although we are constantly engaged in implicit and unintentional action inquiry, we almost never realize or remember in the course of the routines and the interruptions of our days that we may *intentionally* engage in action inquiry. Moreover, few of us are familiar with or practiced in specific strategies and tactics that are likely to increase the efficacy, the transforming power, and the timeliness of our action inquiries. Indeed, the fundamental secret of timely action inquiry is to be awake enough in present time to engage in action inquiry intentionally. As Thoreau once quipped, "I've never known a man who was quite awake." And we find little guidance—whether we look to the world of business practice or the world of academic scholarship—for awakening to and developing intentional, effective, transforming, timely action inquiry in the midst of everyday life. This book begins the lifelong and (from a civilizational point of view) centuries-long process of addressing this gap.

The Three Primary Aims of Action Inquiry

On a subjective, personal level, the value-explicit aims of action inquiry are to generate effectiveness and *integrity* in ourselves. Integrity is generated, not by unvarying behavior, nor by espousing the same principles consistently, but rather through a more and more dynamic and continual inquiry into the gaps in ourselves. Such gaps may appear between the results we intended and the results our performance generates, or between our planned performance and our actual performance, or between our original intentions and our low state of awareness (not quite awake) at the moment of action, causing us to miss an opportunity.

In relationships with family, friends, colleagues, customers, or strangers, the value-explicit aim of action inquiry is to generate a critical and constructive *mutuality*. Power differences and the unilateral use of power by either party reduce the likelihood of trust and honest communication. Mutuality is generated through two dynamics. The first dynamic is an increasingly open inquiry into the play of power between parties, with mutuality as a goal (though often, as in the case of a parent and a small child, a presently felt mutuality can be wrapped within layers of assumed dependence, so that full mutuality may be a generation or more in the making). The second dynamic that generates mutuality, once we recognize the present play of power between us, is more and more creative actions to develop shared visions and strategies, increasingly collaborative ways of conversing, and jointly determined ways of learning the worth of what is created together. If you look back to the short descriptions some of our coauthors have offered about how action inquiry is alive in our lives, we think you will see concerns for effectiveness, for integrity, and for mutuality closely interwoven with one another.

On the still larger scale of organization, society, and the environment, the value-explicit aim of action inquiry is to generate *sustainability*. To be sustainable, organizing structures (e.g., laws, policies, networks, etc.) must encourage effectiveness, integrity, and mutuality, and must also be capable of continuing transformation toward greater social justice and greater harmony with the natural environment, as we will argue and illustrate in the body of the book.

Initially, integrity, mutuality, and sustainability may come across to you as high-sounding ideals with little relationship to the gritty actual power reality of our everyday worlds. This perception exists because we ordinarily understand and experience power in a conventional or cynical way as the ability to get what the power possessor unilaterally wants, without inquiry and irrespective of the overall justice of the outcome.

Action inquiry represents an approach to powerful action that is fundamentally different from modern political/organizational action because it treats mutually transforming power—a kind of power that few people today recognize or exercise—as more powerful than unilateral power. Traditional forms of power, such as force, diplomacy, expertise, or positional authority, that are commonly used unilaterally to influence external behavior may generate immediate acquiescence, conformity, dependence, or resistance. But, by themselves, no matter in what combination, they will not generate transformation. Action inquiry blends different proportions of all these types of power in particular situations, but always in subordination to a rare kind of mutual power that makes both the person acting and the people and organizations he or she is relating to vulnerable to transformation. The promise of action inquiry is a new kind of power—*transforming power*—which, paradoxically, emanates from a willingness to be vulnerable to transformation oneself. You will find many illustrations of this kind of power at work in everyday organizational situations in the body of this book.

Summary and Preview

We have introduced action inquiry as something new. Action inquiry is new in two senses at once. It is new in historical terms in that it brings the modern scientific concerns for *inquiry* that generates valid theory and data together with the modern managerial concern to control and coordinate organizing *actions*. And action inquiry is new in personal terms in that it creates a new and different future in our personal daily lives each time we awaken and intentionally practice it rather than acting unconsciously, habitually, and without inquiry.

To provide an initial sense of the defining qualities of action inquiry, we have proposed that:

1. Every action and every inquiry is implicitly action inquiry.
2. Action inquiry interweaves research and practice in the present.
3. We almost never realize or remember in the course of the routines and the interruptions of our days that we may intentionally engage in action inquiry.
4. Action inquiry seeks to interweave subjective, intersubjective, and objective data—subjective data about our own intent for the future, intersubjective data about what is going on at present from the divergent points of view of different participants, and objective data about what has actually been produced with what quality in the past.
5. The special power of action inquiry—transforming power—comes from a combination of dedication to our intent or shared vision; alertness to gaps among vision, strategy, performance, and outcomes in ourselves and others; and a willingness to play a leading role with others in organizational or social transformations, which includes being vulnerable to transformation ourselves.

Practicing action inquiry can give you an enormous competitive advantage over those not practicing it. Indeed, our experience with the thousands of managers we have worked with is that practicing action inquiry, at first, seems very risky to them but then leads to organizational promotions more rapidly than they can initially imagine. (This unexpected outcome tends to occur first because we *over*estimate the risks of new behavior and *under*estimate the risks of our ongoing habitual behavior and, second, because visible, voluntary, noncompetitive, gap-filling leadership initiatives are relatively rare in organizations today.)

But action inquiry does not actually generate so much a competitive advantage as a mutual, collaborative advantage. Action inquiry becomes even more rewarding as you develop the perspective and skill to encourage others to exercise it as well. The full promise and power of action inquiry blossoms when it is a collaborative engagement that enriches your life in many more ways (in terms of greater mutuality, trust, friendship, and sense of service and shared meaning) than exercising action inquiry competitively will.

This book offers a fresh approach to helping friends, colleagues, work teams, and organizations learn even as they are involved in the cut and thrust of daily action. We offer action inquiry as a highly usable process whereby managers and whole organizations simultaneously learn at several levels and modify their actions as a continual process. This process not only allows us to correct errors before they have negative consequences for business outcomes and trust, but can also be experienced as pleasurable and energizing as a critical mass of colleagues join in, creating a positive climate for ongoing learning.

Our intent in writing this book is to support you to begin or continue your own action inquiry journey. We illustrate the inquiry-in-action process with many more examples, some humble and momentary, some so strategic and artistic and sustained that they have transformed whole lives, whole companies, whole industries, or whole countries. Further, through exercises for Chapters 1, 2, and 3 presented in the Interlude chapter, we invite you to enter into the inquiry-in-action process. We begin with a focus on the individual manager, then expand it outward to teams and organizations, and, finally, to society and human living in general. Welcome to this action inquiry!

PART ONE

Learning Action Inquiry Leadership Skills

ONE

Fundamentals of Action Inquiry

By "action inquiry," we mean a kind of behavior that is simultaneously productive and self-assessing. Action inquiry is behavior that does several things at once. It listens into the developing situation. It accomplishes whatever tasks appear to have priority. And it invites a revisioning of the task (and of our own action!) if necessary. Action inquiry is always a timely discipline to exercise because its purpose is always in part to discover, whether coldly and precisely or warmly and stumblingly, what action *is* timely.

These sentences are easy enough to read and to write, and they make action inquiry seem obviously worthwhile. When don't you want to act in a timely fashion? Yet action inquiry is also the hardest thing in the world to do on a continuing basis (at least so it feels to some of us who've been working and playing with it for three or four decades). The difficulty arises partly because of the unusual degrees of awareness of the present situation that high quality action inquiry requires. The difficulty arises partly because of the many different and potentially conflicting political pressures and standards of timeliness that may be at play in a given situation. And the difficulty arises partly because of how hard it is to develop a taste for making ourselves vulnerable to change at the very moment when we are also trying to get something done.

A small example of action inquiry may seem ridiculously simple. Here is a company president speaking by phone to her special assistant:

> "I'm assuming you are handling the Jones contract. Let me know if you need assistance."

The president makes her assumption explicit and advocates that the special assistant seek her support, if necessary, to assure the job gets

13

done. The assistant may say, "What? I've never heard of the Jones contract." Or, "I thought Paul was taking care of that." Or whatever the truth is, if it is incongruent with the president's explicitly stated assumption and offer of assistance. Many of the day-to-day frustrations of work life can be avoided by such brief assumption-testing action inquiries.

But even such obvious types of checking and inquiry as this president displays are rare in business, professional, and familial conversations. Consider the recent simulated operating room study of medical residents receiving training on how to avoid errors (Rudolph 2003). This study shows that in over 4,000 comments by the lead physician during simulated operating crises, only three combined some direction about what to attend to with an inquiry about what the assistant was learning. This small number occurred in spite of the fact that half of these young doctors were trained in a specific method for inquiring in the midst of action only minutes before the simulation. Yet their much more deeply internalized need to appear independent, competent, and knowledgeable interfered with showing the vulnerability necessary to learn the data that can prevent error (as a number of them acknowledged in postscenario interviews).

A shift in awareness is needed, a shift to a kind of awareness that shows us the opportunity to make a comment like the president's. This kind of awareness transcends the sort of implicit self-image that prevents medical residents from seeking colleagues' help in the operating room and instead attends responsively to the real need both the patient and we have for help. What is this awareness? How can we gain access to it in a timely way?

The Underwater Pipeline Project Manager

For some clues, let's listen in as Steve Thompson, a highly competent and well-paid manager, reconstructs a confrontation with his boss, Ron Cedrick. Steve's team is laying underwater pipeline when a storm begins to blow around their North Sea platform.

British National Oil Company had contracted with Ron Cedrick to construct and install its "single anchor leg mooring system" that can fill oil tankers at sea, eliminating the need for hundreds of miles of pipeline from the offshore oil fields. The initial underwater construction had been completed in a picturesque and protected Norwegian fjord. But we were now saturation diving for 8- to 12-hour periods from aboard a 600-foot derrick ship in the February North Sea, which can be unpredictably violent.

The most critical part of this dangerous procedure is the launch and recovery of the six-man bell through the "interface"—the wave-affected first 25 feet below the ocean surface. Rough seas have separated more than one diving bell from its winch. When this happens, there is little hope of returning the divers alive.

It was my first job as project manager, so it was of particular importance to me that the crew was doing an outstanding job and Cedrick was extremely pleased with our performance. Famously aloof, Cedrick wore a shiny gold metal hard hat. And, no matter how difficult, his projects always came in ahead of schedule.

The bell had just gone into the water for an anticipated 12-hour run when the wind changed direction and was coming at us from the same direction as the moderate swell, just as it does before it really blows. I alerted the shift supervisor to keep an eye on the weather and went up to the bridge for a look at the most recent forecast and facsimile, which confirmed my suspicions.

Just then, Cedrick came up to me, "I personally appreciate the fine job you and your boys are doing and I know it'll continue. I know the weather's getting up a bit, but we have to complete the flowline connection today to stay ahead, so we need to keep that bell in the water as long as we can before we let a little ole weather shut us down. I've seen the respect those boys have for you and I know they'll do what you ask."

"Yes, sir" I responded confidently. What was going on inside me at that moment sounded different, though. The moment I reviewed the weather on the bridge, I became tense with fear. I was afraid I wouldn't have the strength of character to shut down the operation in the face of my overwhelming desire to succeed objectively and in Cedrick's eyes. I was also afraid I would have to deceive my people into thinking that pushing our operating limits was justified.

The outcome was all too predictable. I kept the bell in the water too long. The weather blew a gale. The recovery of the bell through 20-foot seas was perilous. I compromised the safety of the divers and set a poor precedent for the permissible operating parameters. I received no satisfaction from the major bonus Cedrick gave me for "pulling it off"—we did complete the flowline connection. Inside me, the awareness that I had

manipulated and jeopardized the safety of my fellow workers galled my illusion that I was an honest, ethical man.

   After the emergency was over and the mission successfully accomplished, Steve Thompson could simply have congratulated himself for
getting the job done in the face of significant obstacles and for winning
the praise of his superior. Instead, his awareness was alert and vulnerable in a way that revealed a serious weakness of character to him that
few have the strength of character to face. He became aware of a serious
incongruity between his espoused or proclaimed values and his actual
actions.
   We were led into the Steve Thompson story by two questions about
the kind of awareness associated with action inquiry. What is this kind
of awareness that transcends all our implicit self-images that cramp
awareness and prevent us from acting with integrity, mutuality, justice,
and inquiry? And how can this kind of awareness be accessed in a timely
way even in an emergency?
   The case itself shows us no positive answer to these two questions.
Steve did not display such awareness during his encounter with
Cedrick, nor in the action-packed hours that followed. He got the job
done and the divers out safely, despite the turmoil and danger. The story
illustrates a type of awareness in action that puts action first and inquiry
later, or not at all. Steve has a well-honed awareness of how to adjust
himself and his team behaviorally from minute to minute to changing
conditions. In engineering and social systems theory, we call that a high
reliability capacity for digesting and learning from *single-loop feedback*
(information that tells me whether or not my last move advanced me
toward the goal). Reliable single-loop learning is critical for reaching
goals efficiently and effectively, and Steve obviously demonstrated this
quality of awareness in this case.
   By the end of his experience, Steve also demonstrates a second quality of awareness that is much more difficult to describe. It seems something like an awareness that transcends one's self-image, since he sees
his "illusion" about himself "destroyed." But it is not yet an empowering
awareness that allows him in the midst of the turmoil to see a leadership
initiative that generates greater legitimacy as well as efficiency and effectiveness.
   Let us review more closely what happens in Steve Thompson's experience. At a certain specific moment, he becomes aware that there is a
significant disharmony among several of the personal forces that moti-

vate him. There's his desire to please his boss, innocent and constructive enough in itself, you might ordinarily think. Then there's his desire to perform efficiently and effectively, ordinarily considered the *most* constructive of inclinations in a work setting. Thirdly, there's his desire to deserve his team's respect by holding their well-being uppermost. Finally, there's his self-image as an honest, ethical man.

These four good chunks of Steve's soul find themselves in a new and stormy juxtaposition to one another during the outer storm in the North Sea. He reports his inner experience as "tense with fear" and "galling." He describes the outcome as the "destruction" of his "illusion" that he is honest and ethical.

But just a minute—what is really going on here? Is that self-image really an illusion? Isn't Steve's story to himself at the time and when he later writes it up the very essence of honesty? Isn't the whole reflective process that he chooses to engage in afterwards the very essence of ethical inquiry? How else may we develop true, ethical integrity except by the compassionate, unsparing observation of our lack of integrity?

By receiving feedback and reflecting on what he wrote, Steve gradually realized that yes, of course, he possessed a real, and a real strong, ethical concern. Indeed, this concern was motivating his entire self-criticism. He came to realize that two subtle qualities pushed him out of shape at the time of the storm, one by its presence and one by its absence. The quality whose presence pushed him out of shape was Cedrick's clever use of multiple types of power (his legitimate and potentially unilateral power as a superior; his authority and fame as an expert in his craft; and the sheer seductive, man-to-man power of his down-home-Texas-macho talk about "a little ole weather"). At the time of the storm, Steve could feel the effect of Cedrick's use of power on himself, and he could feel the implicit illegitimacy of the pressure. At the same time, however, he could not name what was happening to him, nor imagine a way to defang it. This happens to a lot of us, if not all of us: When certain types of power are directed toward us, we become stunned or hypnotized, unable to articulate to ourselves what is happening to us, and unable to take creative action in response.

The quality whose absence pushed Thompson out of shape was a kind of attention or vision that can impartially observe both the storm going on outside us and the storm going on within, which we can call super-vision.

Single-, Double-, and Triple-Loop Awareness

Systems theory offers a framework for naming and understanding super-vision (Deutsch 1966; Torbert 1973). In systems theory terms, during his crisis with Cedrick and the weather in the North Sea, Steve success-fully dealt with single-loop feedback. He adjusted his behavior through-out the storm in such a way that the men below were recovered safely. But he also experienced a jolt of *double-loop feedback* that he couldn't fully digest. He knew vaguely that this feedback required him to trans-form his structure or strategy, not just amend his behavior. We might say he needed to clarify that when the goals of efficiency, effectiveness, and legitimacy clash in a situation, legitimacy usually deserves to come first, effectiveness second, and efficiency third (because in the longer run, ef-ficiency is only sustainable if it leads to effectiveness and effectiveness is only sustainable if it leads to legitimacy). We might also say that Steve needed to learn that when the existing authority structure (Cedrick, in this case) uses power in a way that threatens the legitimacy of the enter-prise, a counterinitiative based on a kind of transforming power that en-hances mutuality is called for.

But the very notion of transforming power that enhances mutuality is unfamiliar to most people, so it is not surprising that it was unfamiliar to Steve. Moreover, most of us treat our current structure, strategy, or action-logic as our very identity. To accept double-loop feedback can feel equivalent to losing our very identity. We will tend to resist that, unless and until we feel a still deeper spiritual presence within us that allows us to continue to feel ourselves as ourselves even as we try different roles, or masks, or strategies. This deeper spiritual presence or super-vision is not based on a self-image, but rather on experiencing the actual ex-change occurring among the four territories of our experience—our at-tention, our strategies, our actions, and our outcomes. In systems theory, this is called *triple-loop feedback* because, as shown in Figure 1.1, it highlights the present relationship between our effects in the out-side world and (1) our action, (2) our strategy, and (3) our attention it-self. Triple-loop feedback makes us present to ourselves now. (When Thoreau said he'd never met a man who was quite awake, we think he meant he'd never met a man continually present to himself in this way.)

By role-playing alternative actions he might have taken in a training setting, Steve gradually realized that he needed to listen into, but not identify with, many other aspects of the situation of which he'd been im-

Figure 1.1   Single-, Double-, and Triple-Loop Feedback
Within a Given Person's Awareness

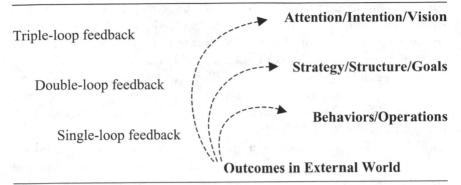

plicitly aware at the time. At first, he thought the only alternative was to have disagreed with Cedrick in a direct confrontation instead of saying "Yes, sir." But he hadn't been completely confident that he would have to bring the team up early at that point, even though the weather report was worrisome. So why risk confronting the boss then?

A simple third alternative, which he next enacted, would have been to respond to Cedrick exactly as he did at the time, but then bring the bell out of the water earlier. In reflection, he realized that, to respond to the real situation in a timely fashion, his awareness at the time would have to have been able to embrace several disharmonious systems of energy—the actual external weather system, the team diving system, Cedric's psychological system, and his own psychological system. For example, his awareness would have to have been able to embrace Cedrick's very real compliment about how well the men thought of Thompson (not just its manipulative context) and to remember and feel clearly *at that time* his own usual sense of himself—that others' respect for him was based on his professional good judgment, not on being a daredevil or a servile, easily manipulated conformist. In other words, to respond to Cedrick exactly as he did at the time, but then bring the bell out of the water earlier, he would have had to feel as he was beginning to feel during the role play—that his power and Cedrick's power could mutually balance and enhance one another, like the balance of powers among the legislative, executive, and judicial branches of the U.S. government.

This power to balance goal-oriented action with inquiry about the goal, in such a way as to also balance the influence of different participants, was illustrated even more explicitly in the third role play that

Steve simultaneously invented and produced as he tried to exercise in-the-moment super-vision. "I'm not sure how much is at stake for you or the company in completing this ahead of schedule," he began tentatively, inquiringly. When the person playing Cedrick in the role play did not answer during a brief pause, Steve continued, "We certainly can leave her down a while, but I'm not sure we'll be able to finish. The boys know I'll push them, but they also know I won't endanger lives. Do you want to stay up here with me to monitor the situation, or do you want me to continue on my own judgment?" Here, Thompson invites Cedrick to legitimize his "ahead of schedule" goals, counterposes it against the good of the divers (another legitimate reality in the situation), and invites Cedrick to have as much influence as he wishes on the unfolding situation, while clarifying Steve's own priorities (including his lack of competitive desire to seize power from Cedrick).

What Steve began to appreciate through these role plays was that he could actively cultivate, not just single-loop learning of new actions to achieve someone else's goals, nor just double-loop learning of new strategies and new goals to fulfill an intuitive vision. Now he found himself engaging in triple-loop learning that intentionally cultivates ongoing super-vision. Super-vision is the quality of awareness that briefly witnessed the disharmony in Steve's soul during the original situation. Flashes of super-vision occur in us so briefly that we often fail to name, digest, or remember them. Had Steve originally been able to tolerate observing the disharmony in his soul and in the wider situation further at the time of the emergency—had he continued exercising super-vision instead of mentally judging himself as irredeemably unethical—that heightened awareness might have made it possible for him to act differently at the time.

Where did these after-the-action awareness experiments during his role plays actually lead Steve? Within months of writing about the incident and doing the role plays, his colleagues were describing him as "a changed man." He was no longer merely a technical ace, in the image of Cedrick, who pushed himself and everyone else to the limit on particular jobs. Steve was now seen, not only as highly energetic and reliable within the boundaries of his assigned authority, but also as a broad-visioned, trustworthy, balanced, and concerned leader on a wider scale. As he emerged from the executive program in which he'd done the writing and the role plays just described, Steve received an offer to join the top management and board of the company, leapfrogging Cedrick, and more than doubling his previous salary.

That is not all. His learning did not promote only his self-interest. Three years later, Steve became president of a competing company. In his new role, he immediately saw an opportunity for corporate action inquiry. His new company had recently lost a major client. Rather than assuming that this was an unalterable event and perhaps feeling superior to his predecessor (certain that he, Steve, would never let a big one get away like that), Steve personally called the CEO of the erstwhile client and learned specifically how his own company had failed (that is, he sought single-loop feedback). He then engaged members of his company in restructuring the systems and relationships responsible for poor performance (that is, he engaged his own company in double-loop learning). Next, he offered the erstwhile-client a new contract that bound Thompson's company to an unusual proportion of the financial responsibility for any failure in timely performance (thus creating a condition that encouraged ongoing triple-loop awareness within his own company while seeking to meet the contract). This time his company met its obligations and regained a significant customer.

Here we see some evidence that Steve went beyond castigating himself to cultivating a more sinuous, just-in-time awareness that generated the exercise of vulnerable, mutuality-enhancing, transforming power under real-time pressures that improved the fortunes of both his company and a client's.

Improving the Quality of Our Awareness by Including Four Territories of Experience

The question is how can you, the reader, as an individual manager (and you do manage at least your own time and actions), go beyond merely passively appreciating the increased effectiveness, legitimacy, and personal sense of integrity that Steve Thompson gradually gained through his writing and role playing exercises? How can you yourself become more aware of, and less constrained by, your own implicit and often untested assumptions about situations you find yourself in?

The first step is to begin to recognize how limited our ordinary attention and awareness is. The second step is to begin exercising our awareness in new ways in the midst of challenging situations.

A good way to begin recognizing the limits of our ordinary attention is to take a moment right now to reflect. We urge you to start a journal, if you do not already have one, for exercises like this one. Think about significant incidents during your lifetime, with another person or with a group, that have had unsatisfactory outcomes. Make a list of a half dozen of these incidents. You will want to include current ongoing issues that you may have at work, or at home with your family or friends, or with some sports team, or church, or other activity you participate in. New insights into any of these issues can be put to work right away since the situation is current. Recurrent difficulties with a particular person with whom you will continue to interact are particularly fruitful to examine closely. (Even though the difficulties are all his or her fault [of course!], still, if you can learn how to act to avoid or overcome them, you will be happier.) Long-ago incidents that you still wonder about, or feel hurt by, are also good candidates for your "unsatisfying incidents" list.

We really encourage you to list several such incidents in your journal. We will be inviting you to journal for yourself repeatedly in the coming chapters. Indeed, Chapter 2 will offer a methodology for studying one or more of these incidents more closely.

Now let's look at how you can experience the limits of your ordinary attention by beginning to stretch it in new ways, gradually creating the capacity for super-vision. First, we rarely exercise our attention to span the four "territories of experience" that we've been discussing in Steve Thompson's story and that are shown in Table 1-1. As a result, our attention simply does not register a great deal of what occurs. Reading this book, for example, you are likely to become oblivious for periods of time to sounds and other events in your environment, oblivious, too, to your own body position and breathing, oblivious even to the fact that this book is a physical object with size, weight, and texture as distinct from the cognitive meaning of the words and sentences you are reading. Being reminded of these facts now may momentarily jolt you into a

Table 1-1 Four Territories of Experience

First territory	*Outside events*: results, assessments, observed behavioral consequences, environmental effects
Second territory	*Own sensed performance*: behavior, skills, pattern of activity, deeds, as sensed in the process of enactment
Third territory	*Action-logics*: strategies, schemas, ploys, game plans, typical modes of reflecting on experience
Fourth territory	*Intentional attention*: presencing awareness, vision, intuition, aims

widened awareness of several territories at once. Can your attention include a sense of the book as object (first territory), a sense of your breathing (second territory), and a sense of the meaning of the sentences (third territory) as you continue to read?

Typically, during our lifetime, our earliest years after we learn language are engaged in learning how to deal directly with the first territory of experience—the outside world—by learning how to run and play games relatively skillfully, putting the basketball through the hoop or the thread through the hole of the needle, rather than the point of the needle into our hand. Next, with our teenage friends and sometimes our parents as sounding boards, we focus more on the second territory of experience—our own performance itself. We learn how to play roles in conventional, preexisting social games relatively skillfully. We may become the listening conflict-reconciler in a torn family, or perhaps advance our own status by trumping lower status members of our peer group. By college age or in our early twenties, many of us turn our primary attention to providing new value by developing creative or problem-solving capabilities in some cognitive field—the third territory of experience—be it music-making or accounting, software development or medicine.

But few of us today go on to the profound field of adult learning wherein we seek to directly engage the fourth territory of experience—our attention itself, our super-vision—with its capacity for intentional movement among the other three territories of experience and across more than one at a time. Have you maintained the sense of the book as object and of your breathing as you read this entire paragraph?

This chapter, and this book as a whole, is an invitation into an executive world of persons such as we and you who increasingly wish to act and to attend inquiringly from moment to moment. At the end of this section, after Chapter 3, you will find a summary of each of the first three chapters and relevant attention exercises to help you transform the idea of action inquiry into the practice and experience of action inquiry. For now, though, we invite you to explore in Chapter 2 how your own personal action inquiry can expand into your conversations on the job and among your friends. Then in Chapter 3, we will introduce the unique power of organization-wide action inquiry.

TWO

Action Inquiry
as a Manner of Speaking

On the basis of Chapter 1, you can now begin to practice action inquiry within yourself whenever you wish (though you may find, as we did in our early years of practice, that you need a lot of support to cultivate this wish). By the end of this chapter, you will have received enough guidance about how to practice action inquiry in conversations to begin practicing the interpersonal quality of action inquiry at work and in other areas of your life. You may even find you would like to share the practices with a select group of friends or co-workers. Just as we saw in Chapter 1 that the primary value for ourselves in exercising personal action inquiry is a deeper sense of integrity, so we will find in this chapter that the primary value for our relationships in exercising interpersonal action inquiry is a deeper sense of mutuality.

Let's begin this chapter by listening in to Anthony as he makes a first try at action inquiry that leads him into a rich vein of leadership learning that transforms his division and his career. Later in the chapter, we describe a specific way of exercising action inquiry each time we speak. And we end the chapter with a specific discipline that small groups who wish to improve their leadership effectiveness can use. But first, let's gain an intuitive appreciation for action inquiry and see how you can practice it no matter what your formal position may be in your organization or family.

Anthony's Action Inquiry Leadership Experiments

Anthony is a staff member in a consulting firm. As a benefits consultant in the Wheeling office of an international human resources consulting firm, he has for the past two years immersed himself in the narrowly specialized world of a very complex method for comparing company benefit programs for large corporate clients. He has become one of the firm's few experts in this method. This role fulfills his personal ambition to "do something unique to differentiate myself."

Now he would like to break out of his cocoon as a specialized individual contributor, and an opportunity to play a more value-added, entrepreneurial leadership role presents itself. This opportunity has two components. Anthony sees a quality improvement opportunity and he has ready access to the office's strategic management team. The organization of the Wheeling office is a nonhierarchical one, with the office divided into 12 teams, each headed by a team coordinator who reports to the office manager. The team coordinators are plagued by a problem that Anthony feels he can help them address: shortcomings in a myriad of administrative functions such as billing, training, hiring and new employee initiation, career tracking, work allocation, and performance review. The team coordinators are supposed to oversee all these functions while simultaneously bringing in new clients and working with ongoing clients. The coordinators are constantly forced to juggle priorities amid tight time constraints. Clients, employees, and the coordinators themselves suffer the consequences.

No one has assigned him this project, but Anthony makes a significant commitment at the outset and develops a plan to help ameliorate some of the team coordinators' problems. First, he will meet with the office manager to discuss the project, then meet briefly with each team coordinator to explain his proposed approach. Next, he will prepare questions for interviews and a survey instrument and will administer both. After analyzing the data, he will present feedback to the team coordinators at one of their monthly meetings. A collaboratively determined action plan will then be developed and implemented. In effect, Anthony has traded in the time he might have spent lamenting the ineffectual situation and blaming others for time that he's put into imagining a creative, inquiring, mutuality-enhancing response.

With his flexible plan in mind, Anthony meets with Don, the office manager. Scheduled for half an hour, this meeting, as Anthony puts it, "blossomed into two hours of discussion about our team coordinator problems and how this project could help address them." An important clarification occurs in this meeting. Don suggests that Anthony should make recommendations to the team coordinators after collecting his data, but Anthony responds that he does not intend to recommend solutions, "but rather to facilitate a collaborative effort involving all of the team coordinators." We see that Anthony is sensitive to optimizing all participants' sense of mutuality.

Anthony proceeds with the survey and interviews. After several further discussions with Don, he decides to survey the team coordinators explicitly on their responsibilities—those they wish to retain, those they would prefer to delegate to their team members, and those they believe should be handled through a centralized office administration.

As Anthony describes his experience:

> My follow-up discussions with the team coordinators were fantastic opportunities to experiment with my behavior on a one-to-one basis. They were very willing to open up and discuss sensitive subjects and were also appreciative of my efforts to make their lives easier.
>
> Each coordinator directs a given consulting specialty. I had to constantly be aware of how to frame questions, which areas to hone in on, which to tactfully sidestep. For instance, on several occasions, I drew a chart with "market growth" and "market penetration" on the two axes (the old star/dog/cash cow diagram). While talking with the coordinator of a health care team, I marked his team in the star category, and a defined benefit team in the dog category. Should the leaders of these two teams have the same set of responsibilities? Perhaps the health care coordinator should let expenses rise to permit getting more revenue, while the defined benefit coordinator should work on cutting costs to increase profit.
>
> In any event, the chart proved to be a perfect arena for using my framing/advocating/illustrating/inquiring skills. You can't just tell a senior manager and expert who's been in the business 25 years that he should change his behavior. But the components of action inquiry verbal behavior came right out of me. "Let's talk about revenues and expenses for the next few minutes (framing). I don't think that two separate team coordinators should necessarily share the same focus regarding profit generation (advocating). Look here on this chart. See how the pension team is at the opposite end of the spectrum from the health care team (illustrating)? Would you have them focus on the same issues (inquiring)?" It was an opportunity to increase the team coordinators' awareness.

In the following, we more closely examine the four different "parts of speech"—**framing, advocating, illustrating,** and **inquiring**—to which Anthony refers in the foregoing paragraph. By way of concluding this story, Anthony suffered an attack of stage fright just before his final presentation at the monthly senior management meeting, not surprisingly in that he was making himself vulnerable by experimenting with new behavior while surrounded by his superiors. Despite this, the meeting itself went well. It resulted in the selection of three teams as pilots to test the notion of delegating coordinating functions so as to encourage leadership skills development by subordinates. Anthony received a promotion shortly thereafter.

Improving the Effectiveness of Our Speaking by Interweaving Four Parts of Speech

What is it that Anthony learns about talking that begins to give him enough confidence to enter unfamiliar and uncertain realms, where everyone is senior to him in formal organizational power, but where he nevertheless speaks improvisationally as if he were among peers?

Speaking is the primary and most influential medium of action in the human universe—in business, in school, among parents and children, and between lovers. Our claim is that the four parts of speech—framing, advocating, illustrating, and inquiring—represent the very atoms of human action. If we can cultivate a silent, listening, triple-loop awareness to our own actions and to a team's current dynamics, as we have just seen Anthony begin to do in the midst of his meetings, we can arrange and rearrange the interweaving of these atoms as we speak, peacefully harnessing the human equivalent of technological, unilateral nuclear power.

During the industrial age and the current electro-informational age, we have become technically powerful, but have not cultivated our powers of action. People who speak of moving from talk to action are apparently not awake to the fact that talk is the essence of action (and they probably talk relatively ineffectively). We are, in fact, deeply influenced by how we speak to one another. The very best managers often have an intuitive appreciation for much of what we are now saying and have semi-intentionally cultivated an art of speaking. However, most of us are rarely aware of how much we are influenced by the nuclear dynamics of conversational action. Instead of attending to the dynamic process of conversation, we focus all of our deliberate attention only on the content of the words being spoken.

Our claim is that Anthony's speaking became increasingly effective as he became present enough to his own ongoing talking to increasingly balance and integrate the four parts of speech. In other words, if you find that your speaking is dominated by one or two of these types of speech, the recommendation is to try adding more of the other types. You can then test these claims by your own conversational experiments.

Here are definitions and examples of the four parts of speech:

1) *Framing* refers to explicitly stating what the purpose is for the present occasion, what the dilemma is that everyone is at the meeting to resolve, what assumptions you think are shared or not shared (but need to be tested out loud to be sure). That is, put your perspective as well as your understanding of the others' perspectives out onto the table for examination. This is the element of speaking most often missing from conversations and meetings. The leader or initiator too often assumes the others know and share the overall objective. Explicit framing (or reframing, if the conversation appears off track) is useful precisely because the assumption of a shared frame is frequently untrue. When people have to guess at the frame ("What's he getting at?"), we frequently guess wrong and, because the frame is veiled, it is not surprising that we often impute negative, manipulative motives.

For example, instead of starting out right away with the first item of the meeting, the leader can provide and test an explicit frame: "We're about halfway through to our final deadline and we've gathered a lot of information and shared different approaches, but we haven't yet made a single decision. To me, the most important thing we can do today is agree on something . . . make at least one decision we can feel good about. I think XYZ is our best chance, so I want to start with that. Do you all agree with this assessment, or do you have other candidates for what it's most important to do today?" (Actually, after you've reviewed the next three parts of speech, you will see that this example of testing a possible frame for the meeting includes all four parts of speech.)

2) *Advocating* refers to explicitly asserting an option, perception, feeling, or strategy for action in relatively abstract terms (e.g., "We've got to get shipments out faster"). Some people speak almost entirely in terms of advocacy; others rarely advocate at all. Either extreme—only advocating or never advocating—is likely to be relatively ineffective. For example, "Do you have an extra pen?" is not an explicit advocacy, but an inquiry. The person you are asking may truthfully say, "No" and turn away. In contrast, if you say "I need a pen [advocacy]. Do you have an extra one [inquiry]?" the other is more likely to say something like, "No, but there's a whole box in the secretary's office."

The most difficult type of advocacy for most people to make effectively is an advocacy about how we feel—especially how we feel about what is occurring at the moment. This is difficult partly because we ourselves are often only partially aware of how we feel; also, we are reluctant to become vulnerable. Furthermore, social norms against generating potential embarrassment can make current feelings seem undiscussable. For all these reasons, feelings usually enter conversations only when they have become so strong that they burst in, and then they are likely to be offered in a way that harshly evaluates others ("Damn it, will you loudmouths shut up!"). This way of advocating feelings is usually very ineffective, however, because it invites defensiveness. By contrast, a vulnerable description is more likely to invite honest sharing by others ("I'm feeling frustrated and shut out by the machine gun pace of this conversation and I don't see it getting us to agreement. Does anyone else feel this way?").

3) *Illustrating* involves telling a bit of a concrete story that puts meat on the bones of the advocacy and thereby orients and motivates others more clearly. For example: "We've got to get shipments out faster [advocacy]. Jake Tarn, our biggest client, has got a rush order of his own, and he needs our parts before the end of the week [illustration]." The illustration suggests an entirely different mission and strategy than might have been inferred from the advocacy alone. The advocacy alone may be taken as a criticism of the subordinate or of another department, or may elicit an inappropriate response. It might, for example, unleash a year-long systemwide change, when the real target was intended to be much more specific and near-term. However, an illustration without an advocacy has no directional to it at all.

You may be convinced that your advocacy contains one and only one implication for action, and that your subordinate or peer is at fault for misunderstanding. But in this case, it is your conviction that is a colossal metaphysical mistake. Implications are by their very nature inexhaustible. There is never one and only one implication or interpretation of an action. That is why it is so important to be explicit about each of the four parts of speech and to interweave them sequentially if we wish to increase our reliability in achieving shared purposes.

4) *Inquiring*, obviously, involves questioning others, in order to learn something from them. In principle, the simplest thing in the world; in practice, one of the most difficult things in the world to do effectively. Why? One reason is that we often inquire rhetorically, as we just did. We don't give the other the opportunity to respond; or we suggest by our

tone that we don't really want a *true* answer. "How are you?" we say dozens of times each day, not really wanting to know. "You agree, don't you?" we say, making it clear what answer we want.

If we are inquiring about an advocacy we are making, the trick is to encourage the other to *disconfirm* our assumptions if that is how he or she truly feels. In this way, if the other confirms us, we can be confident the confirmation means something, and if not, then we see that the task ahead is to reach an agreement. At this point, it is likely to be useful to switch from focusing on one's own point of view and inquire further about how the other frames, advocates, and illustrates the issue we are discussing.

A second reason why it is difficult to inquire effectively is that an inquiry is much less likely to be effective if it is not preceded by framing, advocacy, and illustration. Naked inquiry often causes the other to wonder what frame, advocacy, and illustration are implied and to respond carefully and defensively: "How much inventory do we have on hand?" ("Hmm, he's trying to build a case for reducing our manpower.")

Notice that the central value running through the four parts of speech is *mutuality*. In advocating and illustrating, we present our own current point of view as cogently and persuasively as possible. In framing and inquiring, we extend ourselves as creatively as we can to embrace others' points of view.

But how do we know what to inquire about, or what illustration to use, what to advocate, and how to frame the overall situation on any given occasion? The general answer is that each of these four parts of speech originates from our first-person research into the four territories of experience we discussed in Chapter 1 (see Figure 2.1).

Here is how they come together. To determine what inquiry invites the widest possible shared understanding and coordinated action in the current situation (and to hear the responses clearly), we need to attend

Figure 2.1 How the Four Parts of Speech
Draw Their Timely Content from the
Four Territories of Experience

Framing	Attention/Intention/Vision
Advocating	Strategy/Structure/Goals
Illustrating	Behaviors/Operations
Inquiring (and Listening)	Outcomes in External World

primarily to the external world territory of experience (e.g., "What is it about the business climate now that makes you take such a strong position?"). To determine what illustration is most apt now, we need to attend primarily to the stories that our behaviors tell or embody (e.g., "The fact that you've interrupted me twice and are virtually shouting makes me wonder what is making you angry about this."). To determine what strategy to advocate, we need to attend primarily to the cognitive/emotional territory of experience (e.g., "We may come up with a creative strategy for facing this market if we can figure out a way to advance what we are each fighting for at the same time."). To discover what frame may be most inclusive and well-focused for our common activity, we need to attend primarily to the final territory of experience, the territory of intuitive intentions (e.g., "I'm realizing that if we want to keep growing this company and our leadership team over the next decade, maybe the best gift we can give it is to learn how the two of us and our two divisions can collaborate better. Is that kind of ten-year vision at all compatible with yours?").

Exercising the super-vision to interweave these four parts of speech may seem a poor investment to you because it sounds like a lot of work that provides virtually no unilateral, technical power to get results. Indeed, using inquiry and illustration to discover and tell truths that make us vulnerable to other perspectives may seem deeply threatening to whatever momentum we have developed (or imagine we have developed) in manipulating situations unilaterally. A large part of each of us does not want our momentum interrupted. Therefore, we are hesitant to try a true framing, advocacy, illustration, and inquiry approach because speaking like that may call forth true responses that interrupt our momentum and disconfirm our happy dreams. That is why it is most motivating to start trying conversational action inquiry in situations where we are already dissatisfied with the results we've achieved through our ordinary approach. Then there is little to lose by trying in a new way. But as we have already said, while such interpersonal action inquiry can enhance our joint efficiency and efficacy, the primary value to be gained is increased mutuality. Not until we ourselves transform to the point of valuing mutuality above unilateral control will we become fully comfortable with this approach to speaking.

We will not succeed in framing, advocating, illustrating, and inquiring regularly and effectively, however, until we strongly and sincerely want to be aware of ourselves in action in the present. Nor will we succeed in framing, advocating, illustrating, and inquiring effectively until we strongly and sincerely want to know the true response, *especially* when it questions our current frame, advocacy, and illustration. We may gradually come to feel in our bones that only actions based on truth and mutuality are good for us, for others, and for our organizations. (Developing this feeling is a lifetime journey in its own right, and we explore some of the major stages in that journey in Chapters 4 through 7.)

Not only must we really wish to know the truth about how others are experiencing the situation, but we need to act/inquire in a way that also convinces the other person(s) that we wish to be questioned and even proven wrong. Why? Because people generally are reluctant to disconfirm another person's frame, advocacy, or illustration. To do so directly is often thought of as rude—as making the other "lose face." The more sensitive the question, the more important it is to illustrate why it is important to us to hear a disconfirming response if that is, in fact, the true response.

A Disciplined Way to Practice the Four Parts of Speech

Eight years ago, our associates Erica Foldy, Jenny Rudolph, and Steve Taylor formed a voluntary learning team. It meets once a month to practice action inquiry. They have helped other such groups to start as well. In their version, individuals usually present cases about significant interactions they have had (or that they plan to have). Live cases between the members of the group also occur. In fact, Anthony's story, told earlier in the chapter, was an ongoing action inquiry project that he sought the members' help on. The members of another such group sometimes use the immediacy of e-mail to ask for help with specific challenges they are facing that very day at work.

Rudolph, Foldy, and Taylor (2001) have written one of the few careful descriptions of how this process can work on a given occasion. The rest of this chapter presents a much-condensed version of their description. It illustrates a kind of conversation that directly supports personal self-transformation toward greater clarity, using framing, advocating, illustrating, and inquiring. You, too, can potentially create a small group of colleagues, or of outside the office friends, to discuss cases like the ones we invited you to begin writing at the end of Chapter 1.

The point of working through such a case is to help the casewriter (and others) see how she or he is stymied and to avoid similar problems in the future. The grid (see Figure 2.3) provides one overarching framework that guides this work. Using the tools described in the following, we analyze the case and fill in the grid with observations about Dana's implicit assumptions, actions, and results.

In this particular case, Dana is the director at Action on Changing Technology (ACT), a union-based coalition that addresses the occupational health effects of computer technology. When this conversation takes place, Dana has been the director for less than a year. Anne, the other person in the case, predates Dana at the organization by about a year and a half. Anne hadn't wanted the director position. Anne is very smart organizationally and politically, despite her youth. Dana has a lot of respect for her and relies on her heavily, especially when she first takes the director's post.

Anne and Dana had a very good relationship for the first few months after Dana arrived, but at some point it began to get strained. More and more often now, their conversations reach an impasse. In the following example (Figure 2.2), typical of the pattern, Dana and Anne argue about what sites are appropriate targets for their organization's help. Two other staff members, Miriam and Fred, are present, but quiet, during the following exchange. Read Figure 2.2 now.

The group starts by seeking to learn what Dana's desired results are. What does Dana want to get out of this interaction? The right-hand "Thoughts and Feelings" column of the dialogue (Figure 2.2) often provides clues about the casewriter's desired results.

Dana's right-hand column suggests she thinks Anne's nomination of a target site for an educational effort is wrongheaded. She thinks, "That's not a good idea," and "She's missing the point." In the spoken dialogue Dana attempts to set Anne straight, exclaiming, "The enemy is not the director of Phoning Inc." and when Anne retorts that maybe he is Anne's enemy, Dana's rejoinder is, "But that's not strategic." Note that all these comments, both to herself and spoken out loud to Anne, are brief advocacies related to the *content* of what they may do. In effect, they all come from an attention concentrated in the cognitive territory of experience. None of them relates to the *process* of how each is currently speaking; none of them comes from attention to the behavioral territory of experience at the time of the action.

What is the right sort of target, as far as Dana is concerned? We get a hint that it is not a small, progressive organization when Dana attempts to turn aside Anne's suggested target by saying, "They do good stuff, don't they? They only take progressive clients" and "They're a tiny outfit and they're basically on our side." Note that these comments vary

Figure 2.2   Example Dialogue with Concurrent Inner Monologue

What Dana and Anne Said	Dana's Thoughts and Feelings
Dana: What are some other potential sites?	
Anne: A while ago we talked to some people at Phoning, Inc. Maybe we can check back with them.	That's not a good idea. Why is she suggesting it?
Dana: You mean the telemarketing group in western Mass? They do good stuff, don't they? They only take progressive clients.	
Anne: Well, they don't treat their phoners very well.	She's missing the point.
Dana: They're a tiny outfit and they're basically on our side. Maybe if we had infinite resources, but we don't.	
Anne: I don't see what all that has to do with it. There are workers there working under bad conditions. They could use our help.	Shit, are we going to butt heads again? Her purist politics drives me nuts.
Dana: The enemy is not the director of Phoning, Inc.	
Anne: Maybe he's not your enemy, but maybe he's my enemy!	Why do we get like this? Why does it get so tense? Why do we fall into this pattern over and over?
Dana: But that's not strategic.	

between a rhetorical inquiry (which she answers herself), an illustration ("They're a tiny outfit"), and an advocacy. This whole part of the conversation is framed by Dana's first inquiry about other potential sites.

The learning group notes these patterns and asks Dana if she can clarify why she said these things. She says she wanted to influence the group to identify targets that fit her criteria. Dana could have encouraged all staff members to name potential sites, then framed a subsequent part of the conversation as an attempt to develop shared criteria for a good site. Instead, she is implicitly trying to enforce her own criteria for a good site.

Dana also seems to be bothered by the conflict between herself and Anne. She thinks to herself, "Shit, are we going to butt heads again?" and "Why do we get like this? Why does it get so tense?" When the group queries Dana about this, she says she wants a harmonious discussion that will help the organization move forward.

By this time in the conversation about Dana's case, the irony of Dana's wanting a harmonious discussion in which only her point of view is allowed to prevail is plain to all, especially Dana. In hindsight, Dana notes that she had another goal in the conversation which was less obvious to her at the time and which seems to have been overridden by her desire to have her viewpoint prevail. That other desired outcome was "to have a real dialogue." "What is a real dialogue?" someone asks. Dana says a real dialogue is one in which Anne and Dana share their views fully, listen to each other, and negotiate actively. In other words, Dana begins to realize that she holds an espoused value of mutuality (real dialogue), but that her operative value in the conversation is one of attempted unilateral control.

When we compare Dana's "desired results" with the ones she got, we get a clear picture of the challenge facing Dana. In this case, the actual results are almost the exact opposite of what Dana hoped for. Instead of having her point of view prevail, she and Anne are deadlocked. Instead of real dialogue, they have dueling assertions. Instead of harmony, they have simmering frustration. How did this happen? If we trace counterclockwise along the grid in Figure 2.3 from Actual Results to Actual Actions to Actual Frames to Desired Frames to Desired Actions, we begin to see the answer.

We try to imagine the Desired Actions as concretely as possible. For example, one way for Dana to publicly reflect on her and Anne's conflict and ask for help is to say:

> "I feel in a dilemma here. On the one hand, I really want us to target the organizations I think are right. On the other, when I push my view I think that contributes to a pattern that Anne and I repeat over and over that has stymied us in the past: I say my view, then she says hers, and we don't seem to have much of an impact on each other. I'm not getting my way, she's not getting hers, and we are all just stuck. I think I'm open to influence on what the right strategy is. I believe if we worked together, we might actually come up with a better strategy than the ones Anne and I

Figure 2.3   Case Summary Using a Grid

Dana's Actual Frames	*Dana's Actual Actions*	*Actual Results*
1. Anne has purist politics and these are the wrong standards for the organization. 2. If I'm wrong, then my credibility (as the boss) is shot. If I'm wrong, then maybe I shouldn't be the boss. 3. It's my responsibility to handle this tough strategy question (alone). 4. If I admit I was mistaken, then I lose face.	Advocate own point of view but don't inquire about others' Keep reasoning hidden Appeal to abstract standard of being strategic, about which there is no consensus	Deadlock: Dana's view does not prevail and there is no real dialogue Frustration

Dana's Desired Frames	*Dana's Desired Actions*	*Desired Results*
1. I respect Anne and her views. 2. I'm not solely responsible for the strategic direction of the organization. 3. Real dialogue about strategic direction enhances my credibility. 4. I'm willing to experiment to get a better outcome.	Dana inquires about Anne's view Dana makes her own reasoning public and inquires about other peoples' Dana publicly reflects on her and Anne's conflict and asks for help	Dana's point of view prevails Harmony in the group Real dialogue in the group

are individually carrying around in our heads. Would others of you be willing to give this a try?"

Note that to say any of this, Dana first has to detach from her advocacies in the cognitive territory of experience and pay a new kind of attention to the behavioral territory of experience. What are the advantages of exercising super-vision and saying something like what's just been posed?

This group approach has three advantages. First, it invites the silent Miriam and Fred into the conversation, empowering them, increasing the overall mutuality within the group, and reducing the likelihood of sheer polarization between Dana and Anne. Second, it describes the deadlock in the current *process,* a whole realm that Dana was not directly and explicitly aware of during the original conversation. The third advantage of this approach is that it explicitly invites the use of mutual influence to generate a possible double-loop change in strategy for the organization. If Dana and her colleagues (and you!) are able to learn how to attend to the action-flow of meetings as they occur, then she (and they and you) may be able to help others mired in a similar situation.

We now turn to Chapter 3 to address the question of how *personal* and *interpersonal* action inquiry can expand into *organizational* action inquiry.

THREE

Action Inquiry as a Way of Organizing

In Chapter 1, we illustrated how we can each practice *first-person* action inquiry within ourselves. This is action inquiry in which we seek the attentiveness—the presence of mind—to begin noticing the relationships among our own intuitive sense of purpose, thoughts, behaviors, and effects. In this way we gradually generate increasing **integrity** within ourselves.

In Chapter 2, we examined some up-close illustrations of how we can practice *second-person* action inquiry in our conversations with others. In this action inquiry, we seek to interweave framing, advocating, illustrating, and inquiring to better name what is occurring from all players' perspectives. Thus we gradually generate greater **mutuality** and mutual commitment to whatever conclusions we reach. Moreover, we noted that effective and timely second-person action inquiry requires the participant to exercise first-person action inquiry at the same time.

In this chapter, we introduce action inquiry as a way of organizing people, knowledge, and resources across space and time, with the aim of **sustainability.** We call this *third-person* action inquiry, since it goes beyond ourselves to include others present in the current moment, as well as others who may never come to know one another. This latter group is related to one another over time through an organizational, network, or market structure, for example, the stock market. Toward the end of the chapter we will examine the stock market as a a third-person way of organizing through action inquiry that involves literally millions of people. But before we get to that, we will describe an organizational transformation on a much smaller scale, involving hundreds of people rather than millions—a change at a graduate school of management. And before *that*, we will briefly recount some of the experiences of a three-person partnership during its first year of establishing a business. And before that—indeed, next—we will explain how action inquiry functions as a way of organizing.

The Basic Tasks, Temporal Horizons, and Power of Organizational Action Inquiry

We argue that effective, transformational, sustainable third-person action inquiry requires interweaving the same four territories of experience with the same opportunities for single-loop, double loop, and triple-loop feedback and learning and change as we discovered in first- and second-person action inquiry. As we will show empirically in Chapter 7 when we examine which CEOs are capable of helping their organizations transform successfully, successful third-person action inquiry requires the practice of first- and second-person action inquiry as well.

In third-person action inquiry, we speak of the four territories as **visioning, strategizing, performing,** and **assessing** (see Figure 3.1). Profitability and growth in market share have long been primary forms of assessment for companies in market economies. A loss of profitability should lead either to a single-loop change in operations or to a double-loop change in strategy, or even possibly to a triple loop change in mission.

But, of course, there are other forms of organization than for-profit corporations (e.g., government, not-for-profits, universities, etc.); and there are other forms of assessment besides profitability (e.g., how the organization affects participants' equity, and how sustainable the or-

Figure 3.1 How the Four Territories of Experience Manifest Themselves in First-Person Attention, in Second-Person Speaking and Listening, and in Third-Person Organizing

First-Person Attention	Second-Person Speaking	Third-Person Organizing
Intending	Framing	Visioning
Thinking/Feeling	Advocating	Strategizing
Sensing/Behaving	Illustrating	Performing
Effecting/Perceiving	Inquiring (and Listening)	Assessing

ganizing process is in terms of its effects on the social and natural environment).

Over time, we authors have come gradually to understand leadership and power in terms of action inquiry and the four territories of experience. We claim that organizational leaders at any level must become capable of accomplishing four very different types of leadership if they are to become fully credible and sustainably legitimate, as well as effective in conventional terms and supportive of the personal and organizational transformations necessary to become triple-loop learning systems. We believe leaders worthy of the name must be capable of:

1. *Responding in a timely way to emergencies or opportunities* in the external world, which may arise unexpectedly at any moment.
2. *Accomplishing routine, role-defined responsibilities* in the performing territory of experience in a timely way, typically requiring one week to three months to complete.
3. *Defining and implementing a major, strategic initiative,* typically requiring three to five years and ongoing coordination among the strategizing, performing, and assessing territories.
4. *Clarifying organizational mission and encouraging continual improvement of the alignment among mission, strategy, operations, and outcomes,* requiring 7–21 years because organizational members determine the value of this process and join proactively in the action inquiry process only gradually.

Because the four time spans connected with leadership capabilities interpenetrate one another and influence each other, effective management over any extended period of time requires juggling and balancing all four kinds of leadership all the time. Indeed, on closer observation, each of the four kinds of leadership has both long-term and short-term qualities (e.g., there will be occasions when the success of the longest-term mission depends on one's immediate response to an unexpected opportunity).

Demands relating to the different kinds of leadership can be in considerable tension with each other because tasks relating to the two short-term kinds of leadership are more externally determined at any given time, while initiative toward the two long-term kinds of leadership are more internally determined (if they are being exercised at all). If, at the one extreme, a leader is at all passive in structuring time, the more immediate, more external demands will gain preeminence, driving out ongoing inquiry and strategic initiative. If, at the other extreme, an administrator fails to perform effectively in regard to the two shorter-term time spans, he or she comes to be regarded as unhelpful and unrealistic (in-credible) by children, students, subordinates, peers, and superiors.

Most leaders tend to deal with the tensions among the types of leadership by choosing one activity to focus on as essential. Don't we all know the "Firefighter" who is constantly battling (and often seems to cause) emergencies? And the "Bureaucrat" mired in routine, who resists every kind of change? And "Farsight," the brilliant strategic planner who can't get anyone to cooperate with him? The approaches represented by these caricatures are almost certain to generate greater incongruities among the territories of experience and reduce organizational effectiveness over time. We may find significant tension and incongruity across the four territories of experience when we enter any given leadership role because our predecessor is likely to have exercised a relatively lopsided leadership approach, like these caricatures.

If, however, a leader can actively and consciously juggle and balance the four kinds of leadership, the demands of each time span will increasingly come to complement and support activities relating to the other three time spans. Obviously, though, to do this juggling and balancing requires a continuing effort of awareness to embrace these four territories of organizational experience to begin with. This effort to generate triple-loop learning—super-vision—on an ongoing basis is, simply put, the secret of reliably timely leadership. But few, if any, organizational members may be making this effort. Instead, different members are likely to have radically different views of what is wrong with the organization and how to fix it.

The four time spans of leadership we have just discussed correspond roughly to types of power that different types of leaders customarily use:

1. *Immediate opportunities and emergencies* often, but by no means always, call for the temporary use of **unilateral power** (simply because there may be no time for anything else). Unilateral power is best at temporarily changing the outside world.
2. *Routine, role-related tasks* and *short-term projects* are typically accomplished through two types of power—**referent power** and **logistical power.** Reciprocal reference power or referent power is power generated, not by the power-wielder but by the power-yielder, by the "consent of the governed." It is best at influencing colleagues' specific performances in regard to a given project.

Referent power recognizes that if you tell colleagues what to do, they may resist. If you ask them if they will (use their power to) help you, they are more likely to do so, so long as you reciprocate.

Alternatively, new projects dictated by the promise of greater efficiency within the existing structure (e.g., developing a new sales software system) require the logistical power to create a coherent new minisystem. Logistical power is the power to reason systematically within a given structure to create a new way of accomplishing a desired result.

3. *Strategic planning and implementation* requires something more complex. To implement a long-term strategy requires juggling logistical power, referent power, and unilateral power simultaneously. To develop a truly motivating strategic plan requires a kind of **visionary power** that is both intuitive and purposeful.

4. Finally, *visioning or re-visioning a compelling organizational mission and generating ongoing action inquiry by members that increases alignment among mission, strategy, operations, and outcomes* requires **transforming power** and interweaving all the types of power we have just mentioned in appropriately timely ways.

The Conception, Investments, and Incorporation of a Small Company

Elizabeth, a successful British Web site designer in her late twenties, chooses to do an action research graduate degree at Bath University that involves reflecting regularly for a year with her two new design studio partners about the kind of business they are creating and whether their day-to-day activities actually embody the spirit of their intent.

The three have rented space, networked their computers, and found several different types of business, all related to a theme they begin to develop when they first talked seriously about creating a business together. They coin the term "service design" to characterize a gap in the design world that they hope to fill.

Unlike "product design" or "graphic design" where discrete products are sold, "service design" concerns creating a sustainable (and adjustable) service that can be customized for each individual client. All three partners are attracted by the idea of natural capitalism—the idea of taking a customer-pull approach to business, seeking the best return on investment from all materials involved in delivering the service, and treating earth systems themselves as services we wish to sustain (e.g., "warming services" and "fresh water services"). Their service design aspiration is to play an ongoing role in gradually shifting the measure of affluence in their work and lives from the consumption of things to the continuous flow of value.

These are grand *mission visioning* designs indeed, and the structure of journalizing and public reflection that Elizabeth has taken on as part of her graduate student work creates a heightened potential for engaging in single-, double-, and triple-loop learning—but what do the partners actually do? Although the partners use none of these action inquiry terms, they do begin asking right away how these ideas apply to their *strategies* and *performances* in their very earliest client meetings, which they follow up with immediate *self-assessing* meetings. For example, in meeting with a car manufacturer, whom they envision as potentially shifting toward becoming a "mobility provider," they set a tone of informality and avoid jumping into a set presentation, on the grounds that a formal presentation is a "supply push" method rather than a "demand pull" method. (It is impressive that they are quickly able to see the analogy between the highly abstract "demand pull" idea and their actual sales practice.)

At the meeting, amid jokes and asides, a brief statement about the market gap in service design leads the potential client to whisper about the company culture of "selling metal" and its unsatisfactory attitude toward service. He confides that a recent attempt of his to change the brand culture has been rejected by the board, but that he still regards culture change as necessary for the survival of the business. The result is that in half an hour, the partners have generated a degree of mutuality that has gotten the client to confide in them a good deal about the company and himself. In effect, they have established a strategic ally at the company.

At a telecommunications company, Elizabeth and her service design partners find that the Corporate Social Responsibility (CSR) department is viewed as a public relations or risk management function, rather than as a positive contributor to the bottom line. The partners ask themselves how they can best serve the department and the company as a whole. They create an imaginary future *Financial Times* article reporting an agreement with a major phone manufacturer, initiated by the CSR department, whereby service profits will be shared between the two companies in return for manufacturing phones that can accept software upgrades, rather than requiring new phone handsets. This future product creates a nonthreatening basis for conversation across the company. It has three outcomes. It leads to reconceptualizing the role of the CSR department. It links CSR with profit rather than cost. And it recognizes that CSR is close to the heart of the business, not a public relations add-on.

Reviewing her learning at the end of the first year of business, Elizabeth realizes that she and her partners experienced significant change. In their previous jobs, they were small pawns within large companies, passively riding a wave of change. Now they are actively making change both in their own business and in the role they take as they consult to other businesses. She is taken aback by who is willing to listen to her and by the respect she and her partners receive. She recognizes that this is related to the mutuality they practice in their meetings with clients. She is struck by how continuously fluid she must be in moving back and forth among the four territories of experience, if true interdependence and new value is to be created. Whereas at the outset of this new venture she often experienced considerable tension, wondering if the partners were compromising their mission as they adjusted to specific client demands and market realities, she later realizes that the very movement back and forth from the abstract to the concrete, from visioning through strategizing and performing to assessing and back again, is what keeps them from compromising their values. Although Elizabeth and her partners do not use our term "action inquiry," they do appear to be intentionally practicing what we mean by it.

Managing a School of Management

Now we jump to a larger, more established organizational setting, where one of us (Bill Torbert) entered as graduate dean. So, he will now slip into the first-person to tell a bit of the story in order to illustrate more concretely the challenges of interweaving the different tasks, time horizons, and types of power associated with practicing organizational action inquiry.

By the time I accepted the position of graduate dean at the Boston College (BC) School of Management (now the Wallace E. Carroll School of Management at Boston College) in 1978, I had extensively experimented with action inquiry at the margins of institutions. At BC, I was determined to discover how an environment of ongoing, transforming inquiry could be generated, institutionalized, and sustained over a generation's time. Such inquiry, I knew, would involve a clear-sighted appreciation of power. It would also require an ethical artistry of enactment that not only questioned and challenged myself and others, but also truly accepted all of us as we are at any given time, not just as we might ideally become.

Writing now, 25 years later, the result of the work at Boston College appears to be enough of a success to provide some concrete illustrations of the dilemmas one is likely to encounter in such an effort. I first offer a brief overview of what occurred in this organization over that period. Then I describe some of the critical incidents in greater detail in order to illustrate the interplay of the four time spans of leadership and the four types of power.

Historical Overview

Between 1978 and 1980, the school's faculty invented and implemented a new model of MBA education. It focused on teaching students two types of skills. It taught action skills through team consulting projects, and it taught analytic skills that showed students how to integrate both types of skill under the pressures of live action. At the same time, it invited both students and faculty to examine and improve not just their own effectiveness, but also that of the program itself. In short, the program came to model "continual quality improvement" some time before many U.S. businesses began to try to accomplish the same thing. By 1982, the program rose from below the top 100 to be ranked among the top 30 in the country in a poll of management school deans. By 1987, the steady rise (even during the serious recession of 1980–1982) in average first-year salaries offered by businesses to graduating classes resulted in a ranking among the top 25 programs nationally on this criterion.

The dedication of students to the program was suggested by their successful initiative to create a graduate school seal, with the motto "Through cooperation and integrity, we prosper" (surely a unique sentiment among MBA programs in the first brief Age of Donald Trump). At the same time, recent alumni of the program successfully funded an endowment for the Diane Weiss Presentation Competition. To this day, this event concludes the first year. It is the culmination of team consulting projects with businesses, projects whose aim is the actual improvement of the business, not just a paper about the business. All first-year full-time students participate in this integration of theory and practice unique to the BC program. The competition was endowed in the name of Diane Weiss, a student who had led her team to a first place finish in those presentations, graduated first in her class, and then died of cancer only a year afterwards.

Exercising Power to Generate Organizational Transformation

How did the simple theory of four leadership tasks, time horizons, and associated types of power, presented at the outset of this chapter, help me to play a constructive role in the developments at Boston College?

While acknowledging that there may have been additional factors involved, there is evidence that both my interest in inquiry-in-action and my sense of balancing the four types of leadership and power played a role in the positive outcomes just outlined. In 1978, the question of mission took my attention in search of an analogy that would best capture and interrelate:

1. What the MBA program ought to do for individual students.
2. What the MBA program ought to do for itself to become an increasingly effective organization.
3. What the MBA program ought to do to best represent the university, a Jesuit university.
4. What the MBA program ought to do to strengthen the wider arenas of professional education and of the global political economy.

Asking these questions led me to a series of interviews with faculty members about how their different fields defined effectiveness, how they viewed the school's effectiveness, and how they viewed their own professional effectiveness. These interviews gave me an opportunity to become much better acquainted with my colleagues than I would otherwise have been and showed me how much commitment there already was within the faculty toward action-oriented courses for students at the school. The interviews also revealed a widespread but not heretofore publicly stated perception of institutional inertia at the school. Different faculty members called this atmosphere "a climate of not doing much," "an organizational inferiority complex," "a negative self-concept about research production," and "a pervasive sense of mediocrity." We clearly needed a transformation of this organizational self-concept if we were going to get anything else of consequence accomplished. But how?

I shared this vulnerable organizational self-perception at an open faculty feedback meeting, and the ensuing public discussion galvanized a number of faculty leaders to realize that pet projects and pet critiques of one another should be put aside and that the school should agree on some new initiatives. After years of failing to vote in any new programs, the faculty approved a major restructuring of the MBA program and five other new initiatives during the following six months. This is one example of how an institutional re-visioning inquiry can, at the same time, shape and support specific strategic initiatives and improve the ongoing operations of an organization.

In the meantime, I had discovered that a key motto of the Jesuit Order is the phrase, "Meditation in Action." This motto marvelously expresses a commitment to simultaneously cultivating wider awareness and effective action, and showed me that the Jesuit character of the university was in no sense irrelevant or a potential impediment, but, rather, a strong support for an MBA program that focused on how to cultivate effective action in oneself and others. This sense of mission—cultivating effective action—aligned a need in American management with a characteristic of a Jesuit university, with a need of our particular school of management, and with a perennial concern of students that their education be more practical. For me, this sense of mission provided a thread of meaning and an intentional focus throughout several long years of effort that might otherwise have appeared chaotic and disheartening.

Chaos did threaten from the outset, and emergencies did occur, as they so often do in managerial settings. These realities required the use of other types of power besides the benign power to gather people together to talk. From the day I entered my new position, I discovered that I had inherited a subordinate who was in such a career crisis that she could perform no work, nor reach a clear decision about what she should do. On the day that I had asked her to present me with a written statement of her intention to do the job or else to resign, she handed me a letter announcing the former. After we shook hands and she left my office, I discovered that she had dropped another letter on the floor which announced her resignation. I spent a sleepless night deciding whether for the good of the office and the school I must unilaterally insist on her leaving (since her announced decision to stay was clearly not a solid one), only to discover on arriving at the office the next morning that she had just had a fight with every other member of the office; whereupon the decision that she resign became mutual.

I remember approaching my first, informal public meeting with students looking forward to introducing myself and learning about them, only to discover a united front demanding that a particular teacher be removed from class in midsemester or that their money be refunded. There is no way, short of proving "moral turpitude," to force a teacher out of his class in midsemester. But a series of very careful and very lucky conversations resulted in the instructor's voluntary withdrawal and replacement by a much more competent faculty member. In each of these cases, a mutual inquiry, fused with a refusal to accept face-saving solutions that protected any participants from accountability, generated a solution.

I remember my shock when I learned that one department at the school refused even to meet with me to begin a conversation about reform of the MBA curriculum, on the grounds that I did not have the authority to force any changes. I had no intention of *forcing* any changes, but that department was so adamant about not altering its priorities (or even examining them) that I did ultimately have to arrange a show of force, using both unilateral and referent power, to get a more mutual and, eventually, transformational conversation started. (Indeed, that department transformed from the worst to the best in the school over the next decade.)

As the preceding stories illustrate, my method for handling emergencies amounted to little more than opening my ears very wide, insisting on the scale of the challenge, and refusing to settle for compromises that did not respond to the challenge. But otherwise, I would listen as carefully as possible for plausible proposals and act as mutually as possible. If unilateral action seemed more and more indicated (as in the case of the department that would not meet with me), I discovered that one key was to be open with whoever seemed to be the antagonist about the factors that were leading me toward unilateral action. This tactic invited the antagonist to challenge my assumptions. If my assumptions were wrong, I was glad to give them up, and the other saw that I could be influenced. At the very least, I had offered the other the respect of a consultation and had eliminated the feeling of being surprised or knifed in the back. Thus I generated some sense of mutuality even if I did ultimately take what the other perceived as unilateral action. It took constant discipline and forbearance on my part to learn this lesson, and though it may sound incidental now, I believe this tactic alone increased my managerial effectiveness more than any other lesson I learned.

This approach led to results as diverse as a $100,000 grant from IBM and an agreement from the university administration to grant faculty who taught in a restructured core MBA program a one-course teaching remission for their work together as a team. Starting off with the use of vulnerable, mutually transforming power, but accepting all the types of power as conditionally appropriate, paid significant dividends. For example, there was no question in my mind that the *reciprocal reference power* represented by the consent and support of IBM and the university administration for this new initiative was undoubtedly more meaningful and persuasive to many members of the faculty at the outset than the internal *logistical power* of the innovation itself, or its *visionary power* in terms of meeting the larger challenges facing American management. How could we gradually generate greater commitment to the innovation by the faculty?

An Action Inquiry Team to Champion Action Inquiry

To create a strong and coherent restructuring of the MBA program, I sought the commitment of highly credible members of each department to form a core team that would plan, seek support for, and initially implement the new program. The primary actor was to be a team, acting in a new way. Because there was widespread defeatism about the likelihood that the faculty would approve *any* proposal, I wanted to create the most competent, committed, and credible team possible. This team would not merely argue for, but, more important, model a new way of doing business together. In my consulting engagements with business clients in recent years, I have found that creating a team that enacts what it advocates is the most attractive and persuasive way to generate ongoing organizational action inquiry.

Through the revealing minutes we sent to the rest of the faculty, the core team meetings quickly became unprecedented demonstrations of mutual empowerment and mutual critique. We adopted a process of teaching one another and then receiving critiques of our teaching. The minutes of our second meeting, for example, included the following critique of my teaching effort:

In critiquing Torbert's teaching, the other members mentioned: being overwhelmed by the background materials; confused by lack of discussion of them; too much lecture; insufficient concrete examples; rushed; no use of board, no summary; event more an example of administrative leadership than teaching.

So, although I had not set out to achieve this result when I taught that day, I ended up demonstrating the public vulnerability I believed a leader must show if he or she is to earn the transforming power to influence others in fundamental ways.

There is no doubt in my mind that the critical factor in securing approval of our final proposals was the fact that a highly credible faculty core team that believed in what it was doing interacted continuously with colleagues for the months prior to the vote, and that those colleagues had had abundant opportunity to influence the proposals (indeed, a preliminary design was rejected). Thus, the faculty team and I had exercised transforming power in a way that transformed both our proposal and the school. Also important to the result were many exercises of logistical power, such as the deletion of potentially controversial administrative issues from the proposals presented to the faculty. Thus, the team's blending of different types of power—its exercise of *transforming power,* primarily, of *logistical power,* secondarily, and, finally, of *referent power* (implicit in its members' preexisting credibility)—generated the successful outcome.

The Stock Market as Action Inquiry

Now let us turn briefly to a much larger organizing activity—stock markets. We will explore to what degree they represent a real-time, decentralized third-person action inquiry process.

How does the stock market reflect the four territories of organizing experience: mission re-visioning, strategizing, performing, and assessing? We can immediately grasp that the minute-by-minute changes in stock prices represent the aggregate assessment, by all stockholders who are buying or selling particular stocks at that time, of the effects of all current business and political actions of which they are aware. Most lay investors, as well as many professional investment advisors, focus the research that guides their choices of when to buy or sell what stock primarily or only on the *assessing* territory of experience. They base their decisions on today's headlines, yesterday's price changes, or companies' most recent quarterly results. Also, their research is often not disciplined, cumulative, or self-referential (i.e., they don't look at how they may improve their success by changes in themselves). However, disciplined, cumulative, self-referential action inquiry in the *performing, strategizing,* and *mission re-visioning* territories of experience is possible in relation to stock buying and selling decisions.

In the performing territory, for example, one can adopt as a self-referential performance discipline the rule: "Sell any stock that loses 8 percent of its value." In the strategizing territory, investment professionals can and do offer their clients choices among different investing strategies (i.e., large cap growth, mid cap value, bonds, etc.). And in the mission re-visioning territory, socially responsible investing (SRI) has since the early 1980s been offering an alternative vision of the very purpose of investing. The aim in SRI is not just to maximize the investor's financial bottom line by choosing relatively reliably high-profit-margin companies, but also to optimize a triple bottom line that includes social equity and environmental sustainability as well as financial profit by investing in companies that give a broader attention to all three bottom lines (Waddock 2001).

Economists, finance professors, and Wall Street investment advisors were almost universally dismissive of SRI during the 1980s and early 1990s because it violated neoclassical economic theory and financial portfolio theory. According to short-term, individualistic, rational choice criteria, narrowing one's investment portfolio on criteria other than shareholder wealth maximization could not help but reduce one's financial return. Very few economists and finance professionals could seriously imagine a double-loop change in such theories. (The 1998 Nobel laureate in economics, Amartya Sen [1982, 1987], is one of those few [Klamer 1989].)

So, imagine the surprise of the professional academics and advisors as a majority of SRI firms began offering clients *better* financial returns than the average conventional investment advisor during the late 1990s (Becker 1999; Torbert 1999). Major investment houses suddenly began advertising so-called social funds as quickly as they could mount any facsimile of one. Moreover, between 1999 and the end of 2001, socially screened investment portfolios under professional management grew 1.5 times as fast as all investment assets, topping $3 trillion and accounting for more than 10 percent of all invested funds for the first time (Social Investment Forum 2001).

What has happened? The SRI movement has apparently managed to conceptualize variables that are not directly financial, but that nevertheless are associated with longer-term positive financial results. We can see how this can be so at this time in history in two different but related ways. First, because human economic activity is today measurably depleting our natural resources, the cost of "business as usual" is increasing. Therefore, companies that take the lead in discovering socially and environmentally friendly strategies can potentially reduce their costs. Second, marketing researchers have identified a growing market segment of "green," "cultural creatives" who are relatively wealthy. Therefore, companies that take the lead in discovering socially and environmentally friendly strategies appeal to a growing consumer segment.

Put differently, the socially responsible investing movement is practicing a form of single-, double-, and triple-loop action inquiry. At the triple-loop level, it has articulated a newly re-visioned mission for investing. At the double-loop level, it has generated new strategies for investment advisors, such as shareholder initiatives and dialogues with companies that offer the companies the opportunity to change various policies that will make them more attractive to the growing segment of investors who make decisions in part on such criteria.

Another ongoing double-loop change generated by the SRI movement is the development of new standards and measures to assess companies' economic, social, and environmental performance. In the year 2000, the UN Foundation offered $3 million in support of the Global Reporting Initiative's commitment to develop new global accounting standards and measures (Bavaria 2000).

It is, however, important to conclude this discussion of the stock market and of socially responsible investing with words of caution. There is no silver bullet answer for making money in the stock market. Because SRI funds tend to eschew big oil companies, they also tend toward high-tech companies. Thus, since 2001 the combination of war and recession has reduced SRI financial returns. Moreover, the entire SRI movement is still in its infancy, including all its methods of assessment (even straight financial accountants have been having a good deal of trouble cranking out the true numbers in the late 1990s and early 2000s!). Therefore, there is appropriate continuing controversy about all the claims made in these paragraphs on behalf of socially responsible investing, and the reader is invited to inquire further (e.g., Entine 2003; Waddock 2003).

In the meantime, the Socially Responsible Investing initiative serves as a useful example of how stock market investing activities can transform. From implicit action inquiries focused primarily on short-term assessment data, we are discovering through SRI that investment decision-making can evolve toward increasingly explicit action inquiries that begin to identify firms that proactively seek to optimize a triple bottom line.

*   *   *

The interlude following this chapter offers summaries and exercises related to the first three chapters. Then, starting with Chapter 4, the next section takes us on a lifetime journey that each of us can potentially take toward the capacity for continually digesting and acting on the basis of single-, double-, and triple-loop feedback.

Action Inquiry: The Idea and the Experience

Summaries and Exercises for Chapters 1, 2, and 3

Chapter 1—Fundamentals of Action Inquiry

In Chapter 1, we introduced action inquiry at the personal scale as a kind of super-vision in the midst of action that simultaneously learns about the developing situation, accomplishes whatever tasks appear to have priority, and, if necessary, invites a re-visioning of the task (and potentially of your own self, as in Steve Thompson's case after he began reexamining his experiences in that North Sea storm).

We focused on how action inquiry begins within ourselves, as an effort to become aware of four territories of experience. The story of Steve Thompson in the North Sea illustrated how, in order to exercise transforming leadership in an emergency, we need to cultivate a kind of inquiry in action that allows us to receive and digest three types of feedback:

1. *Single-loop feedback* about results in the outside world that require us to change *behaviors* if we wish to achieve our goal more efficiently.
2. *Double-loop feedback* about what *goals and strategies* we may need to change to become more effective.
3. *Triple-loop feedback* about what *quality of ongoing awareness* we need to cultivate in order to embrace the four territories of experience and test the legitimacy and integrity of our actions.

Through single-, double-, and triple-loop feedback, action inquiry can help us increase the efficiency, the effectiveness, and the legitimacy of our actions, while simultaneously generating an inner sense of integrity. When our actions generate outer efficacy and inner integrity simultaneously, they become timely in a profound way.

But many of you may be wondering how you can begin to exercise your attention differently so that you are actually doing action inquiry, rather than just thinking about it. Here are some personal practices that you can try right away or that you can return to whenever you want to begin making a commitment to personally practicing action inquiry.

Practice Noticing

The attention practice we suggest here concerns the first essential: noticing. As we said earlier, the first step is to begin to recognize how limited our ordinary attention and awareness is, because many things go on in us that escape our awareness. One person exclaimed, on learning about this kind of awareness, "I feel as though I've lived my whole life in a fog!" Some of us have been surprised to discover how many mental, emotional, and physical activities go on inside us that we didn't even know about until we began truly noticing them.

- At home and at work (to the extent possible), set your watch alarm or cell phone to go off every 60 minutes. When it does this, take 30 seconds to notice how you felt mentally, emotionally, and physically at the moment the alarm went off (including any irritation *that* the alarm went off!).
- As you transition from one activity to another, bring the transition into your awareness by noticing how you feel about ending the previous activity and beginning the next one.
- Check in with yourself daily at each meal time and bedtime to identify the moment that was the most satisfying to you since the last check-in, and pause to articulate to yourself what made it the most satisfying. In the same way, identify the moment that was the least satisfying to you since the last check-in, and what made it so. Recall if you were aware of these reactions as the moments actually occurred.
- Develop the habit of noticing how you are feeling after each meaningful interaction you have with another person or persons.

We suggest that you begin by taking on one of these exercises at a time for a week, then trying the next for a week. Initially, you are likely to go whole days without noticing that you have altogether forgotten your commitment to this noticing. That'll tell you something about the fog you're living in! Later, as these practices take a place in your life, you'll experience more and more spontaneous noticings. You may want to copy the list of noticing exercises and put it where you'll see it each day.

By the way, there are no judgments involved in noticing, because it is a neutral activity (or to reverse it: the judgment you may often find yourself making at first, after a moment of noticing, is not part of the noticing [but noticing the judging is, etc.]). Enjoy the discovery process!

Chapter 2—Action Inquiry as a Manner of Speaking

In Chapter 2, we examined how to listen more deeply, both to other people's speaking and to our own, noticing the process of unilateral or mutual influence. We suggested that meaning is either *constructed* or *fragmented*. Meaning is constructed through the weaving together of four "parts of speech"—framing, advocating, illustrating, and inquiring—as Anthony illustrated in his effective intervention in the human resources consulting firm. Meaning is fragmented through the mindless aggregation of advocacies and counteradvocacies.

Action inquiry speech, we said, is itself constructed from our awareness of the four territories of experience. *Framing* focuses our *attention*. *Advocating* focuses our *thinking*. *Illustrating* bases itself on our *sensing* of our own and others' performances. And *inquiring* is properly guided by our *concern for others'* experiencing and for the *impact of our actions* in the outside world beyond us.

Practice Naming

Now you are in a position to practice attending to the four territories of experience and weaving the four parts of speech into your conversations. One liberating discipline for doing so is to meet monthly with a learning team of colleagues or friends who will support your efforts to put the ideas of this book into practice by examining one another's specific cases (like Dana's), and by attending to and intervening in the process of each team meeting.

In particular, we suggest you practice noticing how you advocate what you are feeling in a conversation. In discussing advocacy in Chapter 2, we stressed that the most difficult type of advocacy for most people to use effectively is one that includes how we feel. As you practice the noticing exercises just suggested, you may find that it is hard to even name some feelings for yourself, much less to do so publicly. One person found that it took two days to find words to describe to herself what she was feeling about a complex situation. To the extent we become adept at both noticing and naming feelings that pass through us, we will become more adept at effective advocacy that appropriately uses feelings. As with the practice of noticing, identifying our feelings is a neutral, nonjudgmental process of discovery. Integrate these naming exercises into your daily practice of noticing what goes on inside you.

- Use the following formula to help you get clarity and name precisely for yourself what feelings you become aware of during your noticing exercises, and as often as feelings arise in you.

     "I feel (felt) __(1)__ when __(2)__ because __(3)__."

  1. What word *best* describes the feeling?
  2. What action, incident, or experience evoked the feeling?
  3. What is it that is important to you that the event affects?

- There are many different ways to convey how you feel. For example, if a colleague takes an initiative that the two of you had agreed beforehand you would take together, and you feel angry about it, you may express that anger in any of the following seven ways (as well as many others):

  1. Subject your colleague to the silent treatment.
  2. "Why did you do that? You broke our agreement. I'm not working with you anymore."
  3. With a lilting, slightly comic tone: "That was quite an initiative you took, making that decision that way."
  4. "I feel like you should have waited for me."
  5. "You make me mad when you charge ahead on your own like that."
  6. "I feel angry because you made that decision without waiting for me."

7. "I have some anger about your making an independent decision, because we agreed we'd wait for this information to get here first. I'd like to hear what feelings led you to act as you did and how you feel upon hearing my perspective."

It may very well not be clear just what kind of differences in response we are likely to get to these seven different ways of expressing our anger, but it certainly seems likely that there will be differences. Go back over the past week, starting with today, then yesterday, and so on. What are the various ways you hear yourself expressing feelings?

These directions are offered briefly, but the practice of analyzing your feelings and how you express them deserves a real commitment of time, a good seat, and a journal to record your reflections at intervals. Dedicating time and energy to do so is itself a significant developmental stretch for most of us. Good wishes.

Chapter 3—Action Inquiry as a Way of Organizing

Chapter 3 introduced action inquiry as a way of organizing that seeks to achieve increasing clarity and congruity across the domains of mission, strategy, performance, and outcomes. We used three examples of organizing at very different scales of size, ranging from Elizabeth and her two partners starting a service design company, to an established graduate school of management of some 700 students, faculty, and staff transforming itself, to the gradual development of socially responsible investing as an approach to the stock market over a 20-year period.

We highlighted how multiple tasks, time horizons, and types of power interweave with one another. We also showed in some detail how mindfulness and mutuality in the midst of leadership action helps generate the single-loop, double-loop, and triple-loop learning necessary for timely and transforming action, as well as for ongoing integrity among vision, theory, practice, and effects.

Practice Action Inquiry

At this point, depending on your personal learning style, immediate needs, or other factors, you may or may not have tried practicing action inquiry yet. This practice section is an opportunity to reflect on your relationship with the third-person organization that is this book and to possibly make a single- or double-loop change in your relationship to it. Obviously, we don't have the power to coerce you to change. Nor do we assume that any change is called for. So, the decision you make after reflecting is all yours.

Whether or not you have yet engaged in the noticing and naming practices we have suggested prior to this point, we invite you now to use the following action inquiry process to critically reflect on your personal experience thus far as you read this book. Feel free to formulate your own wording for each "part of speech" as it applies to the four territories of your experience.

Action Inquiry

Subject of inquiry: Encountering the first two suggested practices in this Interlude.

Initial framing: When I encountered the suggested practices, the intention I formed with regard to them was _____

_____.

Advocacy: I decided the best response for me at this time was for me to _____ because _____.

Illustrating: Since then, what I've done is _____.

Inquiring/listening: Are the results of my decision what I expected them to be? Yes ____ No ____

Why or why not? _____

_____.

Am I satisfied with my plan and the way I followed through with it? Yes ____ No ____

After this inquiry do I now want to change my stance toward these practices? Yes ____ No ____

[Potentially] Reframing: At this point, what I want to do with these practices is _____ because

_____.

In conclusion, this process of reflection is leading me to make:

1. No change
2. A change based on single-loop learning
3. A change based on double-loop learning
4. A change based on triple-loop learning in my engagement with this book

Now that we have sketched out in the first three chapters a generic sense of how first-person, second-person, and third-person action inquiry can be practiced, we will start over again. In the next section, we ask how persons can evolve toward this path of timely, transforming action inquiry.

PART TWO

Transforming Leadership

FOUR

The *Opportunist* and the *Diplomat:* Action-logics you probably resort to, but don't want to be circumscribed by

So far in this book, in Chapters 1 and 2 we described examples of action inquiry that beginners may try in relation to particular incidents at particular moments of time (and we are all in some sense beginners in each new situation!). We illustrated with Steve Thompson's and Anthony's action inquiries. Then, in Chapter 3, we introduced a far more complex sense of action inquiry that embraces a highly nuanced sense of how time horizons and types of power may interweave to help persons, groups, and organizations transform. Obviously, there is a huge gap between the elementary action inquiry of asking a question at a useful moment, and the advanced action inquiry of crafting the entire mission, strategy, performance, and assessment processes of the socially responsible investing movement over 20 years.

The Overall Developmental Process

Now, in the next several chapters, we wish to illustrate how challenging it is to transform ourselves and help others to transform toward an advanced capacity for action inquiry. There is no step-by-step procedure to follow that will accomplish this mission in a month or a year. Self-transformation toward fully and regularly enacting the values of integrity, mutuality, and sustainability is a long, lifetime path that most of us follow as we grow toward adulthood, but that very few continue traveling intentionally once we become adults. Each major step along this path can be described as developing a new *action-logic:* an overall strategy that so thoroughly informs our experience that we cannot see it.

We cannot see our own action-logics, especially not at the moment of action when we most need to see them, unless and until we ourselves reach the point along the developmental path where we recognize that the different action-logics that different people hold are among the chief causes of conflict at work and at home. Only then do some of us become dedicated to appreciating our own and others' action-logics, especially in the midst of action. Only then can we invite ourselves and our partners to notice, to name, and to transform our action-logics, at moments when they may be inhibiting good working together, good loving together, or good inquiring together.

Over the next four chapters, we will illustrate each of the central and usually implicit, unquestioned action-logics by which each of us is usually bounded during any particular period of our lives. We will also discuss how we can help others transform beyond a given current action-logic. It is this implicit, unexamined action-logic that most severely limits our effectiveness. We will make the greatest leaps in quality improvement in our own actions when we become aware of these limits and begin to experiment beyond them. If we can become aware of these overarching action-logics in others and in ourselves, we can reduce unintentional conflict and misunderstanding. Indeed, we can even help ourselves and others transform beyond the limits of our present assumptions.

In this and the next chapter, we will describe four different and successive developmental action-logics: the *Opportunist,* the *Diplomat,* the *Expert,* and the *Achiever.* Any one of these four may characterize your overall approach to managing. Developmental theory and research (see the References for citations) offer strong cross-cultural support for the notion that if we transform at all, we progress sequentially through these four action-logics and then on to other action-logics described in later chapters.

We will describe and illustrate each of the first four action-logics in more detail in the following pages, but here we will orient you to them in brief:

1) The *Opportunist* treats the physical or outside world territory of experience as the primary reality and concentrates on gaining control of things there. This action-logic views unilateral power as the only effectual type of power and works within a very short time horizon of discretion,

from hours to days, grasping opportunities and firefighting emergencies to the virtual exclusion of the other three leadership tasks and time horizons. The ***Opportunist*** views timely action as occurring when "I win."

2) The ***Diplomat*** treats his or her own sensed performance territory of experience as what really matters and concentrates on gaining self-control in order to act effectively. To do so, he or she imitates organizational routines and the behavior patterns of high-status group members. This action-logic experiences referent power and the current norms that such power generates most strongly. This action-logic generally focuses on routine tasks and works within a one-week to three-month time horizon. For the ***Diplomat***, timely action occurs when "I" am "on time" for work, for meetings, and in terms of completing routine tasks.

3) The ***Expert*** treats the strategic territory of experience as the primary reality and concentrates on mastering his or her cognitive grasp of one or more particular disciplines (e.g., accounting, engineering, marketing, etc.). This action-logic treats logistical power as most meaningful and most happily works in a six-month to one-year time horizon to accomplish particular projects. For the ***Expert***, timely action occurs when "I" accomplish tasks as efficiently as possible.

4) After the strategy, performance, and outcome territories of experience have been mastered one by one (usually between the ages of six and twenty-six), most people never again transform their action-logic. But a solid minority (about 40 percent) of highly educated, professional adults do transform once more, to the ***Achiever*** action-logic, which works within a one- to three-year time horizon, juggling the shorter time horizons creatively, treating the interplay among planning, performing, and assessing the outcomes as what is really real. The ***Achiever*** concentrates on making incremental, single-loop changes in behavior to eventually reach the planned results. Timely action occurs when "I" successfully juggle the need for occasional immediate wins, observance of agreed-on deadlines, efficient work, and effective outcomes as judged by the market or other constituency.

Developing a hypothesis about your own predominant action-logic and those of your colleagues can help you to relate more effectively to them. It can also challenge you and them to experiment with thinking and acting outside your and their current "box." Here it is important to understand that we are never altogether locked into one implicit way of framing reality. In fact, "locked in" is not the right metaphor for our relationship to our predominant action-logic.

First, each successive action-logic we describe includes all the possibilities of the prior action-logics and a whole new set of alternatives as well. Thus, at each later action-logic we have more degrees of freedom about which action-logic we use when.

Second, the more we come to appreciate our own and others' ongoing experience as evidencing different action-logics, the more we will notice times, usually brief and not yet sustainable, when we are actually experiencing ourselves and the situation in terms of a later action-logic. We will also notice more and more times when we can intervene to help the situation transform toward a later action-logic. These real-life action inquiries have the added benefit of helping us ourselves transform to a later action-logic.

Third, in addition to our primary action-logic, we each tend to have one particular secondary or fallback action-logic to which we retreat when we are under duress—when we feel insecure, ill, angry, or exhausted or when visiting our parents in our childhood home. This fallback position is well worth knowing and remembering at the moment of action in order to avert ineffectiveness and bad feeling. For example, one of the authors has come to realize that he slips into the *Diplomat* action-logic when tired and tends to give away the store, so to speak, to avoid conflict, rather than hold his position. Learning to ask for a night to sleep on the question before making a decision may seem like a simple matter to you, but for this writer it took years of struggle and feels like a major victory.

Fourth, and finally, if we increasingly exercise our attention through action inquiry, we can evolve beyond these four action-logics. Whereas these four action-logics more or less have *us,* the later action-logics are ones that, more or less, we *have*—because the later action-logics are increasingly self-aware and self-transforming. By practicing action inquiry more and more and recognizing that we are operating within changing action-logics, we increase our freedom to choose which action-logic is currently timely.

Diagnosing Our Own and Other's Developmental Action-Logics

But so far these first four developmental action-logics are mere abstractions to you. We think you are most likely to enjoy learning about them by listening in as business colleagues tell stories about diagnosing their colleagues and themselves. Of course, as you read these stories, you can also begin diagnosing members of your own work group or colleagues from other departments with whom you interact most often in order to get your work done (or different members of your family may come to mind). By the time you reach the end of this chapter, you may have an initial diagnosis of your own current developmental action-logic as well.

We suggest that you take three separate pages of your journal and at the top of each list the three work associates (peers, superiors, or subordinates) with whom you would most benefit from a more effective working relationship. Write your own name at the top of a fourth page. As you read this and the following chapters, note which characteristics from each action-logic you associate with each person, with a few words about a particular occasion when he or she displayed that characteristic. You should find that each person displays one particular action-logic predominantly. Although that person will occasionally act in ways characteristic of the earlier action-logics, he or she will rarely show signs of the next action-logic (unless he or she happens to be in developmental transition toward that action-logic) and will almost never exhibit characteristics of the action-logic two beyond. But remember, you are not making a scientific judgment here, only an estimate. And the point of your estimate is not to be right or to pigeonhole yourself or your colleagues. Rather, the point is to test whether your hypotheses about your own or another person's developmental action-logic lead you to choose more effective actions as you work with them. Through your ongoing action inquiry with them, you will gradually become more confident about your diagnostic ability.

Our storytellers are managers or professionals who are learning about action-logics and developmental theory at the time they write their diagnostic stories.

Charles, an *Opportunist*

Kathy, an independent contributor at a large firm gradually diagnoses one difficult co-worker, Charles, as an *Opportunist*:

Charles and I are both at the same job grade, although he has been with the company longer, and I have been on the current team longer. When he first joined our team, he would stop by my desk three or four times per day to ask for work-related advice and design tips. Initially, I was very flattered and found his asking for my technical expertise very ego-satisfying and a boost to my self-confidence.

After weeks and months of more frequent and lengthy stops at my desk, I felt as if he was deliberately manipulating my time. I would work through lunch or stay late to make up for the lost time, initially resenting him, then funneling my resentment towards a system that promotes people on seniority. I now realize that I was externalizing blame rather than recognizing my own cowardice and inability to act.

I did try some experimentation, picking up the phone when I saw him heading in my direction, or asking to see the research he had done and where he was stuck before offering help. When he sensed that I was going to make him work a little, he began asking someone else on the team for help.

Some typical comments made about him by his colleagues include, "I have gotten to the point where I cannot even say 'Good morning' to Charles for fear of hearing the intimate details of his personal life for close to half an hour" and "Kathy, I don't know how you put up with sitting next to him. I sit three desks away from him and I still find it difficult to tune him out."

With the benefit of hindsight, I now think that my spending time trying to help him did him more harm than good because he has since been transferred to another team and has been denied a promotion. He has confided to me that his manager told him he should concentrate more on his work and less on seeking help and on his personal and social life.

From this story, what assumptions do you infer Charles is making about himself and others and about how to relate to them? What does he assume about how to be effective? How does he assume an ethical person should behave? What other patterns do you see in Charles based on Kathy's description? (You may also want to ask yourself whether Kathy's description provides any clues about what Kathy's predominant action-logic currently is.)

Usually, people pass through the *Opportunist* action-logic between about the ages of six and twelve. Through bike riding, knitting, puzzle-solving, and a thousand other activities, they are learning to gain control of the outside world territory of experience. But a certain percentage of adults continue to hold this perspective. They try to make things and people work by manipulating them unilaterally or by making the most advantageous trades possible. Charles flattered Kathy by asking her for advice in exchange for her time and technical help. The ***Opportunist*** manager is sometimes a tactful manipulator, who may even use courtesy as a ploy, but who still views the world as a one-against-all jungle fight. Charles's approach to the jungle is to go to the person who will give him the most for the least cost. He drops that person as soon as the exchange proves unprofitable in the short run. He gives little regard to what others may think of him or to the damage his immediate actions may be doing to longer-term relationships, until something he wants (such as a promotion) is denied him.

As a basis for a management style, the ***Opportunist*** action-logic has bright sides, especially in the short-term: it can cut to the chase in an emergency, it can open unstructured sales territories, and it can courageously embark on paths to adventure. But in the longer term, the dark side tends to show up. The deception and manipulation it will use to gain short-term wins will have longer-term costs in terms of others' low trust. Responsibility for error or misjudgment is a short-term cost that the ***Opportunist*** will typically avoid by not accepting responsibility and externalizing blame.

This action-logic appreciates only the financial and unilateral power aspects of organizations, not the structural and spiritual aspects. It does not value helping managers and organizations to transform and develop. For the ***Opportunist*** manager, it is axiomatic that one must "play one's cards close to the vest," since others are assumed to be doing the same. The Hobbesian equation "might makes right" holds, and the Golden Rule is recast as "He Who Has the Gold Rules." Although in the short run this approach will seem to give him or her an unfair advantage over others, the ***Opportunist's*** career development opportunities are, in fact, severely limited by this action-logic. Whereas managers at later stages can *choose* to act opportunistically on particular occasions, a manager who is bounded by the ***Opportunist*** action-logic has no choice but to act opportunistically on every occasion. Studies of managers in different industries have found that less than 5 percent hold this action-logic (Torbert 1991).

Think of occasions when the three colleagues that you are wondering about, or you yourself, exhibit ***Opportunist*** qualities. To what degree is this a fallback action-logic for you? Or, are you so appalled by this action-logic that you have not learned how to manage someone who exhibits it?

Phil, a *Diplomat*

A supervisor in the parts department of a large manufacturing company gives the following description of his superior:

> Phil, my boss, seems incapable of making decisions on his own and he has even intimated to me that he feels he is a pawn or figurehead and not really in control of his areas of responsibility. Phil is very aware of protocol and observes it meticulously. He is risk averse. He avoids conflict at any expense. I think this is the major reason he feels like a pawn. He has given up so many battles that the idea of fighting doesn't even occur to him.
>
> It is commonly held among my peers (Phil's other subordinates) that he is ineffective in his position. He seems to accept, without resistance, anything that comes from higher up in the chain of command, and this often affects our department in a negative way. Here's an example: we (the parts department) are at the point of entry to the Facilities operational area, which employs over 400 people. I am the first supervisor that newcomers are exposed to. In the recent past we have had numerous hires whom I never got to meet until the night they started. Some of these people are "political appointees." They have been recommended by vice presidents or members of the board of directors. I realize the world is imperfect and that favoritism occurs, but I believe I should be involved in interviewing all incoming employees. I further believe that Phil could at least object to the more blatant cases where political appointees are given regular full-time status (which entitles them to full benefits) while we have people who have been here for months as temps waiting to move up to full time.
>
> Phil has shared with me on occasion things he would like to see happen in our department or has agreed with me about some recommendation I have made to him. But all too often, those discussions end with, "That will never fly," or "The higher managers won't like that." He will then try to convince me not to make waves and to accept "the way things work here." I have no wish to make waves, but I hope I will never become desensitized to the point where I will just accept things that seem so wrong.

What do Phil's guiding assumptions appear to be? The **Diplomat** action-logic focuses attention on controlling one's own social performance and making sure it meets the approval of some or all of one's significant reference groups (family, work team, etc.). Many persons transition to the *Diplomat* action-logic in their early teenage years, and a larger proportion of adult managers are found at this action-logic than at the *Opportunist* action-logic. Studies of managers have found that 24 percent of the first-line supervisors, 9 percent of the junior managers, and less than 5 percent of senior managers hold the *Diplomat* action-logic (Torbert 1991).

For the *Diplomat*, the values of significant others are the highest good. Some thing or some action has value if it is fashionable, if it sells, if it influences others, or if high-status persons treat it as valuable. Behavioral skills—the right moves or words at the right times—are seen as critical for gaining membership, meeting others' standards, and observing the correct protocol.

Like the *Opportunist* action-logic, the *Diplomat* action-logic has its bright side and its dark side. In a positive vein, the *Diplomat* manager can provide qualities of reliability, loyalty, and good will that raise morale and function as organizational glue. And sometimes calling someone a "diplomat" implies that he or she has the exquisite sense of tact that permits both honesty and agreement about the most difficult issues, enhancing the self-esteem and dignity of all parties in the process. But at other times, the implication of calling someone a "diplomat" is that he or she avoids and smooths over all potential conflict, masking both true feelings and objective data in an effort to maintain harmony at all costs. Thus the *Diplomat* can become alienated from associates who, like Phil's subordinate, are put off by the *Diplomat's* dismissal of their concerns and suggestions. (It is a harrowing irony that the *Diplomat* often cannot quite see or comprehend that he or she sometimes creates conflict by the very act of trying to avoid it.)

Diplomat managers do not seek out negative feedback about themselves. Quite to the contrary, they attempt to deflect it. They equate negative feedback with loss of face and loss of status. To tell them that it is constructive because it can help them achieve their goals does not make sense to them. No goal is as compelling to them as the implicit rule against losing face. This aversion to feedback helps explain why the *Diplomat*, like the *Opportunist*, becomes relatively more locked into his or her action-logic in adulthood, as well as more blind to the possibility of other ways of behaving, than persons at later action-logics.

The *Diplomat* manager is as unable to criticize others and to question group norms as he or she is to engage in self-criticism. We see this in Phil, who will not try to correct the apparently unjust handling of so-called political appointees. An organization led by a *Diplomat* will be inhibited from adapting to changing competitive realities or to discovering and creating new strategic opportunities. Subordinates will feel a sense of stagnation and disillusion. They are likely to lower their aims and effort and may even falsify information such as sales or production records in order to "look good."

Challenging and Supporting *Opportunists* and *Diplomats* to Transform

Let us ask, by way of concluding this chapter, what can a leader or coach do to help persons at these two action-logics to become increasingly competent leaders who are increasingly useful to their organization? Refer to Table 4-1 for a summary of the characteristics of the *Opportunist* and the *Diplomat*.

In dealing with *Opportunist* managers and helping them develop, an organization must develop clear, well-defined, relatively just systems both for doing the work in the first place and for evaluating managers' performance. (If these are not in fact clear, the *Opportunist* will likely be the first to notice and try to take advantage.) In particular, the *Op-*

Table 4-1 Managerial Style Characteristics Associated with *Opportunist* and *Diplomat* Developmental Action-Logics

Opportunist	Short time horizon; focus on concrete things; often good in physical emergencies; deceptive; manipulative; views rules as loss of freedom; views luck as central; rejects critical feedback; externalizes blame; distrustful; stereotypes; fragile self-control; hostile humor; flouts unilateral power, sexuality; treats "what can get away with" as legitimate; punishment = "eye for an eye"; positive ethic = even trade; timely action = "I win"
Diplomat	Committed to routines; observes protocol; avoids inner and outer conflict; conforms; works to group standard; seeks membership, status; often speaks in favorite phrases, clichés, prefabricated jokes; face-saving essential; loyalty to immediate group; feels shame if violates norm; sin = hurting others; punishment = disapproval; positive ethic = nice, cooperative; timely action = "I'm on time"

portunist's annual goals and associated concrete incentives (raise, bonus, promotion) must be tightly linked to performance, and the performance goals must include social process goals (how colleagues are to be treated, etc.), since the *Opportunist* has not yet internalized such norms.

The *Opportunist's* manager must not blanch at the possibility of imposing real unilateral penalties for poor performance, including termination, since the *Opportunist* tends to disregard or actively reject verbal negative feedback. Using unilateral strategies to influence someone else to reduce his or her unilateral, nonresponsive behavior is the action inquiry strategy of choice when experience shows that more subtle forms of power (reference power, logistical power, and so on) aren't communicating. Moreover, prior to the first overt move, the manager is well advised to align colleagues with the strategy, for the *Opportunist* often adopts a "take no hostages" attitude about conflict, trying to face the disciplinarian down by quickly recruiting bystanders to his or her banner on the basis of a carefully designed version of events.

This overall strategy may sound heartless and nondevelopmental. However, having experienced how much havoc the *Opportunist* action-logic can wreak within an organization, how well-sealed this action-logic is from transformation, and what has worked in the few instances we are aware of when further development has been elicited, we offer it as the most loving way we know. It may be helpful to think of it as the kind of so-called tough love often recommended for difficult teenagers, alcoholics, or drug addicts.

Organizations interested in creating environments that challenge *Diplomats* to continue developing will do well to structure management development activities around real-time projects in small teams, providing regular practice in specific skills such as *framing, advocating, illustrating,* and *inquiring. Diplomats* feel more at home in small work groups than in formal management meetings. They will reveal more of themselves and form friendships through which they can later potentially be influenced to accept the vulnerability necessary for transformation. Every member in such a team can hold different and rotating leadership responsibilities, with regular peer assessment and feedback guided by a team mentor who does not hold direct authority over the team. This approach may initially sound like an unrealistically large investment by the organization. But such arrangements also lead to reliable high performance in autonomous or semiautonomous project groups, so the investment has multiple payoffs.

Because each of the early action-logics focuses primarily and explicitly on only one of the four territories of social experience, real tensions inevitably arise in project teams with multiple leaders, such as those suggested above. The *Diplomat's* skills in avoiding conflict are sure to be exceeded, if not by the tangible, physical specifics, then certainly by the conflicting action-logics of the participants. This situation can become a transformational experience for the *Diplomat,* if he or she perceives high-status members of the organization as supportive of personal experimentation and transformation, and if he or she is receiving week-by-week assessment feedback and guidance from a team mentor.

Practice Noticing Patterns

As you continue through this book, you will gradually discern which action-logic seems to be primary at this time in your life (perhaps inviting others to help you). We think it is important to emphasize a dynamic we pointed out in this chapter, that we each tend to have a particular fall-back action-logic we act out of when we are under duress. These tend to be unconscious patterns. Whether or not you come to diagnose your current primary action-logic as *Opportunist* or *Diplomat,* it is worth examining the following exercises as opportunities to transform ineffective actions.

- Practice noticing if you have a habit or a pattern of feeling rushed to move into action or speech *opportunistically.*

  1. Start with just noticing if you make rushed or impulsive actions.
  2. Then, notice what feelings accompany such impulses, using the formula we provided earlier.
  3. Then start paying attention to the situations that evoke such impulsive responses in you. When you do the check-ins, begin to inquire of yourself, "What seems to be 'at risk' for me at those times I want to rush in?"
  4. Then start paying attention to the chain of events immediately following any of your "rushing-in" behaviors. Begin to inquire of yourself, "What is the worst that could happen if I put myself 'on pause' next time?" Imagine a chain of events that might follow such a pause.

5. When you have exercised this self-awareness for a while, you will be able to choose when to pause, and timely action inquiry will help you decide a strategy, instead of an unconscious strategy deciding itself for you.

• Practice noticing if you have a habit or a pattern of "stuffing it" (disregarding your own feelings) *diplomatically* in reaction to external events that affect you, especially if they represent possible conflicts between what you and others want or do.

1. When you do your daily check-ins and identify unsatisfying moments you have had, explore your experience for moments you may have "stuffed it."
2. Review the event and identify what you did or said immediately before the other person(s)' unwelcome behavior. What were you actually hoping for instead? How would you have felt if you got what you wanted?
3. What feeling did you "stuff" on getting the response you didn't want? Use the formula we provided earlier if it helps name the feeling.
4. Next, try to notice *when* something affects you in a way you do not welcome. *Beware:* These reactions can go underground so quickly we don't know they are happening. Be vigilant!
5. Our *diplomacy* can be a mask for fear, hurt, or anger we do not healthily express at the time it is aroused. We first need practice unmasking the feelings *to ourselves.* Privately practice the formula for naming feelings each time you do your check-ins, and every time you notice yourself playing the diplomat.
6. When you have exercised this self-awareness for a while, you will be able to choose when and how to voice your reactions to external events, and timely action inquiry will help you decide on a strategy, instead of an unconscious strategy deciding itself for you.

Let us turn next to an examination of the two action-logics where the majority of managers and professionals are found: the *Expert* and *Achiever* action-logics.

FIVE

The *Expert* and the *Achiever:* The most common managerial action-logics

The *Opportunist* and *Diplomat* developmental action-logics are in some ways pre-managerial action-logics. For one thing, few middle or senior managers are, in fact, found to hold them exclusively (see Table 5-1). For another, neither action-logic can reliably use feedback to generate performance improvements. Put still a third way, the *Opportunist* and *Diplomat* action-logics are not yet concerned with generating new systemic value by actions that are timely in the sense of cutting costs through new efficiencies or increasing revenues through new sources of effectiveness. Thus, these two action-logics do not produce many managers, and we can understand why, because they do not produce manager-like actions of forward planning, performance feedback, and operational improvement.

By contrast, as shown in Table 5-1, the *Expert* and *Achiever* action-logics together account for the vast majority of all managers—about 80 percent. These two action-logics are also the first two that begin to value single-loop feedback for improved performance. However, they do so in very different ways, and they do not yet encourage double-loop feedback that contributes to their own or others' development to later action-logics.

Larry, an *Expert*

The same supervisor who described Phil as a *Diplomat* in Chapter 4 offers this description of Larry, a fellow supervisor:

Table 5-1 Developmental
Distribution of 497 Managers
(across industries and
organizational levels)

Opportunist	3%
Diplomat	10%
Expert	45%
Achiever	35%
Later action-logics	7%
	100%

Larry has unquestioned technical expertise in his area and believes himself to be unrivalled in this area as well as in administrative record keeping. He is a perfectionist, even going so far as to criticize one of his employees about his technique of decorating the office Christmas tree.

Larry is very conscientious, has a high sense of obligation to moral standards, and feels this differentiates him from the rest of the group. He strives to outperform everyone around him and is not against pointing out the faults of others. He is almost as unforgiving of his own mistakes, so I guess that's fair. He values decisions based on merit as long as they fit within his guidelines. He would, however, prefer to make all the decisions himself. I work closely with Larry and find that sometimes he will take over a project we are both responsible for and complete it all himself, which makes me look bad and, worse, puts me in a weaker role in the group.

Larry is ambivalent about receiving feedback. He has shared with me a feeling that feedback is not required for him and that it is, in some instances, even irritating to him. He seems to be sure that he knows everything he needs to know to do his job. I am impressed with his planning and organizational skills. He has been a great help to me and I do not want to sound too negative about him, but he is extremely dogmatic. His word is law and is not subject to discussion. "My way, or no way" is Larry's credo. Even though we are peers, he seems determined to maintain a position of total dominance. I have tried to be patient and wait him out, but so far he seems to be unyielding.

The **Diplomat** may come to feel bedeviled by the conflicts between other people's priorities for him (his buddies want him to go out for a beer, his boss wants him to stay late, and his wife wants him home by

6 PM). Eventually, rather than continuing skillfully to meet others' expectations and suffering silently, he or she may desperately seek a more internally consistent, a more reliably value-adding, and a more objective basis for decision making. For the *Expert,* the guide to action becomes a specific craft-logic that yields a single "right answer." This characterization certainly seems true of Larry, based on his colleague's description of him.

The *Expert* no longer identifies with what makes him or her the *same* as others in the group. He or she identifies more with the unique skills that make him or her *stand out from* others in the group. In Larry's case, he takes over, without any discussion, projects for which he shares responsibility with a fellow supervisor. *Experts* depend less on others' judgments of quality, more on their own. They view their judgments as objective based on the mastery of a skill.

For the *Expert,* other people's preferences are treated as variables in a wider situation—usually unimportant variables—rather than as guides to his or her own actions. We say "usually unimportant variables" because in each of the early developmental transformations, the process of deidentifying with the prior action-logic initially leads to a devaluation of what the prior action-logic holds most dear. This process tends to mean that *Diplomats* disdain "uncivilized" *Opportunists* and *Experts* disdain "namby-pamby, political" *Diplomats.*

The bright sides of the *Expert* action-logic include a future-oriented, project organizing and completing approach; hard work for the sheer sake of completing an assignment well; a willingness to receive feedback and learn from acknowledged masters of the craft, though rarely from peers (as in Larry's case); and a kind of authority resulting from his or her expertise that can lead subordinates to strive for the *Expert's* admiration for a job well done (and that can impress even an annoyed peer, as in Larry's case).

Experts' shadow sides include not usually being good team players because their critical demand for perfection within the logic of their particular discipline can come to seem like sheer competitiveness to others. Also, their unwillingness to respond to feedback outside their area of expertise (e.g., to feedback about customer preferences or time-to-market considerations) can make them seem altogether closed to feedback. Again, Larry serves as a prime example. His logic is the *only* logic.

Another shadow aspect of the *Expert* is that he or she may fall victim to self-generated stress. In Chapter 1 we described Anthony, a young manager who for two full years dedicated his efforts to becoming an ***Expert*** in a very complex method for comparing company benefit programs. Anthony testified to the anguish, both physical and mental of his "perfectionist nature." "I would find myself obsessing about minutia in an effort to rationalize every last variation in my results." Anthony's successful experiment with action inquiry gave evidence that he began to develop beyond the *Expert* action-logic toward the *Achiever* action-logic, an accomplishment that only a minority of managers today realize.

But, before looking at the *Achiever* action-logic in more detail, we invite you to stop reading for a few moments and note on your sheets of paper the *Expert* characteristics and illustrations that you are now beginning to appreciate as such in your own action-logic, or in those of the colleagues you are trying to understand better.

Joanne, a Rising *Achiever*

Joanne, the manager we meet next, is explicitly exercising action inquiry in order to enter the *Achiever* action-logic. Like Anthony, who took on the task of helping the senior managers of a consulting firm's branch office change their roles, Joanne is breaking the constraints of the *Expert* action-logic and is beginning to understand and experience things in a new way, illustrating for us how action inquiry can help us transform our own action-logic. The length and detail of her story as well as its fresh, up-beat tone seem to reflect her sense of discovering a new world.

> My job as market research manager for the magazine requires that I be a problem solver and "perfectionist." It is part of my daily routine to delve into why things are the way they are—digging, analyzing, and presenting the results. Comments that people make about me include, "You're really good with numbers," "I don't know how you can understand this stuff." These are comments that an *Expert* would love to hear, and I *have* loved hearing them in the past. But I am now finding this action-logic very constraining. I would prefer to be less detail conscious and be more involved with the overall picture, working towards long-term effectiveness rather than short-term efficiency.
>
> Steve, the marketing director, confided in me that he was interviewing for a different position within the company and, if he were to accept, it would be fairly soon. I felt it was vital that I display more of the characteristics of the *Achiever* stage of development in order to be seriously con-

sidered for the position of marketing director. I developed a plan that included a number of experiments.

My first action on hearing this news was to have a discussion with Steve and ask his advice on the best way to proceed. I said I was very interested in eventually becoming the marketing director. Steve expressed confidence that I could do the job, but his response also confirmed what I already knew: I needed to become more visible to upper management—in general, take a proactive role in increasing my communication with these people.

The next major action that I took was to rewrite my job description. Jim, the publisher, had asked us to send him our job descriptions so he could start thinking about the division of responsibility (now that the marketing director position was unfilled). On Steve's suggestion, I rewrote my job description and included responsibilities of the marketing director that I am interested in taking on. I clearly stated in my letter, "I'm not sure that I've adequately expressed my abilities and interest in the past and am taking this opportunity to do so." I also told him that one of my priorities was to continue to improve my written and oral communication skills.

By taking this action I was letting Jim know that I was making efforts to change my behavior. The letter itself was unprecedented for me. I also opened myself to some self-examination and opened the floor for criticism. My hope was that Jim would realize my level of commitment and assist my development.

There was no direct response to my letter and rewritten job description, but over the past few weeks Jim and the national sales manager have sent me copies of presentations that they liked and have called to solicit my opinion on other presentations. Recently, Jim has asked me to take on the development of the general presentation. I adamantly expressed interest in this project in my letter.

An ongoing action is to maintain daily contact with Jim, the ad director, and with the national sales manager. While this sounds like a small and trivial thing, it is actually one of my most effective experiments. I used to go an entire week or two without speaking to the publisher. By taking this initiative, I've created a chain reaction. My calls to them have started conversations that have prompted them to call me more often. During these conversations I've been able to convey my knowledge on different subjects—which, in some cases, has led to being given responsibility for certain projects or keeping track of certain matters. Another result is that my name comes up often in discussions between these people and other upper-level managers in the company.

Another effective action that I took was to volunteer for a project with which I previously had no involvement. We needed to develop a new rate structure for buying advertising space in our magazine. The project had an almost impossible deadline, but I was able to meet it. It involved working several nights until 9 PM and on two weekends. I felt it was important for this project to go as smoothly and quickly as possible. If there had been delays and mistakes, Jim might not have entrusted it to me again. This was an area he might not have thought I could help with. If I hadn't taken the initiative, he still wouldn't know it.

The next major action I took was to schedule a meeting with Jim to discuss my compensation. In essence I wanted to ask for a raise, but I also wanted to convey that I was confident in my abilities and the contributions that I make and have the right amount of aggressiveness to be successful in marketing. This meeting was my best opportunity to properly apply framing, advocating, illustrating, and inquiring in my conversation. By thinking about these conversational elements, I was able to turn a potentially difficult and tense conversation into a positive and productive meeting. We discussed my reasoning and his and were able to make each other see the other's view on a few issues. He agreed that I was not adequately compensated for my contributions.

In conclusion, I am very satisfied with the progress I've made. While no decisions have been made to promote someone to the position of marketing director, I feel I've made significant progress towards the goal of being that person.

My frequent contact with the publisher and others in the company has helped me to move fully out of the *Expert* stage and into the *Achiever* stage. I receive criticism in a much more productive manner and have changed my focus from short-term satisfaction to long-term effectiveness. The most personally felt progress that I've made, however, is my ability to be an initiator and no longer a pawn.

The *Achiever* is passionate about accomplishing goals. Whereas Joanne heretofore has concentrated on digging into the inner workings of things, mastering the numbers, and presenting the answer, the *Achiever* action-logic is wider in scope. It focuses not just on how things work on the inside, but on how to be effective in one's wider surroundings and on how to help the organization as a whole be effective. As Joanne moves from *Expert* to *Achiever* we see her attention expand beyond digging into research data. She conveys her "knowledge on different subjects" and takes on new kinds of projects, such as recommending a new rate structure. She advocates a promotion for herself from the more technically oriented position of market research manager to the more entrepreneurially and managerially oriented role of marketing director, typical of the *Achiever's* focus on functions that help the organization carry out its established strategy.

Much more than those who hold the prior action-logics, the *Achiever* pays attention to differences between his or her own and others' points of view and places a value on teamwork and on agreements reached through consensus. The *Achiever* action-logic is the first that recognizes the juggling of different time horizons as not just a bother, but, rather, as close to the essence of what managing is. In developing the new advertising rate structure, Joanne illustrates this canny interweaving of time horizons, recognizing that she had to act fast, but also efficiently and effectively to succeed in contributing value.

The *Achiever* welcomes personal feedback and seeks mutuality in relationships with co-workers. In Joanne's case, her associations with other managers are on the rise as she assumes the *Achiever* action-logic. She observes the sharp increase in her frequency of contacts with other managers, noting that her initiative in this area is even beginning to cause "chain reactions." She reasons with her boss on the subject of her salary, emphasizing not just that she got her way, but that mutuality was achieved. Increasingly, she appears to be seeking and valuing feedback.

There can be a flip side, a darker side, to the *Achiever's* way of handling feedback, however. Bluntly, the feedback had better fit within the *Achiever's* already-established scheme of things (his or her action-logic), or it will be rejected. You have probably known examples:

- The project manager asks you along with managers from several other departments to attend a meeting in order to give your department's inputs and comments about how the project is being run. Many changes are suggested, but the project manager accepts only those that are consistent with the basic approach she is already pursuing.
- A friend phones you one evening excited about a new business venture he hopes to launch. He tells you his plans and asks your advice. He asks, in addition, that you invest money in the enterprise to help get it started. You think his plans are not sound. You suggest to him several key questions you feel he should explore before proceeding. You tell him further that you do not have the

money to invest. He is extremely upset with both your responses. He ends the conversation by saying you and he are no longer friends.

In both these cases the *Achiever* takes an initiative and seeks feedback about it. But when the feedback is given it becomes clear that the *Achiever's* effort to achieve is made only in terms of his or her own preestablished focus. The *Achiever* is not prepared to question the validity of the action-logic itself and possibly reframe his or her approach in the midst of action.

The *Achiever's* orientation toward subordinates and superiors is complex. On the one hand, the manager at the *Achiever* stage values and encourages creativity among subordinates and is able to delegate significant responsibilities to them. At the same time, he or she is able to act mutually with superiors, initiating interactions with them, proposing projects, and disagreeing with them. On the other hand, however, the *Achiever's* inability to question his or her own limited conception of the organization's larger goals prevents any serious consideration or acceptance of strategic alternatives that deviate from the current official or tacit regime.

You are undoubtedly aware of many examples of the thought and action of the *Achiever.* In our studies of managers (Table 5-2), *Achievers* represented 35 percent of the total sample. Table 5-2 highlights the particular managerial characteristics associated with each of the two action-logics we have examined in this chapter.

Art's Summary of the Four Action-Logics and a Look Ahead

Now we will revisit the four action-logics we have considered in Chapters 4 and 5—the *Opportunist, Diplomat, Expert,* and *Achiever* action-logics, with one more story. Art is a manager in a business owned by his family. In his story, Art describes transitions he has made through each of the four action-logics. This affords us a review, but also highlights in a remarkably vivid way something we glimpsed in Joanne's story: the potential people have for acquiring successively wider, more inclusive action-logics. Art presents himself as having accomplished at least four transformations, with a fifth possibly underway. The last two paragraphs of his story provide a look at three further action-logics, the

Table 5-2   Managerial Style Characteristics Associated with the
Expert and *Achiever* Developmental Action-Logics

Expert	Interested in problem-solving; seeks causes; critical of self/ others based on own craft logic; wants to stand out, be unique; perfectionist; chooses efficiency over effectiveness; dogmatic; accepts feedback only from objective acknowledged craft masters; values decisions based on technical merit; humor = practical jokes; sees contingencies, exceptions; positive ethic = sense of obligation to internally consistent moral order; timely action = fast, efficient
Achiever	Long-term goals; future is vivid, inspiring; welcomes behavioral feedback; timely action = juggling time demands to attain effective results; feels like initiator, not pawn; seeks generalizable reasons for action; seeks mutuality, not hierarchy, in relationships; appreciates complexity, systems; feels guilt if does not meet own standards; blind to own shadow, to the subjectivity behind objectivity; positive ethic = practical day-to-day improvements based on self-chosen (but not self-created) ethical system

Individualist, the *Strategist,* and the *Alchemist,* which are all developmentally beyond the *Achiever* action-logic. When you reach that point in Art's story, you can look for new themes—post-*Achiever* themes— which we will discuss in greater detail in the chapters that follow. Here is Art's story:

> When I was 15, I worked in my grandfather's store and I evidenced some *Opportunistic* tendencies. I would do things that made me look good at the time, but had poor future consequences.
>
> At 19, when I was in college, I worked for my father who had bought a large auto body repair franchise. My managerial behavior was diplomatic: I wanted everyone to like me and I avoided confrontational situations. But due to the nature of the people who work in that industry I could not, and did not, remain a *Diplomat* for long. Our employees generally had alcohol, drug, emotional, behavioral, social, or legal problems. Many were in and out of court and jail and could not handle their finances from one week to the next. In retrospect, this put most of them clearly as *Opportunists.*

I remember the turning point from a **Diplomat's** to an **Expert's** mind-set, though I had no name for it at the time. The incident was the first time I had to fire someone. After that, my focus was on driving the employees to do the job right. I was very organized, methodical, and procedural, instituting procedures in our shop that were recommended for use across the country. I hated for anyone to try to tell me that there was a different way to do something other than the "perfect" way I was already doing it, though I often would try new ideas after work when nobody was around. I also welcomed and enjoyed people asking me about problems they could not figure out.

I came to a brick wall using this strategy when we could no longer find any new employees because of the low unemployment rate. I was not able to fire anyone for not following the rules because there was no one to replace them.

I find evidence subsequently of the **Achiever** style. Rather than adhering to the strict procedures, I decided to have the goal be to have the jobs done right and that there could be many ways to achieve that goal. I learned quickly the value of flexibility, working with an alcoholic who would often disappear for several days or weeks; a paranoid individual who put a mirror on his tool box so he could see if anyone was watching him; a person I would call hyper who would run through the shop jumping over cars, climb walls, swing from pipes, coming up behind people to startle them; and an employee who, when I asked how he did such a good job, replied that he would just get high and work. Previously, I could easily have fired any one of them, but I learned that each was useful in his own way. At this time, I also sought out critiques on what I did and if there were ways that I could do better. I watched others to see what I could learn from them and found that everyone had something I could learn from.

After a while, I started doing arbitration occasionally, and I think this introduced me to the **Individualist's** sense of multiple action-logics and of the interaction between process and task. The first brief would seem so convincing, then the other brief would change my mind, and then the oral presentations would again change my view of the whole case. It was also interesting to experiment like a **Strategist** with different ways to resolve problems that leave each side feeling as if they have had their say and accepting my decision as fair and reasonable. In dealing with customers and employees, I now use these same techniques strategically.

The next precipitous event, which may be a glimpse of the **Alchemist** stage, happened when a customer was yelling about something to do with his car. It was also during the busy season. I had 15 employees, 75 cars, hundreds of inventory items, and customer inquiries to handle. I remember that while the person was yelling I felt that I was above the situation looking down. I figured out what I should do to correct the situation and then went back down. After this incident, I could do this as needed, separating myself from the circumstances and calmly determining what I should do to control the situation. After several times, I was both amazed and scared of being able to do this.

Art himself identifies some of the themes of action-logics beyond the *Achiever* when he refers to "the *Individualist's* sense of multiple action-logics and of the interaction between process and task," to the *Strategist's* sharing the decision-making process with others, and to the *Alchemist's* experiencing an interplay of detachment from, and committed action in, present circumstances.

Next Steps

We will explore the post-*Achiever* action-logics in more detail in the chapters that follow, but in the meantime, we hope you are beginning to become as fascinated and delighted as Art at the possibility of discovering new action-logics yourself. If you have listed some of your own characteristics associated with various action-logics (or if you do that writing now), you will have taken the first step in the developmental process. Does your list focus heavily within one action-logic and does that action-logic seem like a comfortable but challenging home? Or does it straddle two action-logics suggesting you may be in transformation from one to the other? Or, like Joanne, does your current action-logic seem confining and the next one liberating? Or have none of the action-logics described so far sounded essentially like you, even in combination? In that case you may find yourself better represented in one of the chapters to follow.

At this point, you may be interested in going beyond your own first-person self-assessment of your action-logic to seek second-person estimates from your colleagues or family members, or even take a third-person scientific measure. If this is true for you, we can offer the following suggestions. With regard to second-person estimates, we know of a number of people who have mixed the phrases for all the action-logics taken from the tables in each chapter, put them on a page, and asked co-workers to circle those that they think apply to the person asking. Not only can this generate some rich information for you, but this process also often generates good work-related conversations about one another's styles. And several times the co-workers have all asked for the same sort of feedback, leading to a double-loop change in how the team as a whole operates.

With regard to taking a third-person scientific measure, we can suggest the Leadership Development Profile, the measure on which all of our statistics about managers' action-logics is based. You can learn more about this measure in the Appendix. You can also begin thinking about and actively experimenting with themes that characterize the next action-logic beyond your present action-logic, as Joanne and Art are doing.

These relatively unstructured initiatives are more likely to appeal to someone at the *Achiever* action-logic than to someone holding the *Expert* action-logic, unless the *Expert* is currently feeling confined by that action-logic, as Joanne described herself in her story. Most *Experts* will find themselves making better headway toward transformation by engaging in more structured environments, such as the action-oriented MBA program described in Chapter 3, that will teach, and encourage them to practice discrete action-inquiry skills.

Practice Openness

Both *Experts* and *Achievers* experience distinct and definite kinds of satisfactions that accompany being very skilled and knowledgeable at what they do. Paradoxically, when we hang onto those satisfactions too long, they can close off further learning and development. To open yourself up, practice an open-system action-logic by carrying with you the assumption that there is something new and valuable for you, small or large, that can be gained from absolutely every person you encounter, anywhere. During or immediately after encounters with others, or during your daily check-ins, listen into yourself with sufficient inquiries (such as the three offered here) to discover new pearls of great price for yourself.

1. What is one specific quality about this person that I really appreciate? How might I cultivate that quality in myself?
2. How do I name the specific quality of this person that irritates me? Can I look in the mirror and discover where I also have that

irritating quality? How might I befriend and transform this feature of myself that I don't like very much?

3. With any person, and especially with people who view things differently than I do, I will try the following internal inquiries:

- "That person is so different from me, but knows *something*
  about *something* that I *don't* know or understand. What is one
  item of knowledge or experience that person has, that I don't
  have?"
- "How might this inform and benefit me in one, or two, or three,
  or all four territories of experience?" (Keep yourself "on the
  hook" until you identify *something* about that person's point of
  view or experience that you can benefit from learning about.)
- I will seek out this person and pursue an action inquiry into my
  question. Afterward, I will notice if I feel differently about this
  person.

Notice whether you are attracted or repulsed by these suggested
practices.

Conclusion

Now, we return to the doorway Art has opened for us into a new realm,
the world of the post-*Achiever* action-logics. These action-logics, starting with *Individualist,* differ from the four earlier action-logics we have
focused on in Chapters 4 and 5, in ways that are vital to you as a current
and/or future leader of your organization. Recent research (reviewed in
Chapter 7) indicates that people at the *Individualist* stage and beyond
are likely to be more effective in transforming their organizations than
those whose action-logics precede the *Individualist.* Because of this
significant social benefit to developmental movement beyond the
Achiever stage, we devote a chapter each to the *Individualist* (Chapter
6) and *Strategist* (Chapter 7) action-logics to show how their themes
differ from those of the *Achiever* and to show the kinds of performance
these postconventional action-logics enable.

SIX

The *Individualist* Action-Logic: Bridge to transforming leadership

In Chapters 1 through 3, we said that action inquiry centers on a process of learning. This learning process is not a mechanistic, automated feedback process producing continuous change, but is instead a bumpy, discontinuous, sometimes upending, and transformational kind of learning. This learning affords individuals and organizations a widening and deepening of vision and new capacities for learning from single-, double-, and triple-loop feedback in the moment of action.

In Chapters 4 and 5, we began to illustrate this bumpy lifetime learning process. Virtually every person goes through several action-logic transformations during early life. We begin life in a stage we call the *Impulsive* action-logic, which we do not discuss in this book. The vast majority of us transform from the *Impulsive* action-logic to the *Opportunist* action-logic sometime between the ages of 3 and 6. A very large majority of us proceed to transform from *Opportunist* to *Diplomat,* usually between the ages of 12 and 16. A certain proportion of us transform to the *Expert* action-logic by the time we are 21. Many more of us do so during the decade after we join the workforce.

These transformations are likely to be bumpy because neither we ourselves, nor, frequently, our parents, teachers, or bosses know that we are going through them. Neither they nor we are intentionally guiding us through such transformations with a developmental map, such as we are constructing here.

But even *with* a developmental map, the process is likely to remain bumpy because, like the Escher painting of the artist drawing himself, we are truly redrawing ourselves and all our mental maps in each developmental change. In fact, linear lists of the different developmental frames or action-logics are themselves misleading in that they imply a straightforward movement, with the map itself remaining unchanged. Yet that is not the personal experience of developmental transformation.

Figure 6.1 may come a little closer to conveying some of the experiential qualities of a lifetime path of development. To illustrate the up-ending quality of each change in our basic action-logic, the three transformations between *Opportunist* and *Achiever* are each shown as a kind of backward somersault. Then, the *Individualist* action-logic is shown not as a destination, but as a path that somersaults reflectively through one's previous history and through the growing recognition of alternative action-logics, until one reaches the *Strategist* action-logic (described more fully in Chapter 7). Then the journey from *Strategist* to *Alchemist* is shown as different in kind again. The double-headed arrows between *Alchemist* and all the earlier action-logics suggest an on-going, time out of time process that will be discussed in Chapter 12.

The *Diplomat, Expert,* and *Achiever* follow a progression through what are identified as the *conventional* action-logics. The conventional action-logics take social categories, norms, and power-structures for

Figure 6.1   A Late-Stage Appreciation of the Dynamics and Simultaneity of Different Action-Logics

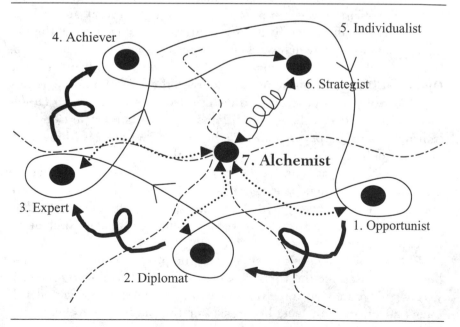

granted as constituting the very nature of a stable reality. We are learning how to relate by gradually gaining increasing skill and control in one territory of experience after another—first, the outside world, as an *Opportunist*; next, the world of our own actions, as a *Diplomat*; then the world of thought, as an *Expert*; and then the interplay among all three as an *Achiever*. As persons operating within conventional action-logics, we typically do not recognize ourselves as seeing ourselves, others, and the world through a particular frame or action-logic. Nor do we realize that our action-logics have been transforming into different ones over the course of our lives. With the longer personal history that we gain by the time we enter our thirties, and with the greater sense of familial, organizational, and societal diversity and change with which our longer history may have endowed us, some of us begin to realize that we may be able to develop some inquiry, choice, and control over the fundamental assumptions we and others make about ourselves and the world we are encountering.

Table 5-1 shows that in the sample of 497 well-educated, working adults in the United States, fully 90 percent score as holding conventional action-logics. Only 7 percent profile at postconventional action-logics, which include the *Individualist, Strategist,* and *Alchemist* stages, referred to as "Later action-logics" in the table. (The other 3 percent profile at the preconventional *Opportunist* stage.) Yet, as we will see in the rest of this book, the small percentage of postconventional leaders have a disproportionate effect on our collective capacities to transform ourselves and our institutions toward greater efficacy, mutuality, and integrity. As we learn more about the advantages of a transformational perspective, more of us may wish to embark on adult transformational journeys.

Postconventional Action-Logics

Whereas the conventional action-logics appreciate *similarity* and *stability,* postconventional action-logics increasingly appreciate *differences* and participating in ongoing, creative *transformation* of action-logics. Thus, the postconventional action-logics are less and less *implicit frames* that limit one's choice, and more and more become *explicit frames* (like this whole theory of developmental action inquiry) that highlight the multiplicity of action-logics and the developing freedom and what we call the response-ability to choose one's action-logic on each occasion.

Furthermore, persons constructing these postconventional action-logics increasingly appreciate that they are exercising forms of power with others in each social interaction. They increasingly recognize that they are either reinforcing or transforming existing action-logics and structures of power as they do so. They see not only that new, shared frames *can* be generated in the present situation, but also that shared frames often *must* be generated, if high quality cooperative work is to have any chance of occurring (because members of the new team come from different national cultures, or have different skills [e.g., sales vs. accounting], or different corporate recognition and reward systems, or different action-logics).

During our journey into postconventional action-logics, we develop the capacity to think intersystemically in action about the different action-logics at play and how they mutually influence one another. No longer is the world a place of discrete objects, like billiard balls on a table, that cause subsequent events unilaterally and sequentially, based on an initially planned strategic act. Instead, causation is recognized as circular, relational, and systemic, and the assessment measures one chooses are recognized as reflecting one's action-logic as well as feedback from the outside world. Now, for the first time, the skills of framing, advocating, illustrating, and inquiring that we introduced in Chapter 2, and the skill of seeking disconfirming feedback become more like principles of discourse than mere skills.

Other related changes occur—the principles by which we aspire to live have a stronger influence; the rules of others become less determining and are increasingly felt as a restriction of questionable legitimacy. At the same time, the question of whether we or our institutions are acting consistently with espoused principles becomes more motivating and more insistent. Likewise, the related question of how to overcome our own incongruities and avoid hypocrisy becomes more urgent. Differences within a person or organization are no longer covered-up or projected onto some external enemy or scapegoat. Instead, they are treated as the raw material for constructing a genuine integrity in action, as Steve Thompson, the underwater pipeline manager, began to do in Chapter 1.

There are many ways to develop heightened awareness of the degree to which we do *not* reliably act in a way that harmoniously accomplishes our intended outcomes. One is to engage in various forms of spiritual practice that aim at generating a heightened ongoing presence to ourselves. Another is to start our own small group where members present and analyze cases about specific efforts to act effectively that have not yielded the intended results (as illustrated in Chapter 2). A third is to write a critical/constructive autobiography, in dialogue with developmental theory (and possibly in dialogue with a mentor or executive coach as well).

Art's autobiographical writing at the end of Chapter 5 gave us a first taste of that activity, and much of the rest of this present chapter offers a fuller example of this practice. One of the authors has guided many people over the past 20 years in doing so. Celia, an African-American executive in her late forties wrote the following "career autobiography" as part of her doctoral program. Her story is an exemplar of *Individualist* self-reflection. As you read her autobiography, you may wish to take brief notes on incidents in your own past life that now seem to you to reflect one or another of the action-logics at work. This reflective practice can help us become more self-accepting of ourselves, as well as more accepting of others whom we today find expressing action-logics that no longer mesmerize and constrain us.

Celia, "Tracing the Roots of My Dream"

Opportunist and *Diplomat*

My years through college were really my *Impulsive* years, and I have decided not to go back that far for this discussion. Rather, I think this discussion starts after college with the *Opportunist* action-logic because I found myself trying to gain a skill and a sense of where my personal power would fit. I was searching for a place where I would feel comfortable. I also see that by doing this kind of assessment, I was blending in to the *Diplomat* frame because I found myself trying to understand others and gain a sense of their cultures and what made people make the decisions they did. I do not see a clean break between these two frames for me.

In reflecting back I realize that the first time I began analyzing the workplace was when I took on my first "real" job. Shortly after I was married, I started my first job at the Riggs Bank in Washington, D.C. I had never before experienced prejudice firsthand, but I sure did there. Tellers would make black customers wait longer for service than whites and would call them derogatory names when they were not in earshot (although sometimes I think the black people *could* hear them). The bank wanted me to move into training, but I had no passion for the numbers and in fact was a terrible teller. The environment just did not suit me, so I moved on.

I became a receptionist for a major communications law firm that was also in the District. I was not challenged by the job and spent most of my time finding out what made the people tick that worked there. My error rate was abysmal and my intention was to pursue a life of mediocrity simply to provide a paycheck.

My next adventure was with the Aluminum Company of America (ALCOA). I was hired into what I understood was a quasi-professional job, tracking government contracts. It was here that I realized that I was basically a rabble-rouser at heart. I challenged secretaries for why they were still "getting coffee for their guy" and managers for why they weren't willing to delegate tasks of any real interest. While the picture sounds somewhat dismal, I did learn a great deal. After I was finally out of the clerical functions, I was going to the Hill to Senate and House hearings on various things that affected the aluminum industry. I loved this part of the job and writing reports on trends for the plant managers.

Next, I was interviewed by the American Federation of State, County, and Municipal Employees (AFSCME) for the administrator position to one of the directors. The culture of AFSCME fit me, and I was molding my actions to succeed in the union. This was the first acknowledgement or even understanding that I was cut out to be an agent of change. I loved working for AFSCME. It became a real cause for me. I learned about ways to help employees gain fairness from their employers and the power of collective bargaining and written contracts. I became a labor zealot.

I met Alex in Boston in 1976, the weekend after the 4th of July. He was in charge of a SWAT-like team that was put together to settle a strike of the Massachusetts State Employees over contract negotiations. He pulled the whole initiative together and really created a strong presence with the government officials and the union members. Our story is history from there. We moved to Virginia when the strike was settled and a solid union was built. Here we worked for the national headquarters of AFSCME, traveling all over the country either managing organizing drives or settling strikes. Shortly after that we both officially divorced our respective spouses and married each other.

Expert

I took a stand about myself when I met Alex. This was a turning point in my life. Alex was a mentor to me. No one has had a more profound influence on my life. He helped me understand the personal power that I had and gain confidence in myself to pursue my own dreams. He is the person that taught me how to present my ideas with passion. He showed me that I could stand on my own and build a life that I wanted and not one that someone else expected for me. Alex was and is a true leader. People gravitated to him. He had a mission and he was pursuing it aggressively. He is about building people-focused workplaces where wages and working conditions are fair and conducive to productivity. Prior to this point I was very conventional and married to a guy I knew I never should have married. There was no passion for life, and my first husband had no vision for his future. Had I not met my second husband, I probably would have stayed in that dissatisfying relationship much longer.

I believe that I was moving into the Expert stage because I was taking charge of myself and beginning to master myself and my outside world. Prior to this I was unsure of myself and often did not feel competent. I was the youngest of a family of very high achievers. My mother's favorite statement about me was that I was the "loving one," implying that I lacked the genius of the others. Meeting Alex brought me into my own. I was going to do things now because I thought they were right for me not because others thought so.

My life for the next few years became one of exploring the new me. I was far enough removed from my immediate family that I could really find out who *I* was. I was also madly in love with Alex. I was continuing to develop a deep passion for the trials of workers and becoming really focused on the inequities of the workplace. However, another perspective was emerging—the political nature of institutions, both labor and companies. Many things were done in the name of good for the worker that were often more good for the union and its long-term survival and less for the worker. I saw corrupt union officials and managers who would stoop to almost anything to maintain their power.

Regression to Earlier Action-Logics

Alex was eventually recruited from this position to head up human resources at the Office of Social Services in New Jersey. I was offered a position with a joint labor/management committee to help establish areas of partnership between labor and management—although those words were not used then.

I threw myself into this job. I had a rough beginning. In retrospect I believe that I had dropped back to the **Diplomat** frame as I was trying to adapt to this new work environment. At times I think I was also operating from an *Opportunist* perspective. Both of these approaches probably made it harder for me than if I had known about these differences and had the foresight to stay in the *Expert* mode.

I also had not made the mental change from being adversarial to collaborative. I was confrontational in style, I talked *at* people to convince them rather than to bring them in, and did not know how to listen in constructive ways. I was threatened if someone challenged my point of view and I tried to argue them over to mine. I was angry because no one thought the work we were doing in the pilot employee involvement efforts was significant.

My husband, however, was off in his own world at this time. I never knew or asked what was consuming him and did not want to know. I believe that he was taken by the power of his job. This was a dark period for me. I considered getting a divorce, but I truly loved Alex and could see us together. Life without him did not seem like a viable option. We needed to work this through. To this day I am not sure he knows how serious this dark year and a half was. I still see vividly what was going on and feel my loneliness. This whole period after the pilot fizzled is what I would characterize as a period of dormancy.

Transition Toward Achiever

What should I do? I needed to believe that I was smart enough to be successful, but what did I need to do to grow? I decided to go to graduate school. If I could not get real fulfillment on the job, I would learn more so I could contribute more. Somehow Alex came back into focus for me—he was there again. Maybe this is because I got focus for myself. He drove me to take the GREs and waited for the exam to be finished. He cheered me on when I thought I did not do well (which I did not). He supported me all the way in getting through my master's degree. It seemed as though every day I was applying to the workplace something I had learned in school. I graduated with flying colors, which was totally affirming to my ability. It restored my self-esteem.

My role became an internal consultant to state agencies. I worked with senior managers who wanted to change the way they lead their organizations and try different models. I started to move into the maverick situation again. I had a passion for organization development. I was, however, much less dogmatic and more facilitative and interested in discovery. It seemed like such a natural progression from where I was. Again, I was out front of my colleagues. This time, though, I was not scared to be. I was pursuing a dream that fit and I knew was my destiny.

During this period my mother died very unexpectedly. This had a profound impact on me. I was unprepared for how much I would mourn her loss. Maybe it was because I was finally coming to grips with our relationship. I was learning so much about myself and how to build positive relationships—those based on dialogue and understanding and not debate—that I was finally able to dialogue with her and not feel threatened or put down or defensive. Here, I got a first *Individualist* taste: my mother's perspective was no longer oppressive and to be avoided. Instead, her perspective and mine now seemed deliciously different and to be savored. But she died before I could really come to closure with her on our relationship. I think she will never know how significant she was in shaping my life. Perhaps that is why I resented her so often. I think I cried for my mother every day for two years, usually when I drove to work by myself. She always flooded in. In many ways she kept me going because she would have been so proud of me getting my master's.

From here I landed my dream job. I became the director of quality for a state agency. I was part of the executive team and in charge of consulting to that team relative to total quality system implementation. I had been working all this time for an opportunity of this magnitude. I was calmer about the role I was playing and I did not need to be so central as I had before. I was more secure about myself, who I was and what I brought to the table. But all exciting periods end. The ending here was hard again. The commissioner changed due to a change in the political environment and the emphasis on organizational change and quality diminished. I was crushed. I still could not quite get full endorsement. It was time again to move on. It moved me to the next plateau of learning, but before this happened I again went into dormancy.

The Individualist Journey

Alex again faced career change, and this time it was not so positive. I always had faith that he would regroup, and he did, but this time it was more of a struggle. I was now in limbo and so was he. The halcyon days were in the distance. But I realize now what strength we both have together. I could no longer stay with the state both financially and because the luster was gone. Alex was no longer there and the joy of being in the same business was gone. We were in a financial upheaval and something needed to be done. I was moving from holding the secondary career to holding the primary career. I was not prepared for this change, but in looking back it seems my whole life was about coming of age for myself, coming to really be me and making my dream come true.

I was canvassed by several firms in New York City for potential positions. After consultation with my husband I decided to venture forth. In truth, I was flattered by the potential, but also scared. Moving from the public/labor sector to the private/management sector would mean a whole lifestyle change for me that I was not sure I was prepared for. At any rate, I went to the interviews and cried all the way home because I knew that I was going to be offered a job and would be making a critical change in my life. The first job fell through, and I was crushed. I had worked all the issues through in my mind and with my husband, and we were ready to go.

My old job became unbearable. Fortunately, more offers were coming my way and I received a wonderful offer from Chemical Bank. I landed a job at a vice-president level heading up professional development for one division.

Being at Chemical was like I always belonged there. I knew what to do and how to do it. I knew how to pull together a department and how to deal with the executives in the company. In reality I had been dealing with executives all my life—my husband was one and in many ways so was I. I quickly moved into the role of strategist to the business heads after I launched a successful executive development program. The business relied on me for quality improvement advice, and I was slotted to become the quality officer for the business after I had completed my tour of duty at the head of professional development. I was doing global initiatives, working with the sales force to improve their performance measures and streamline their pipeline reporting process. It was really a dream job and I was doing well at it.

Then the merger hit and all things creative and strategic of the sort I was working on came to a screeching halt. At this time I came across the Executive PhD Program I later joined and began to collect further data on it. Headhunters were also calling, and I had time to look at other opportunities.

Today, as an internal consultant, I am less at the center of client system and more at the boundaries helping them discover for themselves. This is a real growth point for me. I no longer need to be as dominant as in the past, I have fewer answers and many more questions, and the questions center around the clients' discovering their own strengths. I am more fluid in how I approach things. I see things more from a strategic point of view. I also recognize the power of dialogue and the negativity of debate. Ultimately I would like to run my own business.

As her story ends, we see Celia moving from being more of a junior to her husband and her mother toward full seniority, becoming the primary career person and the senior generation in her family. She is also moving from being more of a zealot to being more of a facilitator of collaborative inquiry, even in a business environment that does not conform to her values. In this we hear resonances with the **Strategist** action-logic that we will explore in Chapter 7.

It is particularly interesting that, as she closes, Celia is considering leaving big business to create an environment more attuned to her own priorities. In our work, we see an increasing number of managers profiling at this **Individualist** action-logic, and they are frequently people who have recently left inside jobs to take a role in small consulting firms both where they have more control over their working environment and where their primary job becomes listening deeply into others' worlds in order to facilitate transformational change. This trend may be influenced by the decreasing job security in firms worldwide. It may also derive from the increased interest in our own psychology, which, in turn, may be influenced by the postmodern, expressive trends in popular culture and technology. Or, are more and more of us responding to the dramatic signs we are receiving in the post-9/11 era that the environmental, political, business, and spiritual worlds are a systemic whole, that is calling us to optimize a triple bottom line—economic profitability, political mutuality, and ecological sustainability—rather than simple-mindedly taking sides?

Having read Celia's story, you have likely begun to form some impressions of the kinds of thoughts and actions that are characteristic of the **Individualist** action-logic. Once again, we offer a summary of characteristics in Table 6-1.

Summary

The dawning of awareness of postconventional understanding may be a confusing time for us. The **Individualist's** dark side includes troubled feelings of something unravelling or needing resolving, along with a sense of paralysis about how to move, because we have not yet developed postrelativistic principles.

Table 6-1 Managerial Style Characteristics Associated with the *Individualist* Developmental Action-Logic

Individualist	Takes a relativistic perspective; focuses more on both present and historical context; often aware of conflicting emotions; experiences time itself as a fluid, changeable medium, with piercing, unique moments; interested in own and others' unique self-expression; seeks independent, creative work; attracted by difference and change more than by similarity and stability; less inclined to judge or evaluate; influences by listening and finding patterns more than by advocacy; may become something of a maverick; starts to notice own shadow (and own negative impact); possible decision paralysis

Yet this is also likely to be a time of renewed freshness of each fully tasted experience, of dramatic new insight into the uniqueness of ourself and of others, of forging relationships that reach new levels of intimacy, and of perusing new interests in the world. Excitement alternates with doubt in unfamiliar ways. If this sounds like a contradictory jumble, as the ups and downs of Celia's story sometimes seem, then this is a fair representation of the *Individualist's* experience. Looking back at Figure 6.1, you will see that there is no stopping point for the *Individualist,* and that he or she is in part engaged in a journey that reevaluates all prior life experiences and action-logics.

The *Individualist* is a bridge between two worlds. One is the preconstituted, relatively stable and hierarchical understandings we grow into as children, as we learn how to function as members of a preconstituted culture. The other is the emergent, relatively fluid and mutual understandings that highlight the power of responsible adults to lead their children, their subordinates, and their peers in transforming change.

From the point of view of conventional-stage employees, *Individualist* managers tend to provide less certainty and firm leadership. This is in part because the *Individualist* is aware of the layers upon layers of assumptions and interpretations at work in the current situation.

Practice Immediacy

Just as the *Individualist* action-logic is a bridge to transforming leadership, there is a certain capacity for in-the-moment immediacy—for awareness and choice and artistic practice in the present—that is a bridge to the finely tuned performance of timely action inquiry in the later, postconventional action-logics. We suggested earlier that you experiment for one week with each new practice we offered before trying the next practice. If you have done this, you will have accumulated a number of practices to employ throughout your day. Now, you may be ready to start paying attention to how you are developing more immediacy with them.

- When your watch alarm goes off each hour for your noticing exercise, does it take less and less time (we started with 30 seconds) to notice how you feel mentally, emotionally, and physically?
- Has it become automatic to notice how you feel as you transition from one activity to another?
- Do you find fewer and fewer surprises as you do your check-ins at meal and bed times?
- Do you find it takes less time to accurately name, for yourself, how you feel about things as they happen?
- Do you find yourself naturally incorporating how you feel about situations as you are advocating?
- Do you find yourself noticing rushing, stuffing, and closed *Expert* reactions sooner after the events that evoked them? Or even *as* they are evoked?
- Do you find yourself resisting others' points of view less often, and expressing curiosity about their points of view more often?
- Does there seem to be less fog in your awareness? (Or does there seem to be more fog because you are more aware of how often you are foggy?)

The Next Step

The **Strategist** action-logic, to which we turn next, is the first general response to the question of how to lead timely and transforming change in a mutual way that invites and even sometimes challenges others to join in the leadership process. Most persons at the *Individualist* action-logic are eager to continue transforming in this direction.

SEVEN

The *Strategist* Action-Logic: Developing transforming power

A principal feature of the *Strategist* action-logic is self-awareness in action. It not only intuitively recognizes other action-logics and itself as action-logics, as does the *Individualist,* it also intuitively recognizes all action as either facilitating or inhibiting ongoing transformational change of personal, familial, corporate, or national action-logics. If we are aware of ourselves in action in the present and among others who may be framing the situation based on entirely different action-logics, participating in both incremental and transformational change, then the central question becomes: What action is timely now to whom?

The *Strategist* is fascinated by the possibility of a certain kind of timely action that is recognizable as "on time" in the *Diplomat's* sense, as efficient in the *Expert's* sense, and as effective in the *Achiever's* sense, and that can *at the same time* support one's own, or another's, or an organization's transformation. A key here is that there is a voluntary quality in a system's transformation. Timely action by others can support our own transformation by giving us well-framed double-loop feedback, yet at the same time each of us can only increase our freedom and individuality by choosing to digest that feedback and transform. At the same time, we are more likely to digest such feedback and choose the vulnerable path of transformation if we experience our colleagues acting in ways that open them to possible transformation as well. Hence, the little-known and rarely practiced power to transform is a mutual, vulnerable power, disciplined by careful, inquiring attention to the timing of each of the interacting persons, groups, organizations, or regions.

Of course, most people scored as Strategists by a measure of developmental action-logics, such as the Leadership Development Profile that underlies the developmental studies mentioned in this book (see the Appendix for detail), do not explicitly speak and think in the developmental terms we use in this book. Nevertheless, they tend to appreciate the need to change with the changing seasons, either intuitively or based on related theories (e.g., Shakespeare's "ages of man," or the Hindu life cycle, or Confucian discipline ["at fifty I learned to listen . . ."], or Erikson's theory of development). For example, someone at the *Strategist* action-logic is likely to sequence the strategic decisions somewhat as follows: first, to negotiate salary and conditions with an apt sense of *Opportunist*-ic self-enhancement and self-protection; second, to adopt a more *Diplomat*-ic orientation in the first months on the job, learning about the new culture, including its vulnerabilities and susceptibilities to leadership; then, third, to choose areas to exercise their *Expert*-ise to make standout value-added contributions that lead to promotion; and so on.

Keenly aware of multiple viewpoints, the *Strategist* is well equipped to maintain institutional and personal connections with subordinates. He or she will tend to intuitively blend the kind of top and bottom line performance *Achievers* expect, with the high quality standards the *Expert* respects (without the unintended effects of fear and competitiveness that an *Expert* boss tends to generate), and still find time to share family stories with the *Diplomat.*

Another way of expressing the new step the *Strategist* takes is not just to accept individuality (as the *Individualist* does), but to welcome evolving individuality in the context of mutual relationship. Implicitly if not explicitly, the *Strategist* becomes increasingly attuned to the developmental process, recognizing that others (as well as teams and whole organizations, as we will explore in Chapters 8 through 11) have developed as a result of their past experiences and that they need the opportunity to develop autonomously toward integrity, mutuality, and sustainability. Accompanying this recognition is a willingness to let others (such as our subordinates or our children) make their own mistakes, but to do so in the context of developing greater alertness and capacity for single-, double-, and triple-loop self-correction. However, the *Strategist* is also aware of the limits to autonomy, realizing not only that emotional interdependence is inevitable, but also counting personal ties among increasingly autonomous friends to be among his or her most important treasures. In the context of this new appreciation for mutuality, the development of explicit mutual visions, charters, and contracts at the outset of relationships and organizing processes becomes increasingly significant.

Unlike the *Achiever,* the *Strategist* is open to the possibility of rethinking and even altering his or her viewpoint and purposes in a situation and helping others to do the same. The *Strategist* consciously seeks and chooses new ways of framing opportunities, dilemmas, and conflicts that accommodate the disparities, paradoxes, and fluidity of multiple points of view. From the *Individualist,* the *Strategist* inherits the ability to acknowledge and deal with inner conflicts, such as conflicting needs and duties. But, whereas the *Individualist's* relativism can make him or her feel paralyzed by such conflicts, the *Strategist* comes to appreciate the tension of opposites as paradoxical and seeks resolutions that transform the very differences that initially seem irreconcilable.

Persons operating from the *Strategist* action-logic truly lead, whatever their organizational rank or role. They focus their own and colleagues' attention on whether mission, strategy, operations, and outcome are in conflict with one another and might be aligned more coherently. The *Strategist* will develop ways to detect disparities between mission and strategy, strategy and operations, and operations and outcome so that ineffective and unethical processes can be corrected. The *Strategist's* sensitivity to systemic disparities includes a keen awareness of inequities in race, ethnicity, class, gender, and development among colleagues and subordinates. This perspective is consonant with a global rather than an ethnocentric vision and demands that the *Strategist* make every effort to redress social inequities in ways that promote personal and institutional development, rather than generating *Diplomat*-like dependence on government aid.

The *Strategist's* expressions are spontaneous, combining genuineness and intensity. Feelings are expressed vividly and convincingly, including sensual experiences, poignant sorrows, joy, and delight. Expressions often have a light touch, including fantasy, sensitivity, and existential humor. The *Strategist* and the still-later postconventional action-logics become increasingly sensitive, not just to how the past influences the present, but also to how our current actions, including our words, affect the present and the future.

The person with the *Strategist* worldview sees purpose in life beyond meeting his or her own needs. Continuing development of self and others is a primary concern. The *Strategist* also seeks to discover what he or she does uniquely well. This person is involved in a personal quest—a life work—with a sense of vocation. This quest may be focused within the workplace, outside it, or both, for conventional work/family boundaries mean less than the relational principles the **Strategist** wishes to practice. The question of identity for the **Strategist** includes the question of his or her social and spiritual vocation.

Here, we will tell only one exemplary close-up story of a rising **Strategist**. Sharon, a team leader in a large consulting firm, provides a striking example of the mutuality a **Strategist** can feel and exercise, even with a boss who has a longtime reputation for top-down, unilateral decision making. She discusses her differences with her boss, who is not, Sharon explains, the type who is accustomed to candid discussions of differences with his subordinates:

> I was working with a manager that I knew had a style very, very different from mine. I knew if I was going to be promoted to manager in this make-or-break year, it was crucial that I get this guy on my side, that I make him see I was ready to be manager.
>
> He was called "the assassin." He was known for picking people off in that critical year. I figured the only way I know how to approach this is to talk to him about it—be honest and get things out on the table that no one talks about. So I said, "Steve, I am scared to death of working for you this year because I know you don't promote people. I know you think I'm screwing up because it's different from the way you do things, but trust me. It will work. I know it."
>
> He was very task oriented. He wanted to look at budget analyses and all this sort of junk, and I keep telling him, "Steve, there are six people on this project. I don't need to look at a written report to tell you what's going on." I think that was the pivotal point for me in changing because I realized we had two different styles. His had worked for him for a number of years. I could learn from him, but I could never be that way. And that's when I realized my style was no less valid. My way was not the wrong way. I don't need to continue looking for "the" answer.
>
> I had several conversations with him about our differences. I don't think any staff person had ever before confronted him on his evaluations of them or his approach. I just kept pointing out to him, "Steve, we're different but trust me. I have delivered everything on time, haven't I?" And he would have to say, "Yes." "My project team is happy?" He said, "Yes." I said, "See, it's not that I do it worse, it's that we're different, and it's not that I can't learn from you."

I think he got a lot from me. Everyone told me, "Sharon, what did you do to Steve? He gave you an 'Outstanding'. He stood up and supported you."

Significant here is the way Sharon addresses the differences between her boss's action-logic and her own in conversations with him. In action inquiry terms, she combines advocacy and illustration of her views with explicit recognition of the differences in their frames and with inquiry in the process of testing and building her commitment to a style of working. She does this even with a subject previously considered unmentionable in her organization, her boss's evaluation of her. She does not refrain from discussing this subject when her principles demand that she discuss it.

Despite Sharon's exemplary story of exercising transforming power, the *Strategist* stage is not without potential shadows and turmoils. The ability to see multiple points of view in conflict, and others acting in ways that reinforce the conflict, can lead to suffering. Awareness of the play of power in general and the strength of transforming power in particular can veer in the direction of obsession. Also, the sense of developing a personal wholistic theory of how to generate change, a theory that integrates broad historical and organizational currents with personal practices, can lead to grandiosity and ego-inflation if it is not humbled by the kind of ongoing spiritual practice that shows the difference between the *Strategist's* theories and the other three territories of experience. Table 7-1 summarizes the characteristics of the *Strategist* action-logic.

Table 7-1 Managerial Style Characteristics Associated with the *Strategist* Developmental Action-logic

Strategist	Recognizes importance of principle, contract, theory, and judgment—not just rules, customs, and exceptions—for making and maintaining good decisions; high value on timely action inquiry, mutuality, and autonomy; attentive to unique market niches, particular historical moments; interweaves short-term goal-orientedness with longer-term developmental process-orientedness; aware of paradox that what one sees depends on one's action-logic; creative at conflict resolution; enjoys playing a variety of roles; witty, existential humor; aware of and tempted by the dark side of power

A Research-Based Look at the Strategist

Research has begun to confirm that people who hold later action-logics do indeed tend to be more effective managers and more transformational leaders. Our own research specifically points to a link between the post-*Achiever* frames and a manager's tendency to redefine problems and to propose collaborative rather than unilateral action in responding to problems.

In one of our studies, we placed 49 MBA graduates in a simulated management setting called an "in-basket" exercise (this was in the mid-eighties, well before the age of e-mail). According to the exercise, they had been hired to replace a manager who had died in an accident. They must still complete another week at their former employer, but they are responding to 34 letters, memos, reports, and phone messages they find in their predecessor's in-basket on a Sunday afternoon, before they have met their new colleagues. Because each subject responded to the same set of 34 items, we were able to apply statistical tests and found that those who measured at postconventional action-logics by the Leadership Development Profile redefined problems in response to more of the in-basket items and made collaborative action proposals in response to more of the items than did those who measured at the *Achiever, Expert,* or other earlier frames.

To find out more about *Strategists* in action on the job, we did a follow-on study. We interviewed 9 men and 8 women who held a range of positions, mainly in service industry firms, including 5 in financial institutions, 2 in research firms, 2 in hospitals, and 4 in consulting firms. The other 4 worked in manufacturing firms. All held advanced degrees, mostly MBAs. Nine held managerial positions, including 1 chief operating officer and 3 functional area heads. Four were in specialist or individual contributor positions (such as financial planner or loan officer), and 4 were consultants. Fifteen of the 17 were in their thirties, with the median age being 36, and the median length of work experience being 10 years. Figure 7.1 shows how the sample breaks down in terms of participants' action-logics. We separated the transcribed interviews into two groups, "conventional" and "postconventional."

We discovered that there were indeed important differences in the ways the conventional and postconventional professionals thought, spoke, and acted at work. We found the differences to be particularly striking in three major arenas: their ways of exercising leadership, their

Figure 7.1   Action-Logics of 17 Study
Participants

Post-conventional	Strategist	6	10
	Individualist	4	
Conventional	Achiever	5	7
	Expert	2	

relationships with their superiors, and their ways of initiating action when proposing ideas or programs.

How Strategists Think and Act

Leadership Practice

- *Strategists* are more likely than *Achievers* to undertake double-loop learning, designing situations where others can be the origin of causation, where tasks are controlled jointly, and where others may make choices and take risks.
- *Strategists* make more frequent and more conscientious efforts than *Achievers* (a) to understand subordinates' frames, inquiring about them rather than dismissing them; (b) to form an integrative awareness of these frames, including discrepant frames; and (c) to use them as a basis for synthesizing new shared understandings.
- *Strategists* are more likely than *Achievers* to test the limits of their organizations' and their superiors' constraints and to create new spheres of action for their subordinates and for themselves.

Relationships with Superiors

- Both *Strategists* and *Achievers* see it as appropriate to influence their superiors' beliefs, goals, and actions.
- *Strategists,* in influencing superiors, are more likely than *Achievers* to undertake a negotiation among initially diverse frames to create a new shared frame, while *Achievers* are more likely to assert their own view as superior and beyond question.

- *Strategists* are more likely than *Achievers* to identify their perceptions as perceptions, rather than as immutable realities, and to discuss differences in perceptions explicitly with their superiors.
- *Strategists,* more than *Achievers,* base their actions on principles rather than rules, even when those principles are at odds with rules established by their superiors.

Action Initiatives

- When their actions are inconsistent with their own principles, *Strategists* are more likely than *Achievers* to notice the discrepancy and act to reduce it.
- *Strategists* are more likely than *Achievers* to view their action processes as unique rather than generalizable and rule-governed.
- *Strategists* are more likely than *Achievers* to to see that their effectiveness lies in setting a stage—a frame in which their own as well as others' aims can be expressed—rather than rushing into getting their own solutions and processes adopted.
- *Achievers* gain acceptance for their own goals by using their awareness of others' points of view as a guide. They see implementation as a linear move toward the goal. *Strategists,* however, use their awareness of others' points of view to question and revise their own goals, as well as to test whether their perspective influences others. They see implementation as an iterative, developmental process involving creation of new shared understandings, leading to the repeated reframing of problems.

Taken as a whole, these statements argue strongly that the capacities managers need, in order to create settings in which they, their colleagues, and their organization as a whole can transform, require a developmental shift of perspective beyond the *Achiever* action through *Individualist* relativism to the *Strategist* action-logic.

Just how dramatically true this turns out to be gradually dawned on us during a decade of studying our own consulting efforts to help companies, colleges, and health care organizations transform. We turn now to an overview of the different outcomes that resulted when CEOs who held conventional developmental action-logics and CEOs measured as *Strategists* tried to lead organizational transformation.

Studying Organizational Transformation Efforts

For 10 years, three of the authors and one other consulting partner participated in and studied 10 organizational development efforts, spending an average of 4 years with each enterprise. The organizations included both for-profit and not-for-profit enterprises, ranging in size from 10 to 1,019 employees, with an average of 485 staff members. They represented numerous industries, including financial services, automotive, consulting, health care, oil, and higher education.

All of the 10 CEOs and many members of their senior management teams completed the Leadership Development Profile. Five of the CEOs measured at the postconventional action-logics (four at *Strategist,* one at *Alchemist*); and five measured at conventional action-logics (two at *Achiever,* two at *Expert,* and one at *Diplomat*). In all five cases in which the CEO was found to be at the a postconventional action-logic, the organization transformed in a positive way—the businesses grew in size, profitability, quality, strategy, and reputation. Several became industry leaders. Moreover, trained scorers agreed that that these five CEOs supported a total of 15 organizational transformations (indeed, all but one of the postconventional CEOs supported at least two transformations during the years we worked with them).

Conversely, the five cases of organizations with pre-*Strategist* CEOs, yielded no organizational transformations on average. In one case there was a three-stage regression; in two cases there was no change; and in two cases there was positive organizational transformation. In the three cases with no positive transformation, the organizations experienced crises and highly visible performance blockages.[1]

This finding is further strengthened by another analysis of the data. Two of the four consultants were measured at the *Strategist* action-logic and the other two were measured at the *Alchemist* action-logic (to be described in Chapter 12). According to our developmental action inquiry theory, those who develop beyond the *Strategist* action-logic exercise action inquiry more and more continuously and increasingly appreciate the intersystemic complexity of acting in a timely fashion, as well as the moment-to-moment paradoxes of exercising "vulnerable

---

1. The correlation between later CEO stage of development and positive organizational transformation is statistically significant beyond the .05 level and accounts for an unusually large 42 percent of the variance by the Spearman Rank Order Test.

power" in order to do so. Thus, we would predict that the **Alchemist** consultants should be more effective than the **Strategist** consultants at supporting pre-**Strategist** CEOs to help their company transform. Our data bear out this prediction. The **Alchemist** action-logic consultants played the lead role in the two cases where pre-**Strategist** CEOs participated in successful organizational transformation (as well as in one of the two cases where there was no change).[2]

To see more clearly how and why different leadership action-logics have different effects on organizational transformation, let us contrast some actions of one of the **Strategist** CEOs with some actions of the **Diplomat** CEO.

One **Strategist** CEO in our study openly presented his weaknesses and shortcomings as a leader to his senior team during a time of organizational crisis. Based on this openness, others took a similar risk, and the team was able to assign responsibilities that eliminated potential blind spots, challenged each another to develop new skills, and provided regular feedback on each other's performances.

Contrast this action to the one **Diplomat** CEO in our sample companies. He was so unwilling and so unable to work constructively with any negative feedback from colleagues and from the market that eventually his entire strategic planning team resigned. After we consultants also failed to influence him, we recommended that he resign. When this also failed, we then recommended to the Board Chair that he replace the CEO. When our recommendations were not accepted, we ourselves resigned. The organization continued to lose money and reputation until the CEO was finally replaced.

In this example, the **Strategist** who makes himself vulnerable to transformation, generates voluntary transformation in others rather than mere external conformity and compliance (or else resistance). In contrast, the **Diplomat** CEO is so deeply committed to maintaining peace and saving face in each particular meeting that he cannot see or name his own vulnerability, much less actively invite his colleagues to help him correct it.

Looking a little more closely at the three examples in which the or-

---

2. Thus, if we add together the developmental scores for the CEO and the lead consultant in each of the 10 cases, and if we correlate the rank order of the resulting numbers with the rank order of the number of successful transformations achieved by each organization, we find that this correlation is significant at the .01 level and accounts for 59 percent of the variance.

ganizations did not transform in a positive direction, we find that in each case, the pre-*Strategist* CEOs had increasingly distanced themselves from the consultant and from senior management team members who measured at the *Strategist* or later stages. In one case, the CEO alternated betwccn, on the one hand, highly valuing his internal consultant/senior manager and the change process and, on the other hand, trying to displace her from the senior management team altogether while freezing the change process. As a result, the organization did not transform during this period (the consultant/senior manager won a civil suit against the CEO, he retired, and the senior manager went on to take a CEO role in a different organization).

A closer retrospective look at the two anomalous cases where a CEO operating at a conventional action-logic *did* support positive transformation is also interesting. In both instances, the CEO treated the outside consultant and the one or more team members measured as *Strategists* as close confidantes and gave them wide leeway in influencing the content and timing of different interventions.

In one of these two positive cases, there was a tragic later chapter (after the original research had been completed and reported as in the preceding text). The CEO, who had been scored at the *Expert* action-logic originally, and who had learned many collaborative skills, such as framing, advocating, illustrating, and inquiring, and had created multiple leadership roles for each team, became CEO of another, much larger organization during a merger. Although he may have evolved to the *Achiever* action-logic during our work with him (we do not have a second action-logic score for him), he had certainly not yet evolved a *Strategist* sense of timing and reframing, as events showed. In the new setting there was little trust and no history of senior management development as a team. Nevertheless, rather than discovering what actions would be timely and creative in the new setting, this CEO tried to reproduce what had worked in the previous organization where there was high trust. The organization regressed, lost hundreds of millions of dollars, the CEO became isolated, and he was fired.

Conclusions

So, what do the results of our three very different studies of *Strategists*—our in-basket laboratory experiment, our interview study, and our long-term action research field experiments with 10 organizations—suggest for other organizations that may be embarking on, or are in the midst of, a transformation process?

First of all, they indicate that although **Strategists** will tend to be agents for constructive change at whatever level in the organization they occupy, any business that is serious about achieving organizational transformation should carefully consider the significance of the CEO's action-logic in particular. The results of our field experiments suggest that at least initially, the CEO's support is necessary in order to create a culture in which change can start anywhere within the organization and that only a CEO at the **Strategist** action-logic can reliably do so.

This finding is strongly reinforced by Jim Collins (2001) in his recent book *Good to Great.* Collins isolated 11 companies that transformed from good to great in terms of market share and financial performance and then sustained the new levels of excellence for long periods of time. He found the quality of engagement of their CEOs, which he summarizes as a paradoxical blend of "humility and fierce resolve" (a **Strategist's** integration of inquiry and action?), to be a critical factor in all these sustained organizational transformations. Although he is unable to explain the qualities of these CEOs in theoretical terms, we suggest they sound developmentally like **Strategists** and recommend that interested readers consult his book and see for themselves.

Practice Reframing

Now taking one form of action inquiry (or often several) as a leisurely discipline one chooses to cultivate, the **Strategist** seeks to invite inquiry into more and more moments of life. Whether it be through song or dance or a sport, through meditation or prayer or journal keeping, through carpentry or sewing or cooking, through poetry or a musical instrument or theatre, the **Strategist** seeks out practices intended to heighten awareness and attunement at each moment.

Likewise, in moments of professional or familial tension among our own, others', and our institutions' different agendas, the **Strategist** wonders how to reframe the dilemma and the assumptions that obstruct resolution. The following exercises can help.

- Try using developmental theory to help characterize the situations you encounter and the strategies you design and see to what degree it converges with or extends your intuitive sense of timing.

The next section will introduce you to the realm of team and organizational dynamics. Continue to hone your capacity for immediacy in noticing the developmental dynamics going on in you and around you.

- Be conscious and intentional about inquiring into your own, others', and institutions' framing of any problematic situation in which you find yourself. Notice the familiar starting assumptions with which you operate, and question them, turning them inside-out, and follow the new logics that result from doing this.
- Where paradoxes and polarities are evident, take time to play with them alone and with others, peek under each of their assumptions, try replacing them with others and discover where it takes your imagination.
- If you've tried several different ways to resolve a situation with no success, ask yourself what's the *last* thing you would ordinarily do right now and seriously consider doing it. (The last thing we would do in a situation does not fit our action-logic about what the situation requires, but our current action-logic may be precisely the cause of our repeated inability to resolve the situation.)

The Next Section

In the face of perpetual transition in the churning global economy of the early 21st century, the great challenge is how to interweave productivity, inquiry, and transformation in the short and long term, both individually and corporately. This challenge of transforming our predominant global action-logic toward the *Strategist's* collaborative inquiry mode is at least as great as the global *Achiever* struggle to gain unilateral political, economic, and technological control over nature and society that has preoccupied us for the past 500 years. As more and more of us become aware of the dignity of mutual, transformational relationships, rather than unilateral, exploitative relationships, within organizations and countries, between men and women, and between society and nature, we will become increasingly inspired to devote our daily lives to these means and these ends.

Up to now, we have discussed how action inquiry leads us in this direction at the individual level. Starting in our next chapter, we begin to examine how teams and whole organizations can transform through these same action-logics. Sometimes they evolve slowly, sometimes they

engage in intense episodes of action inquiry to transform from one action-logic to another. We show how they can gradually evolve into learning organizations that continually interweave productivity and inquiry.
As the evidence from our research studies in this chapter has illustrated,
the **Strategist** is committed to catalyzing such ongoing organizational
transformation. Thus, in moving into the next section, we are not moving beyond the **Strategist** action-logic, but more deeply into its day-to-
day organizing concerns.

PART THREE

Transforming Organizations

EIGHT

Transforming Meetings, Teams, and Organizations

In Chapters 4 through 7, we have been talking about taking an action inquiry approach to transforming the action-logics guiding our own practice. Of course, our own practice in an organization involves us with other co-workers, so a large part of what we have discussed so far has concerned how to diagnose colleagues as well as ourselves and how to experiment with acting differently with our superiors and subordinates. But the focus has fallen consistently on how each of us can improve our own practice through action inquiry.

In this section of the book, we shift our focus to the questions of how to lead teams and organizations through developmental transformations. This shift in focus is subtle but important because we are not shifting the focus *away* from the individual to the group and we are not shifting the focus simply because we think it's a good idea to cover these topics. We are shifting the focus to the group and organizational scales because that is what you and any other individual who goes very far in your own practice of action inquiry will want and need to do. In fact, as we have seen in a general way at the end of Chapter 7, **Strategist** CEOs become highly effective at leading organizational transformation, in part because they are less attached to their own frames and, therefore, more aware of how people, organizations, and societies journey through different frames and action-logics over time.

In other words, by turning to the development of learning teams, learning organizations, and the learning society, we are continuing to focus on how you, the individual, can conduct action inquiry. But now the arena of your action inquiry can begin to expand beyond your exercise of leadership in changing your own practice to include your exercise of leadership in transforming a group's or organization's practice. You begin to appreciate how people and organizations are either transforming toward greater integrity, mutuality, and sustainability or not. As you become increasingly aware of incongruities among your (or their) principles and your (or their) practice, you become increasingly committed to the moment-to-moment action inquiry of reentering the four territories of experience whether on the personal, the team, or the organizational level. Through observing the many points of view and action-logics at work in any given situation, you cease to cling to your own initial point of view.

Just as people who evolve toward the later action-logics become more and more skilled at exercising action inquiry in the present, so also groups and organizations can be helped to transform toward becoming "learning organizations." Learning organizations, like the **Strategist** at the individual level, intentionally and explicitly seek out single- and double-, and, eventually, triple-loop feedback and change. But, just as the movement to the postconventional action-logics is no simple, one-time transfer for a person, the same is true for organizations. Multiple transformations are necessary before an organization's action-logic intentionally supports the personal transformation of its own members, as well as the ongoing transformation of its teams, its new divisions, its strategic partnerships, and so on.

Moreover, there is a sense in which organizational transformation is more fragile than personal transformation. Short of an extraordinary accident or illness, individual persons tend to maintain an action-logic once they win through to it. But an organization's board can oust its CEO and senior management team, or sell the company to a competitor. In such cases, the governing action-logic of the organization may regress virtually overnight. (Strategic mergers can also be intended to help the core organization transform culturally in a progressive developmental direction, as in the case of Carly Fiorina's HP/Compaq merger, but progressive transformation requires more than one night!)

In learning organizations, openness to questioning exists, assumptions are tested, seeming mistakes are rarely punished but are a basis for further learning, new knowledge is shared, and new knowledge is gained collaboratively. In short, inquiry, and specifically developmental action inquiry, becomes an activity of the organization. Sometimes, this begins with a small group of inquirers operating within a larger organization that is not initially friendly to this open-ended learning process. We have seen a number of cases where these "learning cells" (sometimes no more than three people meeting for lunch every other week) have come in time to influence the larger organization. (What organizational institutions support collaborative inquiry in very large organizations is a major mystery that the world as a whole faces today. The U.S. Constitution, with its supposed "balance of powers" among a principled, reflective branch [the judiciary], a diverse, proposing branch [the congress], and an action-oriented, performing branch [the executive], is a rare example of a large and long-lasting organized collaborative inquiry.)

One of the largest organizations in the world began from the humble beginning of a small group of devoted inquirers. We are referring to Alcoholics Anonymous and all the other 12-step groups that the AA approach has since spawned. Alcoholics Anonymous began as a conversation between two people who wished to change their behavior.

Alcoholics Anonymous is a learning organization in the sense that it supports individual people in reforming their lives when they are down and out. It is a good example of a learning organization in that it demonstrates how eager the individual member must be for transformation in order for developmental change to occur. Granted, we cannot directly generalize from Alcoholics Anonymous to the organizational situations most of us inhabit at work and in our leisure. We rarely inhabit organizations where everyone shares the same intense motivation to transform in a particular direction, and where there is no other order of business but personal transformation.

We also recognize that Alcoholics Anonymous is not focused on organizational learning and transformation—on creating a learning organization—but, rather, on individual learning and transformation. However, this very mission made its early leadership extraordinarily vigilant in guarding against bureaucratization as it grew. So, for our present purposes, the example of Alcoholics Anonymous is very useful as a pointer toward a kind of organizing that encourages both personal and organizational transformations along the path toward personal development and a learning organization. Indeed, Alcoholics Anonymous exemplifies the **Social-Network** type of organization that parallels the **Individualist** frame at the personal scale (see Table 8-1). Like a large international conglomerate that allows its subsidiaries to retain their corporate identities and individual strategies, Alcoholics Anonymous allows its thousands upon thousands of separate meeting places wide autonomy.

More generally, the key to effectual action inquiry, as we have so far described it, is developing a personal attention and interpersonal conversations that interweave the four territories of experience. In the same way, becoming a learning organization entails interweaving action and inquiry throughout the four territories of organizational experience: visioning, strategizing, performing, and assessing. Some readers will remember SAS airlines, vision/motto "Moments of Truth." "Moments of Truth" meant that the presence and openness to inquiry of all SAS personnel in each live encounter with a customer or colleague determined whether the encounter was successful and effective. This vision potentially generated triple-loop feedback for its employees, transforming their attention each time they remembered it as they interacted with the public.

In the realm of strategy, for many years 3M set a strategy of increasing a division's funding if it increased the percentage of its return on investment from recent innovations. This approach made 3M a hub for combining inquiry and action in productive innovation. At the operational level, the case of a small software company that we examine in Chapter 9 will illustrate how meetings can simultaneously encourage frank inquiry and dialogue along with decisiveness. Finally, assessment processes such as 360-degree performance feedback, or triple bottom-line measures of companies' financial, social, and environmental effects, document personal and organizational outcomes in complex, diverse ways that support single-, double-, and triple-loop inquiry and change, and, thus, sustainable improvements in productivity.

Our question is, how does any particular organization evolve to the point of interweaving action and inquiry across all four territories of visioning, strategizing, performing, and assessing?

Parallels Between Personal and
Organizational Development

In answer to this question, we present in this chapter a way of understanding organizational development as a sequence of transforming action-logics, analogous to personal development. As with individual persons, a given action-logic may characterize a given meeting or project, or a whole organization over many years. Within the overall organization, particular projects or divisions may represent leading or lagging developmental tendencies. Similarly, your own department or a team or task force may transform from one stage of development to another during a single meeting or over the course of several meetings.

Table 8-1 indicates how the two theories of development at the individual and the organizational scale are directly analogous to one another. (You will note that we show an early childhood action-logic—the *Impulsive*—that we did not mention in earlier chapters, since we found no managers in our large samples at either of these.) Table 8-2 describes the unique characteristics of the first seven organizational development action-logics in a little more detail. (We defer discussion of the eighth action-logic at both the personal and organizational scales until Chapters 12 and 13.)

Now we offer a few comments on each stage, in order to highlight the personal–organizational parallels in Table 8-1. Then, we give some concrete illustrations of particular meetings and of whole organizations moving from one organizational action-logic to another.

Let us start with a brief comment on the parallel relationship between the *Impulsive* stage of personal development and the *Conception* stage of organizational development. Just as very young children are highly imaginative and express many impulses (e.g., to become an artist, or a nurse, or a professional athlete) that they do not necessarily follow up on in their later life, so do adults frequently fantasize with friends about organizations they would like to create (e.g., to market a baby stroller that can be folded up and would have made today's visit to the city easier), but then do not necessarily follow up on. In retrospect, when one in every ten thousand or so such conversations eventually evolves into a major organization, as Alcoholics Anonymous did, the founding of the organization can be traced back to such incidental or passionate or calculating conversations.

The parallels between the next three personal and organizational development action-logics is less obvious. When we described the *Opportunist,* the *Diplomat,* and the *Expert* in Chapters 4 and 5, we were describing not children in the normal process of development but, rather, adults in organizations who are still motivated by relatively early action-logics. Therefore, we can see the rigidities and limitations in their effectiveness quite easily. By contrast, when we discuss organizations at these three early action-logics (in this chapter and in Chapter 9, see also Table 8-2), we describe them in their natural developmental process (i.e., in their "childhood"), so the positive attributes of each action-logic will be more obvious than its shortcomings (*Investments, Incorporation, Experiments*).

Let us now, therefore, track the similarities between people and organizations at each of these three action-logics. Both the 8- to 12-year-

Table 8-1   Parallels Between Personal
and Organizational Developmental Action-Logics

Personal Development	Organizational Development
1. Impulsive	**1. Conception**
Impulses rule behavior	Dreams about creating a new organization

(*multiple, distinctive impulses gradually resolve into characteristic approach [e.g., many fantasies into a particular dream for a new organization]*)

2. Opportunist	**2. Investments**
Needs rule impulses	Spiritual, social network, and financial investments

(*dominant task: gain power [e.g., bike riding skill, capital] to have desired effects on outside world*)

3. Diplomat	**3. Incorporation**
Norms rule needs	Products or services actually rendered

(*looking-glass self: understanding others' culture/expectations and molding own actions to succeed in their terms [e.g., a marketable product]*)

4. Expert	**4. Experiments**
Craft logic rules norms	Alternative strategies and structures tested

(*intellectual mastery of outside-self systems such that actions equal experiments that generate new ways of doing business*)

5. Achiever	**5. Systematic Productivity**
System effectiveness rules craft logic	Single structure/strategy institutionalized

(*pragmatic triangulation among plan/theory, operation/implementation, and outcome/evaluation—single-loop feedback acted on unsystematically but regularly*)

6. Individualist	**6. Social Network**
Reflexive awareness rules effectiveness	Portfolio of distinctive organizational structures

(*experimental awareness that diverse assumptions may complement one another both for inquiry and for productivity*)

7. *Strategist*
Self-amending principle
rules reflexive awareness

7. *Collaborative Inquiry*
Self-amending structure matches dream/
mission

(self-conscious mission/philosophy, sense of time/place, invites conversation among multiple voices and reframing of boundaries—double-loop feedback occasionally acted on)

8. *Alchemist*
Process (interplay of
principle/action) rules
principle

8. *Foundational Community of Inquiry*
Structure fails, spirit sustains wider community

(life/science equals a mind/matter, love/death/transformation praxis among others, cultivating interplay, reattunement and continual triple-loop feedback)

---

old child at the ***Opportunist*** action-logic and the organization at the parallel ***Investments*** action-logic seek resources from the environment and capabilities with which to manipulate the environment. At best, the child has a bike to learn to ride and parents who are also making inspirational and social network investments in him or her (e.g., offering the child support of some kind and exposure to good teachers). Similarly, wise organizational founders and wise venture capitalists will be concerned with the inspirational resonance and profundity of the organization's mission and mentors, as well as the social, professional, and business alliances that can support the organization during its passage through the ***Investments*** action-logic. However, if the organizational founders are themselves still arrested at the ***Opportunistic*** action-logic of development, they will act as though tangible financial resources are the only significant investments needed. Such an organization may appear very successful in terms of financial backing in the short term, but the lack of network resources and inspiration will result in lower commitment by all stakeholders and will stunt its development in the longer term. Many dot-com companies with significant venture financing during the late 1990s never reached the break-even point.

Given some resources and natural abilities, a person who transforms to the ***Diplomat*** action-logic during the early teenage years and the organization that transforms to the equivalent ***Incorporation*** action-logic are both learning how to operate successfully according to the rules of their social milieus. We call these "peer groups" in the case of teenagers and "markets" in the case of for-profit companies. In both cases, there

Table 8-2   Characteristics of Each Organizational
Developmental Action-Logic

1. *Conception*	Dreams, visions, informal conversations about creating something new to fill need not now adequately addressed; interplay among multiple founders; working models, prototypes, related projects, or business plans developed. Critical issues: timeliness and mythic proportions of vision.
2. *Investments*	Champions commit to creating organization; early relationship-building among future stakeholders; peer networks and parent institutions make spiritual, structural, financial commitments to nurture. Critical issues: authenticity and reliability of commitments; financial investment appropriately subordinated to structural and spiritual investments.
3. *Incorporation*	Products or services produced; recognizable physical setting, tasks, and roles delineated; goals and operating staff chosen. Critical issues: display of persistence in the face of threat; maintaining or recreating consistency between original dream and actual organizational arrangements.
4. *Experiments*	Alternative administrative, production, selection, reward, financial, marketing, and political strategies practiced, tested in operation, and reformed in rapid succession. Critical issues: truly experimenting—taking disciplined stabs in the dark—rather than merely trying one or two preconceived alternatives; finding a viable, longer-lasting combination of strategy and structure for the following stage.

are many difficult moments, and neither the young teenager nor the young company may have the persistence to succeed. Or, both may lose their honor (sense of self-respect based on loyalty to a constructive mission) in their eagerness to conform to the demands of their milieu.

Failure to meet the demands of the larger milieu may result in a person's lifelong membership in a dependent and possibly illegitimate underclass. For example, a disproportionate percentage of people in jail measure as *Opportunists*. In the case of an organization at this stage,

5. *Systematic Productivity* — Attention legitimately focused only on systematic procedures for accomplishing the predefined task; standards, structures, roles taken for granted as given; marketability or political viability of product or service, as measured in quantifiable terms, the overriding criterion of success. Critical issue: whether organization remembers analogical concerns about congruity from mission through outcomes during this emphasis on deductive, pyramidal systems.

6. *Social Network* — Strategic or mission-focused alliances among portfolio of organizations, with strong value on maintaining distinctive traditions, craft-orientations, and relative financial autonomy. Critical issue: will organization regress or progress in economically adverse conditions?

7. *Collaborative Inquiry* — Explicit, shared reflection about corporate mission; open interpersonal relations with disclosure, support, and confrontation of apparent value differences; systematic personal and corporate performance appraisal on multiple indexes; creative resolution of paradoxes-inquiry/productivity, freedom/control, quality/quantity; interactive development of unique, self-amending structures appropriate for this particular organization at this particular historical moment; critical issue: will organization sustain collaborative inquiry as it grows through hiring, merger, or strategic alliances, or will it revert to conventional *Systematic Productivity*?

failure usually means outright economic failure or else a very contingent survival in a small local niche. Success in meeting the demands of the milieu at the price of one's honor also has a significant dark side: it makes development to further stages much less likely.

Young people who are able to break the (*Diplomat*) mold of their immediate social milieu (which sometimes happens by leaving home and high school peers for college) begin to seek out something more consistent to subordinate themselves to than the helter-skelter, conflicting demands of their significant others. They are seeking a more purposeful, skill-based way of organizing their lives and a more objective way of measuring their relative success at doing so. The teenager who says, "I like track better than soccer because in track you are measured by your actual time in the event, whereas in soccer it's whether the coach likes you" is expressing her growing attraction to the *Expert* action-logic of doing well in terms of objectively measured standards and her rejection of the *Diplomat* stage logic of doing well what will gain another person's approval.

This movement from *Diplomat* to *Expert* action-logic parallels an organization's movement from *Incorporation* to *Experiments*. The *Expert's* experiments toward excellence in any given skill involve a series of semidisciplined stabs in the dark. An organization transforming toward the *Experiments* stage at best conducts such experiments in all realms of its business, from the way in which it conducts its accounting (typically moving from the cash to the accrual method at this point and from manual, paper records to computer systems), to the very fact of engaging in proactive marketing rather than simply servicing clients who come through the door.

Like people, organizations very often halt along the path to becoming learning organizations when they reach what could be transformational opportunities and challenges. Instead of transforming, they defend their current culture and structure and become rigid, lose their identity in a merger, or go out of business. Paradoxically, huge and highly successful companies, like Digital Equipment Corporation (DEC), are as much subject to this threat as less successful ones, because successful companies are more likely to remain proudly identified with their current procedures. But each developmental transformation of a company's culture requires learning the opposite skills from the previous action-logic. (For example, the odd-numbered organizational action-logics in Tables 8-1 and 8-2 demand relative centralization, whereas the even-numbered action-logics demand relative decentralization.) Thus, DEC exemplifies a company that, guided by its powerful, scientifically oriented, *Achiever* action-logic founder/CEO Ken Olsen, remained at the decentralized *Experiments* organizational action-logic even after it had become the second-largest computer company in the world and died for its loyalty to its principles (Schein 2003).

Understanding and Leading Meetings as Developmental Processes

We can view each new project or new product, each new team or task force, each new agenda item, meeting, or series of meetings as a developmental process. Microspirals of development in single meetings nest within wider project, departmental, and organizational cycles. To get a more lifelike picture of how even a single meeting can transform through several organizational action-logics, let's listen to a top management team member of a Fortune 100 company who, without ever having thought of himself as using developmental theory, in fact manages team meetings in a manner that parallels the early stages of organizational development we have just been reviewing.

This senior vice president has an undergraduate mathematics background, with an interest in the Pythagorean theory of the octave as the organizing structure for color (the seven colors of the rainbow), for sound (the musical octave), and for human activities such as meetings (his own application). Of business meetings, he says (with our organizational action-logic names added in brackets):

The first note "do" is the leader's vision for the whole meeting. It has to be both crisp and inspiring. It's got to surprise people just a little—jog them awake, make them reconsider what they came in prepared to do. [*Conception*—generating a surprisingly creative new vision]

"Re" is the first response, the first chorus from the group. The leader has got to allow for this if he wants a creative, committed meeting. How he choreographs that first response determines how far the meeting can go. [*Investments*—helping others to join and own the issue]

"Mi" is the first concrete decision of the meeting. If it's taken early on and makes sense to everyone, there's a general loosening up, and the rest of the meeting is likely to fly. [*Incorporation*—something being produced; the vision becoming real]

A lot of meetings end with one or more decisions like this, but if you want to do something qualitatively different again, like coordinate among different decisions, you strike the next note "fa." "Fa" is primarily the group's note again, so the leader's structure should be something that brings out the chorus, something like breaking into subgroups on different issues. [*Experiments*—exploring many implications of the vision]

He goes on to discuss the rest of the meeting octave and concludes:

But the actual meeting can also be viewed as the middle part of the octave ("fa," "sol," "la") between the two intervals. In this larger perspective, the pre-meeting preparation is the first part of the octave and the post-meeting follow-up is the final part.

This final paragraph of the executive's vision of how meetings are best conducted illustrates the notion of overlapping or nested developmental processes that we mentioned earlier. You are welcome to compare back and forth between Table 8-2 and the executive's description of each musical note in a well-run meeting to see to what degree they parallel one another. But our point is less that there is a perfectly precise parallel and more that this illustration brings to life the general sense of how a meeting can be viewed developmentally.

Imagine how much more interesting and productive business meetings in general would be if more executives were this creative in managing them!

Conclusion

The very brief references to well-known organizations offered in this chapter, along with the slightly more detailed notion of how to sequence a particular meeting that we have just examined, illustrate the parallel relationship that exists between personal and organizational development. In Chapter 9, we will look at several detailed examples of small companies transforming from one organizational action-logic to another. This examination will give us a more lifelike picture of these early organizational action-logics and of how an organization can transform from one to another. Gradually, we will begin to develop the capacity to read meetings, teams, and organizations developmentally, along with a sense for what kind of intervention at what time can play a catalytic leadership role in supporting organizational transformation.

NINE

Facilitating Organizational Transformations

M ultiple developmental processes at different scales (personal, team, organizational, national, etc.) influence one another, either interrupting, inhibiting, or encouraging the developmental process we originally focus on. Can we see these interweaving developmental processes in action and intervene to help whole organizations to transform from one developmental action-logic to another?

In this chapter, we first examine a small software company that is stuck between the *Investments* and *Incorporation* action-logics. Then we describe a new merger among three small residential health care companies at the *Incorporation* action-logic, where the challenge is to transform to the *Experiments* action-logic. We conclude with an energy company, where the challenge is to transform from *Experiments* to *Systematic Productivity.* Each case illustrates how a consultant's intervention can create a temporary *Collaborative Inquiry* learning organization within the company, with a great deal of feedback and creative, collaborative decision making, as a vehicle for encouraging each organizational transformation.

Intervening to Help a Small Software Company Transform Itself into Profitability

A small software company has burned through its initial round of venture financing, with net revenues for its products not yet foreseeable on the horizon. The partners are seeking a second round of venture capital, and everybody at the company knows they must make a breakthrough in marketing and sales. Yet, this bottom-line, relatively objective negative feedback alone, as stark as it is, is not propelling the company into a new operating pattern.

An organizational consultant who takes a developmental action inquiry approach is invited to help the company over a two-day period on a Thursday and Friday. He approaches the assignment with the sense that he must engage in an interviewing and meeting process that discovers what disharmonies among the corporate dream, the leadership's strategies, and the day-to-day operations account for the company's continuing losses. But more important, this research and intervention process must discover a positive way to reframe or restructure the situation with the senior leadership team so that it comes to enact vision, strategy, and operations more harmoniously.

> On the first day the consultant interviews the top management (the president and the three vice presidents for production, marketing, and sales) of the computer software company, which numbers 35 employees in all. The president is a generation older than the three vice presidents, and the company is a partnership between the president and the vice president for production. Together, the two of them developed the initial product. In the three years following its founding, the company has produced a large number of high-quality products, but they are not selling well. The consultant discovers numerous problems that have remained unresolved for a long time. Neither mission nor market is well defined. Pricing is a subject of acrimonious controversy. Employee morale is fragile because it is unclear whether competence or nepotism is the basis for rewards (one partner's daughter is the VP for sales and the other's best friend is an employee). Decisions are not driven by any internal sense of mission; they are made only when situations deteriorate into external emergencies.
>
> The bottleneck in decision making appears to be the relationship between the two partners. They respect one another and attempt to share responsibility as though equals. But they repeatedly fall prey to differences in age, formal role, and managerial style. The president plays the role of optimistic, appreciative, absentminded father. The vice president plays the role of pessimistic, sharp, rebellious son.
>
> Having interviewed the senior managers individually during the first six hours of his two-day visit, the consultant is next slated to meet with the two partners to set the agenda for the next day's senior management retreat. But based on what he has heard, the consultant fears that the agenda-setting session and the retreat may themselves fall prey to the

partners' well-intentioned wrangling and indecisiveness. In his 10-minute walk around the outside of the building prior to the session, the consultant engages in the first-person action inquiry of intentionally bringing his attention first to his breathing and then, following that, to the vividness of the outside world, then to his feelings, and, only when he has established an ongoing circulation of attention, to what he now knows about the company.

He decides that the partners' pattern of behavior must change before any other productive decisions are likely, and that he should invent an initiative to help this begin to happen immediately, if possible. Quickly and impressionistically, he applies developmental theory to the company as a whole, to the individual partners, and to his two-day intervention to help him generate design ideas for his meeting with the partners, only moments away.

Applying the developmental theory to the company as a whole (refer to Tables 8-1 and 8-2), the consultant sees the organization as spread-eagled across the fluid, decentralized *Investments* and *Experiments* stages, still living off venture capital on the one hand, while on the other hand experimenting with a whole line of products. At the same time, the company is failing to bite the bullet and meet the limiting, centralizing, differentiating demands of the *Incorporation* stage—the demand, in short, for net revenues.

Applying the developmental theory to each of the partners as individuals, the consultant wonders whether the junior partner is an *Opportunist*, given his seeming self-centeredness and irritability, or an *Expert*, given his technical creativity in designing new software products and his doctoral degree. Recognizing that he is working with scant data, the consultant chooses to err on the upside. (Erring on the downside can insult the client and hurt the relationship, whereas the client will typically not even recognize an upside error, allowing the consultant to adjust with little loss.) Thus in this case, the consultant estimates that the vice president is in transition from the *Expert* to the *Achiever* stage of development, both itching for and resisting the true executive responsibility that a person at the *Achiever* relishes. Similarly, he wonders whether the president is a *Diplomat*, given his affable, seemingly conflict-avoiding style, or an *Individualist*, given his appreciation of individual differences and lack of need to hoard power. The consultant estimates that the president is in transition from the *Achiever* stage to the *Strategist* stage, ready to give up day-to-day executive responsibility in favor of an elder statesman role of mentoring his junior partner and godfathering the company's research and development function (indeed, the president has spoken wistfully of his preference for the VP R&D position).

Applying the developmental theory to his own two-day visit, the consultant interprets the initial interviews as the *Conception* stage of the intervention. In this light, the agenda-setting session with the two partners may represent the *Investments* stage. If so, the question is how to restructure his consulting style at this point from a more passive, receptive interviewing process to a more active, intervening process that models the new investment the partners must be willing to make in decisiveness if they are to achieve the rapid major changes necessary in the organization as a whole. This reasoning convinces the consultant that he must attempt to reframe the partners' expectations and pattern of behavior from the outset of the agenda-setting session. In particular, he decides to recommend at the agenda-setting session that only the partners and the consultant participate in the retreat and that whatever decisions the partners reach the next day be put in writing with definite implementation dates. This smaller retreat makes crisp decision making more likely, especially with regard to restructuring senior management, which the consultant now views as important. He believes the vice president for sales should be demoted, as will be explained in the following. And he believes the two partners must redefine their relationships.

With regard to redefining the partners' roles, the consultant believes the company needs a single decisive executive for the *Incorporation* stage. By chance, both partners have used the image of ballots to describe their relative power within the company in their initial interviews. The president, referring to their equal salaries and to his style of consulting his partner on all significant decisions, speaks of the partners as holding "ballots of the same size" in company decisions. The vice president sees the president as having the larger vote. The consultant now reasons that if the two switch their formal roles, at least as a serious role play for this one day, the president should still see their votes as equal, while the vice president should see his vote as having become larger. Thus, the twosome will become more powerful, but only if each accepts the developmental challenge inherent in the change. For the new roles will only work if they help each executive to move to a wider action-logic—the decisive presidential role helping the *Expert* move toward the *Achiever* action-logic.

More immediately, the mere fact of having the two officers reverse roles for the agenda-setting meeting and the day-long retreat should alter their usual dynamics and put them into a posture of simultaneous rehearsal and performance conducive to action inquiry. Of course, the consultant himself will be in a similar posture as he makes this unexpected suggestion.

The consultant begins his feedback/agenda-setting session with the two partners by proposing that the vice president either resign or become president. This puts the vice president in the action role right away, rather than his usual role of reacting to the president. Although quiet, the president seems ready to play this game. On the other hand, true to his customary opposing role, the vice president objects to rehearsing as president. After considerable probing by the vice president to explore the consultant's reasoning, the two senior officers agree to this serious game.

Now the vice president (in the role of the president) acts decisively rather than reacting combatively. He and the consultant propose various changes, with the president (in the subordinate role) making constructive suggestions and raising questions. The two partners reach written agreement on six major organizational changes the next day, including pricing and focusing on only one of their innovative products. The first of these changes is implemented at lunch that day. The vice president for sales, who is the president's daughter, is invited to join them. The partners discuss the major changes they are considering, and ask her to accept a demotion, and work under the vice president of marketing. She agrees, expressing both her disappointment that she has not been able to help the company more and her relief that her duties will be more circumscribed. Showing that they have by no means altogether lost confidence in her, the partners ask her whether she is willing to take the lead that very afternoon in communicating the new reporting arrangement to the vice president of marketing, as well as informally communicating the other two decisions they have made that morning to other company members. The sales manager enthusiastically agrees.

The following Monday, the written agreement describing the six changes, signed by both partners, is in all company members' mailboxes when they arrive. A company-wide meeting at the end of the following day visibly confirms the partners' agreement and allows for questions and discussion of the implications. A month later, all the changes have been implemented. Two months later, the company completes, six months ahead of schedule, a first of its kind product for a definite and large market. The company fails to get a second round of venture financing, but sales revenues begin to exceed costs for the first time in the company's history due to the new product.

In the meantime, the vice president decides not to become president. The president stipulates that henceforward he will draw a higher salary and exercise the managerial authority of CEO on a day-to-day basis. Another three months later, the vice presidential partner decides he wishes to become president after all and negotiates the change with the other partner.

This case illustrates how developmental analysis of an organization can help to bring its primary issues and priority decisions into focus. It also illustrates how a leader (in this case, the consultant) interweaves developmental issues at the personal, interpersonal, and organizational scales. On the personal scale, the consultant engages in a triple-loop attention-clearing exercise at a critical moment in his information gathering, followed by a double-loop effort to conceptualize everything he has learned about the company up to that point into a theory/strategy for redesigning the rest of the consulting engagement.

Next, he generates an interpersonal action inquiry process among members of the company, particularly the partners and the sales vice president. The role-reversal role play the partners engage in and the goal of reaching written agreements makes this a more immediate and intense action inquiry than it otherwise would have been.

Over the next several months, the intense interpersonal action inquiries transform the way the company as a whole operates in terms of new product development, sales, and revenues. We can also see that over time, the vice president evidently continues an active inquiry about the leadership role he wishes to embody, possibly transforming from the *Expert* to the *Achiever* action-logic.

You may feel a little mystified why the decision to demote the sales vice president worked out so well. The various tactics and strategies involved may have sounded quite risky and the positive outcome in this case may sound lucky. However, during the initial interviews, the consultant learned that both partners, as well as both the marketing vice president and the sales vice president, were all in favor of the demotion. Up to that moment, however, none of them had viewed the issue as discussable, so none was aware that there was unanimous agreement.

The sales vice president was aware of and embarrassed about the negative feelings of others in the company concerning nepotism. She had, in fact, joined the company as a favor to her father at its outset at a very low salary. When the older and more experienced marketing vice president joined the company at a much higher salary after venture financing was obtained, the partners made her a vice president to compensate for her low salary and to give her more credibility with potential customers. She felt unhappy and isolated within the company and not sufficiently competent to hold her position. She wanted to seek advice from the marketing vice president and also to start a part-time MBA program. But she didn't have time for the latter, and she was afraid that she would be rebuffed by the marketing vice president and would also be letting her father down if she asked for help.

All this emerged during her interview with the consultant, after he guaranteed that he would use whatever information she offered only in ways that would increase trust in the company while simultaneously protecting the confidentiality of each individual. When the consultant later met with the partners, he included the issue of "favoritism" as one of the eight major issues requiring resolution and suggested that the demotion of the sales vice president was a step no one he had interviewed opposed. The partners feared she would be hurt by this move. The consultant challenged them to consider whether she was being hurt by the current arrangement and whether the demotion might actually improve her situation. The partners quickly figured out how this might be the case.

Next, the consultant suggested that the luncheon with the sales vice president and the invitation to her to share the results informally would be a powerful way both for the company to be positively primed for a new era and for her to begin regaining "face" with her colleagues. Again, the partners feared the sales vice president might feel forced to accept the invitation and might be hurt in the process. Now, the consultant challenged the partners not to choose inaction in the face of fear, as appeared to be their habit. Rather, he advocated that they practice framing the invitation and inquiring of the sales vice president in ways that would assure that she would *not* be forced to accept the invitation. Then they could ask her both how she viewed the risk of being hurt and whether she wished to assume the risk. During the luncheon, the two most tentative and nervous members of the quartet were the partners who were practicing this new skill of "vulnerable power."

Transforming a Company That Grows Suddenly by Acquisition

In order to become better acquainted with the different organizational action-logics and with the type and time of intervention that can help a particular organization transform, let us now follow a merger of three small organizations as they each transform from their separate *Incorpo-ration* experiences to a shared *Experiments* action-logic (see Table 8-2 to remind yourself of the characteristics of these two stages).

A small, but rapidly growing company has recently become geographically dispersed because of two acquisitions of other small companies by its president. The president asks a consultant to design a two-day quarterly retreat for the 40 managers who constitute the top three layers of man-agement of the new multisite organization. "The people equation is the most difficult, recurrent, and intractable issue," says the president, "and we need our managers to have new core competencies that include recog-nizing and taking responsibility for the impact their actions have on one another, not only in the same office but at the other sites, and for the or-ganizational values that their actions are creating." The president pro-poses a lecture/discussion of the consultant's theory of managerial and organizational development and some skill-building sessions.

The consultant doubts that just talking about transformation will make much difference. Instead, she interviews six members of the orga-nization by phone and learns about some significant issues the president has not mentioned, probably because he's not aware of how much they af-fect others. For example, one of the two new acquisitions is a predomi-nantly minority group, and it's currently more isolated from the other two subgroups than they are from one another. Secondly, the other managers are very uncertain whether they can trust the CEO who's physically im-posing and quite gruff. The consultant returns to the president with a plan for the two days that interweaves managerial and organizational learning in ways that, if successful, will create strong ongoing relation-ships across the newly merged organizations rather than just talking about transformation. Instead of pure skill-building sessions, the consultant proposes (and the president agrees after some concern about the risks) that the staff meet in four cross-functional/cross-locational groups of ten to develop new ways of organizing in the four areas that the interviews have indicated are of greatest concern: (1) budget development, (2) re-cruiting and training, (3) internal communications, and (4) meeting man-agement. Senior management is asked to be prepared to make binding decisions with regard to the proposals at the end of the retreat (and such decisions are, in fact, made at the actual retreat).

Each of the groups of ten is to be managed through five leadership roles, and each leadership role will be held by two members. Four of the leadership roles are "Meeting Leader," "Decision Clarifier and Codifier,"

"Process Facilitator," and "Clown." (The "Clown"'s express function is to make "outside the box" comments, use humor, and turn suggestions inside-out in order to see whether they are thereby improved). Members are to be assigned roles that their fellow group members judge are most developmentally provocative for them. For example, at the retreat, the president later finds himself assigned a "Clown" role, and plays it so well that several extravagant stories about his performance quickly make the rounds!) The fifth leadership role is the "Expert and Follow-Through" leadership role. The two persons with the most influence over the ultimate implementation of any changes in that area play this role.

Without reproducing here any of the detailed supports provided, the schedule in outline calls for an initial presentation/discussion, led by the consultant, that connects the managerial and organizational development theory presented in this book to the history and dilemmas of the organization. The consultant suggests that the three independent sites have each been operating at the *Incorporation* action-logic, and that the new multisite company will require a frame change to the *Experiments* action-logic with cross-site decision-making teams on major issues and a lot of experimenting on everyone's part, such as this retreat as a whole involves.

Next, the conference splits into the four topic areas. In each case, one subgroup of five is to develop a set of proposals in one hour, while the other subgroup of five observes their role-mates and gives five minutes of feedback at the end of the first half hour and again at the end of the hour. After a short break, the observers and the actors switch roles, with the same feedback arrangements, and the new actors come up with a different set of proposals for the same concern (e.g., budget development). After another short break, the entire group of ten develops an agreed-upon proposal. These organizing processes provide individual managers with an unusual amount of immediate feedback about their leadership choices, while at the same time increasing the likelihood that divergent views on the organizational issues are developed, considered seriously, and resolved.

The next morning, each of the four groups makes 10-minute presentations to the other 30 managers, followed by 5 minutes of discussion and concluded with written feedback from all 30. The groups are given half an hour to digest the feedback they have received. Then the entire group reconvenes for 2-minute comments by their (senior management) "Follow-Through" leaders on how their proposals have been influenced by the feedback and what they are committing to do as of the next day in the office. The consultant next leads a discussion debriefing the entire exercise and then leaves the room while the management group develops feedback for her.

At the end of the actual meeting, the feedback to the consultant includes suggestions such as "we needed more leadership for the group assignments at outset," as well as positive comments such as "great to see branch participation without corporate interference," "meetings in this organization will never be the same again," and "the progression of program was great and the lack of structure strengthened learning." On a scale of 1 to 7 (where 1 means "Time wasted," 4 means "As good as an average quarterly retreat," and 7 means "Best quarterly retreat ever"), the 40 participants rate the consultant and the retreat 6.5 on average. Major changes in all four areas of concern follow.

As you can probably see, almost every activity at the 40-manager retreat represents *Experiments* stage organizing on the part of the participants. Everyone experiments with new meeting roles, none more so than the president in his "Clown" role. Everyone experiments a great deal with giving and receiving feedback, from the determination of what role each is to play, through the feedback to the consultant at the end. Moreover, all four efforts to create new organizational structures in the four areas of concern represent disciplined stabs in the dark. The methods of rapid group decision making are new to the organization as well.

What may be less obvious is that the organizational characteristics of the retreat itself represent a distinctive action-logic that is more paradoxical and subtle than the *Experiments*-stage logic. You may have noted that the structure for the retreat is quite complex, yet the participants claim at the end that "the lack of structure strengthened learning." This and the next case represent brief exemplars of later action-logic organizational processes that can stimulate a particular organizational transformation. Our examples suggest that an invited consulting intervention is more likely to generate an organizational transformation to the degree that the consulting intervention itself represents a postconventional action-logic.

Transforming a Corporate Parent Company

Now let us turn to an example of an organization transforming from the *Experiments* action-logic to *Systematic Productivity*. Referring back to Table 8-2 as you read, look for evidence of this movement.

Eagle Energy has become quite complex in terms of legal structure during its *Experiments* stage, in an effort to maximize the entrepreneurial freedom and initiative of every member of its senior management. As a result, the corporate structure shows a not-for-profit parent company and an umbrella for-profit subsidiary containing seven subsidiary companies. Each of the seven vice presidents of the for-profit company serves as president of one of the subsidiary companies. Each subsidiary president has developed his own profit-sharing formula with the umbrella company, based on whatever chips he has to work with and hard bargaining. Each such bargain is viewed as relatively illegitimate by other members of the senior management "team." The vice president and chief financial officer of the umbrella for-profit company is the only woman among the ten senior managers, the only person who is widely trusted, and the only person who is not president of a separate entity.

This jerry-built structure reinforcing cowboy opportunism rather than developing any coordination or team spirit is outflanked. In a desperation move, the president of the umbrella for-profit negotiates the 50 percent sale of the whole company in order to raise new and absolutely necessary capital. The new 50 percent partners agree to grant the company operating freedom, but demand careful accounting of revenues and costs and a return on their investment proportionate to the net revenues of each subsidiary. This apparently minor demand, along with the new capital controlled by the president of the umbrella for-profit, gives him new forms of effective control over the presidents of the subsidiaries. But it simultaneously increases their distrust of him.

A consultant who works with the developmental theory presented in this book is hired to assist the senior team in a retreat that is explicitly intended to restructure the company internally to fit its new ownership status and capital structure. From the first luncheon with the entire senior management to determine whether every member can accept the consultant, the consultant is aware of the high level of tension and distrust. Exhibiting a macho hostile humor typical of the *Opportunist* action-logic, one member recommends that the consultant pay for the opportunity to work with the group, rather than being paid, since he has not worked in this industry before and will, therefore, be learning. The consultant earns a round of laughter by parrying in kind with the comment that he thought the mark of a good consultant was how much he can charge to learn. After a slight pause, he continues by saying nonchalantly that at least he's learned how to talk to more than one person at a time without causing instant distrust—a trick which he understands most of them haven't picked up yet. This generates another round of laughter, the president suggests this is good evidence of the consultant's ability to hold his own in this crowd, and with a clinking of glasses, the consultant is hired.

The consultant proposes that he begin with a round of one-on-one interviews, followed by feedback from him to each individual. At the retreat, each member of senior management will be asked to discuss the feedback he or she has received and to set two goals for personal behavior change, before restructuring of the organization is discussed.

The interviews with, and feedback to, each individual permit the consultant to develop some trust with each member. This approach simultaneously lets the vice presidents know how others view them and where there is collective agreement about the future of the organization, while simultaneously preventing any dysfunctional group dynamics to interfere. It is during these interviews that the consultant begins to see that the chief financial officer is the person with the best relationships in the group, the one who focuses most impartially on the welfare of the organization as a whole, and the one who seems most strategic overall.

During the feedback to individuals, the consultant explores how willing each member is to acknowledge others' issues with him and to set significant personal change goals, which they will share with the group as a whole. He also explores how willing all are to cede some of their autonomy to a more centralized organizational structure, characteristic of the *Systematic Productivity* stage of organizing. In particular, the consultant probes members' reactions to the suggestion that emerged from the initial interviews that the chief financial officer be promoted to executive vice president of the umbrella for-profit corporation. This suggestion is widely agreed to, either because persons genuinely trust her and respect her competence, or because they see her as a buffer between themselves and the president of the umbrella corporation. (The consultant chooses not to make explicit that the suggested promotion emerged through his listening rather than through what anyone said.)

During the first day, the retreat is highlighted by astonishingly revealing comments by each member, along with commitments to change aspects of behavior that others would never have predicted they would acknowledge, much less change. This openness only happens, however, after the consultant is initially challenged about why the group should start with "touchy-feely" behavioral issues before dealing with the "infinitely more important" structural and financial issues. The consultant responds that the group is, of course, free to redesign the retreat as it wishes and that he himself would not usually lead with such a personal activity, but that the trust in the group is so low that he is personally convinced that no lasting progress can be made on the objective issues without a new kind of spiritual investment by each member. This challenge and response seems to bring the stakes into focus for everyone.

During the second day, the retreat is highlighted by a series of consensual agreements. The first is to promote the chief financial officer to executive vice president. The second is to centralize accounting and budgeting. The third, which provokes the longest argument, is to do away with the separate stationery for each subsidiary highlighting its president and to substitute a single version of corporate stationery that lists all the vice presidents on the team as, first, senior vice presidents of the umbrella for-profit and only secondly as presidents of their own subsidiaries.

It is difficult to stress strongly enough how essential the new executive vice president's overall style and specific actions are to the success of this day and the later success of the reformed company. As soon as she receives her mandate from the group, at the outset of the day, she proposes the importance of centralizing accounting and finances. Because of her past record of trustworthiness, reasonableness, and competence, the group comes to agreement on this without undue difficulty. Then, when the stationery issue becomes divisive, she adroitly highlights what an important symbolic issue it is and says that she views the decision as a vote of confidence or no-confidence in her ability to make the newly centralized organization work.

The consultant continues in an occasional coaching relationship to the new executive vice president. Six months later, the consultant meets with her and the senior vice presidents for a one-day retreat. Three months after that, the senior vice president who had been least willing to accept the leadership of the executive vice president takes a position with another company. The executive vice president, in turn, takes over the presidency of his subsidiary as well as continuing to serve as executive vice president of the umbrella for-profit.

In 24 months, the organization has generated enough net revenues to be able to buy itself back from its 50 percent partners.

In this case, we see that each subsidiary corporation, true to the *Experiments* stage, had become a distinct, almost completely decentralized experiment, with very little trust or cooperation among the parts. So little trust or cooperation, in fact, that the consultant chooses to maintain the decentralization in the early phase of his relationship to the company. During this period, he builds trust with individuals and discovers the one member with good enough relationships to serve as the hub of the more centralized organization needed for the *Systematic Productivity* stage. Indeed, there is so little trust and co-operation at the outset, that the consultant designs a retreat format that asks each person to offer a gift to the group (their willingness to make a difficult behavior change) before the group tries to make any collective decisions.

We can trace how the consultant recapitulates the developmental action-logics during the retreat. First, the consultant puts heavy emphasis on sharing the developmental theory as a new vision of what the next stage in this company's history ought to be about (recapitulating *Conception*). In particular he wants to legitimize the notion of greater corporate centralization, which has heretofore been anathema to virtually all the members. Next, in order to develop the trust necessary for more interdependent work, the consultant puts heavy emphasis on the inspirational gifts members need to offer (in this case, each member's commitment to a difficult behavioral change) (recapitulating *Investments*). Finally, the consultant puts heavy reliance on creating a very specific hierarchical structure with heavy reliance on a single leader (thereby recapitulating *Incorporation*). The executive vice president's experiments over the next year represent the *Experiments* substage of this company's transformation to the *Systematic Productivity* stage.

Conclusion

The cases presented in these chapters are meant to help you imagine what stage of development currently characterizes your company or department or work team. They also suggest the kinds of pressures, questions, and values that may make a time ripe for developmental transformation at the organizational level, as well as what kind of sustained action commitments may be warranted to promote successful organizational transformation.

Chapter 10 continues this conversation. There we will first discuss the environmental conditions that today lead many larger companies to the *Social Network* action-logic of organizing. Then we offer an in-depth case of an organization transforming from the *Systematic Productivity* action-logic through a *Social Network* phase toward the postconventional *Collaborative Inquiry* action-logic. This transition parallels the move we examined in Chapters 5 and 6 from the *Achiever* through the *Individualist* to the *Strategist* frame on the personal scale. Just as few managers develop to the *Strategist* action-logic, few organizations develop to the *Collaborative Inquiry* stage. Yet this is the first stage at which the organization begins to develop an explicit, ongoing transformational learning capacity.

TEN

The *Social Network* Organization and Transformation Toward *Collaborative Inquiry*

In Chapters 8 and 9, we have followed a number of the steps through which any organizing process evolves if the objective is to create a genuine learning organization. Ultimately, a genuine learning organization truly encourages the practice of developmental action inquiry among all its members and is actively open to reexamining and transforming its own assumptions about its environment, its structure, and its strategies.

But, even though those previous chapters describe five steps along the path toward a learning team or organization—*Conception, Investments, Incorporation, Experiments,* and *Systematic Productivity*—there is a very significant sense in which a team or organization only reaches the threshold of becoming a learning organization *after* completing these five steps. Occasionally, an organization is shepherded through one early transformation or another by executives or consultants, as illustrated in Chapters 8 and 9. But most organizations, like most people, evolve through each of these early developmental transformations by a process of more or less traumatic trial and error that is never named, never explicitly recognized as a transformation of assumptions and action-logics, and never undertaken with the intention of eventually establishing a learning organization.

In his book, *Finite and Infinite Games,* James Carse (1986) writes: "A finite game is played for the purpose of winning, an infinite game for the purpose of continuing the play. Finite players play within boundaries; infinite players play with boundaries." This imagery is apt in describing the evolving action-logics. Up through the ***Achiever/Systematic Productivity*** action-logic, we are playing within boundaries for the purpose of winning. By contrast, the postconventional action-logics, starting with the ***Individualist/Social Network*** action-logic, are playing with boundaries for the purpose of continuing the play.

Even idealistic, mission-driven companies and not-for-profits are, during their development to the ***Systematic Productivity*** stage, typically based on the assumptions:

1. That the mission is known
2. That the organization's challenges are:
   a. To find the right structure and strategy to accomplish the mission
   b. To overcome external competition or external political blocks to accomplishing the desired outcomes

Beyond the ***Systematic Productivity*** stage, however, an organization, like a person moving through the ***Individualist*** stage toward the ***Strategist*** stage, begins to recognize the multiplicity and dynamics involved. At the ***Social Network*** stage, a holding company often mixes and matches a portfolio of operating companies through a constant process of buying, selling, and redirecting their capital assets. During the past generation, we have experienced a great deal of experimentation in the business world, with a kind of portfolio approach to managing, whereby a parent holding company, either actively or passively, manages dozens or even hundreds of operating companies, sometimes within a single industry, other times across industries.

At the ***Social Network*** stage, senior managers of the holding company tend to be relativistic about the overall mission of the enterprise and about questions of "right" strategy and structure. They engage in double-loop learning and problem solving. They aspire to be "agile," meaning attentive and responsive to the market. In practice, this approach often means that they shift their liquid capital toward investments that in the short-term appear likely to generate the highest profits, while reducing investment in companies and projects that cannot match the company's designated "hurdle rate." They give little attention to the peculiarities of different industries, regions, or longer time horizons. This outlook is a kind of ***Opportunistic*** relativism characteristic of global finance capitalism.

But, like a person moving through the ***Individualist*** toward the

Strategist action-logic, a team or organization can move beyond this *Opportunistic* substage of development toward the *Social Network* action-logic beyond pure financial relativism. A *Social Network* organizational action-logic can also be motivated by a sense of mission and values that transcend financial value. Single-loop profitability (or positive fund balance, in the case of not-for-profits) remains a significant short-term measure of viability. It also is a means by which the organization can continue to focus on more fundamental double-loop and triple-loop values. These may include increasing mutual equity among current members (both economic and political equity), increasing intergenerational sustainability (both organizational and environmental sustainability), or increasing timely, transformational inquiry.

For example, in Chapter 3 we introduced the development of socially responsible investing. SRI optimizes three bottom lines—financial, social, and environmental—through network organizations like the Social Investors Forum, the Coalition for Environmental Responsibility (CERES), and the Global Reporting Initiative (GRI). As we pointed out in Chapter 3, socially responsible investing (SRI) raises a basic question about the very purpose or mission of business. In this sense, the entire social-investing subindustry is a learning process organized in response to a question. Only in the transition to *Collaborative Inquiry* does the purpose and process of establishing a learning organization typically become self-conscious. Thus, the SRI field as a whole begins to enact the *Collaborative Inquiry* action-logic.

The motivation for developing toward *Collaborative Inquiry* comes from a dawning recognition that the organizing mission is actually a mystery that requires the practice of action inquiry—continual researching and reformulating—if members' actions are to be truly guided by the mission. At the same time some organizational members may begin to appreciate that there are inevitable systematic gaps between the espoused mission, values, and strategies of organizational members, on the one hand, and their actual patterns of practice, on the other hand.

Therefore, there is not only a mystery about what an organization's mission really means, but there is also a mystery about how to recognize and correct the incongruities that tend to grow between espoused directions or priorities and actual practices. In other words, what motivates organizational transformation toward *Collaborative Inquiry* is the growing recognition among some members who are willing to take leadership responsibility that it is not only the changing external environment that creates new problems for the organization, but its own way of operating.

Significantly, the original and largest company dedicated continually to SRI, Trillium Asset Management, is structurally arranged as a *Collaborative Inquiry* organization in three ways. It engages in collaborative inquiry with its clients, discovering what values they wish to support and investing in appropriate companies. It also engages in collaborative inquiry with companies about their practices (e.g., influencing Wal-Mart's international labor practices). And it engages in collaborative inquiry from top to bottom of its own company hierarchy because it is a worker-owned company in which the employees are also shareholders.

Why Organizational Change Practices Often Become Ineffective Fads

Ever since the 1950s the attempt to seriously address the mystery of mission and the incongruities that arise among mission, strategy, operations, and outcomes has led to a variety of organizational change and managerial education ventures—to T-groups (sensitivity training groups), to the whole field called OD (organizational development), to QWL programs (quality of working life), to TQM (total quality management), to Process Re-engineering, and most recently to the use of whole systems interventions such as Real Time Strategic Change, Future Search, and Appreciative Inquiry.

The developmental theory we have been discussing can help us to understand why these approaches so often become disappointing fads. One reason is that in order to become marketable on a larger scale, each innovative approach to *Collaborative Inquiry* develops through its own distinct stages until it reaches its own *Systematic Productivity* strategy and structure. Because the specific innovative strategy and structure of, say, TQM or Future Search is different from a client company's strategy and structure, it may help that company make one significant transformation in its manner of operating. But it does *not* transform the whole company into a *Collaborative Inquiry* stage learning organization that continues to research its mission and correct incongruities among mission, strategy, operations, and outcomes.

A second, related reason why these well-known managerial education ventures fade after sometimes having an initial impact on the organization is that only organizational members who themselves transform to the *Strategist* stage (or beyond) fully appreciate the value and the logic of *Collaborative Inquiry* process. (As shown in Table 8-1, the

Strategist and *Collaborative Inquiry* stages are parallel or analogical action-logics). Therefore, only managers at the *Strategist* stage and the still later stages are able to implement *Collaborative Inquiry* on a continuing basis. As we have seen earlier (Table 5-1), more than half of the managers we have measured score two or more stages before the *Strategist* stage, and far fewer than 10 percent of managers measure as *Strategists*.

Thus, the task in helping an organization transform to the *Collaborative Inquiry* stage is not only to transform the structure of an objectifiable social entity, but also to transform the consciousness of many of its members. We do not know what proportion must become *Strategists* or how many times a day they must combine the four parts of speech in their conversations or seek double-loop feedback before the organization can reliably be expected to maintain itself at the *Collaborative Inquiry* stage. But, based on our study reported in Chapter 7 about the CEOs of 10 companies attempting to transform, we are convinced that the proportion of the senior management team that is operating at the *Strategist* stage, and whether the CEO is a *Strategist*, makes a disproportionate difference. Since each personal developmental transformation can take several years, and since the person developing must first discover the internal motivation to do so, it would seem astonishing to us if a company could increase its proportion of *Strategists* from, say, 3 percent to, say, 10 percent in less than five years.

Let us listen in to a consultant who is himself measured at the *Strategist* action-logic describe some of his efforts to help management teams transform to the *Collaborative Inquiry* action-logic:

> To inquire in action is just to be more sensitive and alive to the muchness of the moment. When I open the front door of my home and gaze into the wooded valley, with what do I connect? I have had a few experiences of working with management teams or voluntary learning groups that become capable of performing at a level that radically transcends that of most groups. These groups move from practical to emotional to spiritual questions and are able to see the connections among them. Sometimes the challenges are raw, and the disagreement very uncomfortable; yet the group sustains the quest to turn conflict into understanding and understanding into action.
>
> As a consultant this has a very clear consequence for me—I increasingly often seek to raise uncomfortable inquiries into what the leaders and organizations that I work with are doing. This does get me into trouble

and, although I never enjoy trouble, it is generally good trouble to cause. I was recently working with a brewing company. They have a particular brand of very strong, cheap lager that is widely consumed by alcoholics. Some days office staff of the company have to find their way through the winos and their cans of lager in order to access a side door of their building. I wanted to know how company members felt about this and what sense the organization made of it. This was not a comfortable conversation, and some senior managers simply rejected it. My credibility was damaged. But these are vital questions for the long-term sustainability of the company, and the sense of detachment that I have in inquiring mode is so helpful to raising them.

Very few companies have the vision, the will, or the resources to evolve to the **Collaborative Inquiry** action-logic. Consequently, the typical training processes that are developed for the company's employees aim to instill **Expert/Experiments** skills or **Achiever/Systematic Productivity** skills. These are useful in their own right, but they will not generate transformation beyond the **Achiever/Systematic Productivity** stage.

Figure 10.1 highlights the radical difference between the reality of the **Achiever/Systematic Productivity** action-logic and the reality of the **Strategist/Collaborative Inquiry** action-logic. The horizontal line rep-

Figure 10.1   Achiever Sequential Awareness vs. Later-Stage Simultaneous (and Sequential) Awareness

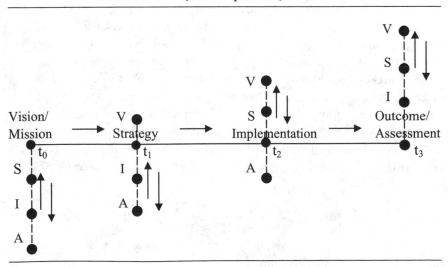

resents the limited *Achiever* awareness of an organizing process as an historical progression from abstract initial vision to final assessment based on concrete outcomes. The horizontal and vertical lines together represent the added dimension of awareness that the *Strategist* begins to cultivate. The vertical line represents the kind of four-territory awareness we have been discussing throughout this book, focused on whether mission, strategy, performance, and outcome are harmonious or incongruent in the present. Another way of describing this figure is to say that the horizontal line represents the territory of experience that is most explicitly being shaped at a given time, while the vertical line represents an awareness of the currently implicit territories of experience as well. This additional dimension of awareness, which includes single-, double-, and triple-loop feedback, only becomes fully internalized as an ongoing practice in a person during the transformation beyond *Strategist* to the *Alchemist* stage (that we will introduce in Chapter 12).

The *Strategist* begins to appreciate first that there is a nameable, systemic, historical dynamic to action and that sensitivity to timing can make one's actions more effective. The *Strategist* is able, in effect, to "see" the horizontal line of history because he or she cultivates at least moments of "vertical" experiencing during which he or she escapes identification with the horizontal and can take a point of view on it. Thus, the *Strategist* is able to systematize "horizontal" history and also to get inklings that reality is not only sequential, but also, in an even more profound sense, "vertical" or simultaneous, including all four territories of experience at once.

So, the person operating at the *Strategist* action-logic has an implicit sense that there is better or worse planning, implementing, and effectuating going on even at the time when visioning is the central task. The moment-to-moment awareness that spans these four simultaneous territories of experience enables the possibility of "seeing" when actions and effects become incongruent with mission and strategy. Only such an awareness of incongruity permits self-correcting in real time at the moment of incongruity. Only a person exhibiting such awareness and self-correction is likely to be trusted over the long run to lead the process of generating a self-correcting, continual quality improvement process organizationally.

Sun Health Care's Journey from *Experiments* through *Systematic Productivity* Toward *Collaborative Inquiry*

Now that we have suggested in general terms what the difficulties of transforming toward the **Collaborative Inquiry** stage of organizing are, let us gain a more concrete sense of what can be involved by following one company's adventure in this direction.

This company is an HMO (health management organization) that we will call Sun Health Care, headquartered in the Southwest of the United States. Founded in the early 1980s, Sun's growth really took off in the early 1990s, showing first respectable and then enviable retained earnings while growing at twice the average rate of the industry as a whole. The organization was involved in a continual quality improvement program for four years during the early nineties, then merged with another HMO and became one of the top-ranked HMOs in the United States in 1998.

Sun Health Care had produced a small profit even in 1988 when many HMOs suffered considerable losses. From 1989 to 1993, Sun's enrollments grew over 20 percent annually on average, more than double the industry average, through increased penetration of its original service area and expansion to contiguous regions. At the same time, its net worth grew to 12 times the 1989 level. In 1993, an impartial consumer satisfaction survey showed Sun as tied for first place nationally in terms of consumer satisfaction. A national industry ranking of overall performance showed Sun as the smallest and youngest HMO among the top 10 nationally. And an employee climate survey conducted by a large firm specializing in such surveys showed the most significant improvement from one year to the next ever found by that firm.

The natural question is, "What happened within Sun between 1989 and 1993 to produce the balanced and positive results just enumerated?" In 1989, the president decided that senior management should develop a formal strategic plan because the organization's size and growth seemed to warrant it, because he wanted the senior group to act more as a team than as division directors, and because he wished to influence his two boards of directors (a corporate board and an independent physicians' board) to think more strategically. After interviewing a number of consultants who might help the senior management in developing its first formal strategic plan, the president engaged one who emphasized the importance of developing a mission statement that recognized the importance of clients and employees as well as of physicians and profits. This consultant also emphasized the importance of helping the senior management team members evolve, not just to the point of planning together, but to the point of implementing the plan together effectively, and of continuing to work together in a strategic manner. In other words, the consultant was advocating the simultaneous (or "vertical") development of multiple territories of experience: visioning, strategizing, and implementing.

The plan that evolved included objectives related to profits, enrollment growth, cost control, expansion analysis, employee development, and quality improvement. The company also hired a new manager to create an internal employee development department.

Equally important, the process of developing the plan included study, feedback, and discussion of the views of the senior team's members about one another's performance and relationships. The president learned that he could improve the levels of initiative, shared understanding, and commitment to follow through among team members by managing the team meetings in a more collaborative fashion. The team members became aware that one member whom they had somewhat isolated because of his many initiatives was not so much a self-serving rate-buster as they had inferred. In fact, the president said he wished other team members would act more like that individual. To a significant degree, this vice president could be viewed as a model member of a more peerlike team where not just the president, but all team members could legitimately take initiatives. These changes in the way the president learned to lead the senior management team and how the team itself behaves prepared the team to be effective in implementing the new strategic plan.

Overall, then, the company appeared to be transforming away from a more informal, decentralized form characteristic of the *Experiments* stage of organizing. Prior to the development of the strategic plan, the company had operated without an explicit mission that embraced its major stakeholders, without a strategic plan, without an organized senior management team meeting process, and with vice presidents who saw themselves preeminently as department heads. Like the last company described in Chapter 9, Sun Health was evolving from the *Experimental* action-logic toward the *Systematic Productivity* stage of organizing—toward a more focused form. It is important to note that, contrary to the usual experience that greater centralization disempowers participants because their jobs become narrowly and bureaucratically defined, this way of vertically aligning mission, strategy, and action process empowers members of an organization.

Indeed, the process of developing the strategic plan, much like the interventions described in Chapter 9, itself had a ***Strategist/Collaborative Inquiry*** quality about it. When the consultant left the organization on completion and adoption of the plan, however, the shared leadership structure for the senior management team soon fell into disuse, with the exception of the president's ongoing efforts and successes at guiding meetings in a more collaborative manner. So, the senior management team settled into a strategically directed ***Systematic Productivity*** manner of operating, and the ***Collaborative Inquiry*** aspects of the consulting intervention receded from view.

From Systematic Productivity *to the* Social Network *Action-Logic*

After the consultant left, the quality program, initiated by the company as one of its newly adopted strategic objectives, combined departmental operational studies and work redesign and based both on TQM principles. An external company was initially hired to support this process, but the new manager of employee development (who was measured at the ***Strategist*** action-logic) led the way in taking full ownership of the quality improvement process into the company. He and his colleagues transformed the prefabricated work redesign methodology into a training process suited to this particular company and to the departmental redesign teams, as well as to the cross-functional new product and cost containment teams.

At the same time, the company was offering doctors the choice of organizing themselves into joint ventures. These joint ventures monitored their own costs with the incentive of sharing in increased net revenues. Soon they were offering doctors collegial review, better returns, and lower costs. As a result, these doctor-led networks organized into joint ventures grew rapidly, and those who continued as independent practitioners were left to question what form of organization served them best. From a developmental point of view, this structure is a particularly interesting ***Social Network*** approach that allows everyone a free choice about how to organize. Although management (and an increasing number of doctors) believed that the joint venture form was, in fact, the wave of the future, combining greater efficiency, greater profits, and peer control rather than third-party control, management did not unilaterally mandate this choice for all the doctors, but instead created an ongoing choice-making situation.

Let us pause to reflect another minute or two about the developmental characteristics of the choice between independent practice and joint ventures that Sun Health was offering the doctors in its network. Some of you may be imagining that we are implying that any of the doctors who were not yet choosing the joint venture form of organizing in favor of their independent practices were mere chumps, and you may be wondering why the HMO did not simply mandate the joint venture form for all its docs. Here is a developmental analysis of the situation. Let us begin by reminding you that a good 30 percent of these docs already owned two homes and a sail cruiser with bedding for six, or the equivalent, and could afford to retire any time. Thus, if the question were to become whether they preferred to retire or to learn new billing procedures, new habits about how much time to spend with each patient, and new ways of teaming with younger colleagues who would probably act superior to them, retirement might well seem the obvious rational and emotional choice. If the HMO tried to force these docs into joint ventures, they might well retire or join another HMO network, robbing Sun Health of some of its best practitioners and generating some hostility among them.

At the same time, each new joint venture leadership team was doing its best to engage a few of its most efficient (least hospital days per patient) and most effective (heaviest specialist case load) colleagues to join it. Thus, a doctor at the *Achiever, Individualist,* or *Strategist* action-logic who wished to work for another 20-or-so years and with a positive efficiency and effectiveness record, or a willingness to join on condition of transforming his or her practice, would be an early candidate to take the lead in creating or joining one of these peer-regulated, high-profit joint ventures under the HMO's wing. Thus, the choice process made it likely that the early joint ventures would draw willing and competent practitioners who were open to teaming and feedback, increasing the likelihood that the joint ventures would establish a positive track record.

Meanwhile, doctors at the *Diplomat* or *Expert* action-logics who wished to work another 20-or-so years, but did not wish to change their patterns of practice, often persuaded themselves that efficiency and effectiveness measures were created by evil forces bent on destroying good medical practice. So, they would initially tend to resist joining the joint ventures. As the greater capitalization, marketing prowess, and efficacy of the joint ventures gradually reduced these independent practitioners' client pools and relative financial success, more of these doctors would try to join joint ventures. But these new joint ventures would face a much tougher battle. They were late entrants, with members with worse efficiency/effectiveness records, with leadership styles less attuned to learning from peer and client feedback. On the other hand, the doctors joining them would be more likely to realize that they really had to change their patterns of practice if they were to succeed in the new professional environment and would waste less time fighting the new procedures than they would have had they been forced to join initially.

In many ways, the choice Sun Health offered its doctors was a perfect example of the *Individualist/Social Network* action-logic. It offered each doctor a free choice, which would initially be dictated as much by the structure of the doctor's action-logic (as well as by his or her particular circumstances and history at the time) as by the structure of the social choice. At the same time, the history of participants' early choices eventually invites all of them to transform their action-logic. Ultimately, the inquiry is taken as far as each participant chooses. With each moment-to-moment choice, we either widen the scope and deepen the intensity of attention our action-logic permits, or we further imprint our current action-logic on our lifetime body of practice (though few of us are present enough to ourselves in most moments even to recognize that choices are being made).

Meanwhile, as each year passed, the senior management team was transforming the strategic planning process from a top-down, departmental process to a yearly, bottom-up, interdepartmental process. Each succeeding year's plan included more detailed objectives and accountability for interdepartmental cooperation. Performance measurements of member growth, member satisfaction, and profit were identified and publicized throughout the company. The high morale and pride of company employees was tangible to anyone who entered their office spaces.

Jogging Senior Managers' Awareness

Nevertheless, the senior management team was not entirely prepared for the degree of controversy that began to develop as more and more departments undertook reorganization. All of the reorganization plans highlighted the critical nature of interdepartmental cooperation (*Collaborative Inquiry* between departments). But two of the seven vice presidents and their departments were increasingly experienced as roadblocks to interdepartmental coordination and as less collaborative within the senior management team. Interestingly, both believed themselves to be strong proponents of the quality program as a whole and of interdepartmental cooperation. Their differences from the rest of the team were highlighted by the president's new, more collaborative style of running meetings.

One of the two was seen by others as too frequently "oppositional" at the meetings, slowing down team decision making to an exasperating degree. The other was seen as taking an independent, "cowboy" attitude and not contributing sufficiently to the senior team. Both were seen as encouraging an attitude of superiority, priority, and entitlement within their departments, rather than an attitude of cooperation and service. The "oppositional" vice president had generated a great deal of irritation and resentment, and the president was considering firing her. The "cowboy" vice president stayed out of other people's way and ran his own show, and the issues surrounding his performance were fuzzier, so he was easier to tolerate. Also, he was a cheerleader within his own department, commanding enthusiastic loyalty among many of his subordinates.

At this point, the president appears to be faced with two choices:

1. Continue struggling to work with both vice presidents, perhaps strongly reprimanding and warning the "opposer" and rapping the knuckles of the "cowboy"
2. Fire the "opposer"

However, the actual scenario departed from the probable. The president sensed that neither of those initiatives would be consistent with integrating action and inquiry, or with exercising transforming power, or with generating an opportunity for developmental transformation on the part of either vice president. If you were in the president's position and had these transformational purposes in mind, what would you do? Is there a way of "jogging" these vice presidents' awareness in such a way that either one or both may choose to *transform* (not merely feel forced to *conform*) his or her leadership style, so that it more nearly re-presents *Collaborative Inquiry*? Or to put the same thing differently, is there a way to go beyond the sort of choice a *Social Network* action-logic organizing structure offers to a *Collaborative Inquiry* structure that, while leaving the participant full freedom of choice, nevertheless also clearly wishes to reward the development of later action-logic capabilities?

We invite you to reflect on this question as we continue this story in the next chapter, where we illustrate how ongoing mini-collaborative inquiries in the course of ongoing business can gradually transform the very way we do business altogether. In addition, if you participate in any work team, larger organization, or family with significant conflict among some of the members, you may want to take 10 or 15 minutes to contemplate anew what you can do. What actions would you consider taking if your aim is to integrate action and inquiry, to exercise transforming power, and to encourage developmental transformation in your own situation of significant conflict?

ELEVEN

The Quintessence of *Collaborative Inquiry*

The Sun Health Care Journey Continues

From the perspective of the *Strategist/Collaborative Inquiry* action-logic, the story we began in Chapter 10 about the disharmony at Sun Health between the majority of the senior management team and the "opposer" and the "cowboy" is not necessarily bad. At the time, the president realized that the "opposer" generated inquiry by her opposition, even if she often did not help such inquiry to reach closure in mutually agreeable action. Firing her could potentially send two negative messages to the company: (1) critical inquiry is not encouraged and (2) people who do not conform to the preferred managerial style will be dealt with summarily. Both these messages would directly contradict the development of a transformational learning culture.

Moreover, lower-level managers were being asked to transform their managerial styles from superior/supervisory assumptions to collaborative/facilitative assumptions (supervisors' titles were literally shifting to "team facilitator"). Thus, it would be consistent to offer vice presidents the opportunity to transform their styles (if, on further inquiry, they required transforming). Such an exercise would also give the senior management group as a whole the opportunity to learn how such transformation could be facilitated on an ongoing basis. And, if the exercise were to succeed in some sense, then it might become a story that inspired loyalty to the leadership and imitation of its members' willingness to transform.

To help structure and conduct this new action inquiry, the president again retained the consultant who had assisted the strategic planning two years earlier. The initial investigation indicated that, on the one hand, the "opposer" had indeed lost the trust and patience of all direct associates. Views of the "cowboy," on the other hand, were highly variable and not as raw.

What the "Opposer" Did

The reactions of the two vice presidents to the feedback about their performance were different from what might have been predicted. The consultant suggested to the "opposer" that even if her opposition may have been justified in particular instances, she was not opposing effectively, so it would be both in her and the company's interest for her to learn to play new leadership roles. This way of jogging the vice president's awareness—by framing a potential collaborative inquiry between herself and the company—apparently both made sense and appealed to the "opposer," who agreed to surrender her customary role ("surrender" was the word actually used). With the consultant, she crafted a three-page plan of action for the next six months, which they proposed first to the president and then, incorporating his modifications, to the senior management team. Her willingness to make herself vulnerable by reframing her purposes and actions and by submitting herself to peer assessment provided a novel spark of action inquiry in the management team.

Despite its collective irritation and initial skepticism, the team responded by agreeing to make the effort necessary to engage in the action inquiry process. It did this for several reasons. The assessment of the problem had been very frank. The proposed goals and coaching procedures were very clear. The vice president was committed, and the evaluation process was explicit (which put the burden of proof on the vice president). In so doing, the senior team was embarking on a (potentially) transforming *Collaborative Inquiry* adventure.

The early weeks of implementation of the plan involved great effort on the part of almost all on the senior management team. Despite her best intentions, the vice president repeatedly acted in ways that others interpreted as oppositional. The consultant emphasized that it was essential to give her immediate concrete feedback when others perceived her as deviating from her new commitments. After about the fourth concrete instance of immediate feedback, the vice president appeared to finally understand just what behavior worked (in the sense that other team members saw it as a positive, good-faith experiment) and what behavior didn't work (in the sense that others saw it as more of the same old tendency to oppose). Thereafter, this issue effectively was resolved, although other aspects of the erstwhile-opposer's style still irked her peers on occasion.

What the "Cowboy" Did

By contrast, the "cowboy" resisted both the validity and the significance of the performance feedback about himself. People's perceptions were wrong, he felt, and his style was, in fact, optimal for the organization. In this case, unlike the previous one, the feedback of others' perceptions had not immediately evoked a re-framing response. This vice president initially responded defensively.

"If this is true," the consultant asked, still hoping to encourage the vice president to engage in a collaborative inquiry with the rest of the team, "will you participate in developing a process with me whereby other members of senior management can come to appreciate your efficacy and perhaps amend their own approaches?" "No," the "cowboy" responded confrontatively, "that's their problem, not mine."

Pausing briefly and looking down reflectively, the consultant asked, "Can you see how this response may support the view that you are not collaborative in your relations with your peers?"

"I can't believe you're trying to trap me in word games!" the vice president responded heatedly and woundedly, thus effectively trumping the consultant for the moment and validating any inference one might have made from his previous comment that he was not motivated to play this game, whatever it was. With such free choices do some moments of incipient collaborative inquiry end.

(We may note in passing that the consultant's final question is really a condensed re-framing, advocacy, and illustration, all formed into an inquiry. The consultant was left to wonder whether, despite his conscious constructive intent in asking the question, as well as his intentional slowing of the pace toward a more reflective tone, there may not have been an unconscious combative confrontativeness to the question that reduced its transformational power.)

A few days later, this vice president met with the president on a separate matter. He intended to fire one of his managers for "gross insubordination." What was the evidence, asked the president. The vice president described a pattern of behavior, based on hearsay, supplemented by a memo by this manager to the human resources department questioning the justice of a corporate decision. The president said this evidence was not unambiguous enough to justify firing. In fact, it was not clear the manager had done anything inappropriate whatsoever. He added that he believed other senior managers held a significantly different interpretation from the "cowboy" of the same events.

Then and there, the president called the rest of the senior team in for an impromptu meeting, and several of them confirmed that their information from several sources indicated the problem was with how the vice president had acted, not how the manager had acted. The vice president was not able to find a constructive way of using this feedback either, later describing the event, during an interview with the consultant, as a humiliation at which "I got my brains beat in." The consultant interviewed both the vice president and the manager he had wanted to fire, and found inconsistencies within the vice president's own story and no basis for firing the manager.

The president continued to try to work with the vice president, but the "cowboy" became increasingly suspicious that his job was on the line. Several weeks later, the president asked him to perform a task that the vice president quickly asserted he could do "standing on my head." The president responded in a pleased tone that this was good because it would increase the senior management team's trust in the vice president. To this, the vice president responded angrily that he should have received a major bonus for his previous year's work rather than being tested in this way and that they should discuss a separation package together. At this moment, both men had to part for other meetings, so the matter was left hanging.

The president related the event to the consultant over the phone, adding "I'm sure he'll change his mind when he thinks it over." "Why do you want him to change his mind?" the consultant responded. "You've repeatedly integrated action and inquiry in your engagements with the vice president, like when you called in the other senior managers for the impromptu meeting. By contrast, the vice president's response has been both uncollaborative and uninquiring since the issue of his performance first arose. You've been searching for convincing secondhand evidence that the vice president is effective or ineffective—for example, sales figures. But it seems to me we now have a plethora of firsthand evidence that the vice president does not integrate action and inquiry, does not collaborate well, and is not engaging in a learning process with regard to his own performance."

Whereas secondhand evidence is always subject to alternative interpretations, this firsthand evidence struck the consultant as less ambiguous because it offered a simultaneous view of the vice president's vision (not becoming vulnerable to inquiry), strategy (alternating between compliance and angry rejection), action (noncollaborative), and outcomes (no signs of learning). The question was how to weigh the relatively unambiguous firsthand, in-the-present observations from the president's and the consultant's own interactions with the vice president in contrast to relatively ambiguous secondhand information. Not wishing to pressure the president into a decision, the consultant urged the president to take 15 minutes of quiet, meditative time alone at the end of the phone call to see whether a clear conviction about the proper course of action announced itself.

Immediately following this period, the president sent a message to the vice president inviting him to meet again in order to work out the details of his resignation, separation agreement, and announcement to the company. Twenty-four hours later, the vice president was no longer working at the company. After his departure, a systematic pattern of misrepresentation about senior management decisions to the "cowboy's" former subordinates was discovered and corrected.

One Hurdle Cleared

What was the president becoming clearer about and more committed to during this experience? Perhaps he was realizing the true challenge of organizational transformation to the *Strategist/Collaborative Inquiry* action-logic: paradoxically one must practice collaborative inquiry in order to gain the capacity to practice collaborative inquiry. The president was becoming aware that the challenge is not just generating improvements in organizational outcomes, but also continual improvement in leadership awareness and practice, so that each leader's performance truly embodies the vision and strategy associated with the improved outcomes. To engage in transformational improvement in real-time senior management encounters requires integrating action and inquiry and exercising mutual, vulnerable transforming power, as the oppositional vice president and the team had done with one another. She and the team transformed from a limited and limiting awareness of outcomes (the things she was complaining about and her status as "opposer") to the simultaneous awareness of vision, strategy, implementation, and new outcomes needed to produce jointly the six-month plan of action. They had played with and transformed the boundaries of the game they had previously been playing. The logic of the *Collaborative In-*

quiry stage of organizing can only flower and flourish within a company if it is regularly practiced in small encounters such as the difficult ones just described. And, as stated before and illustrated by the case of the "cowboy," collaborative inquiry does not unilaterally force a particular solution.

None of the other senior executives, including the president, would have predicted at the outset of the inquiry regarding the two vice presidents that the "opposer" could or would transform as radically as she did, or that the "cowboy" would resist and resign as he did. Because of the action inquiry procedures, however, and the clear initiatives by both vice president's (one transforming, the other resigning), the outcomes knit the senior team together more strongly. Once again, however, the team as a whole did not adopt the **Collaborative Inquiry** logic as its general mode of operating. Instead, as if relaxing after a difficult trauma, it returned to its **Systematic Productivity** mode.

As for the "cowboy" who had in effect refused to play *Collaborative Inquiry* and had resigned, two years later he called the CEO to thank him for his efforts. The former vice president reported that his wife had immediately criticized him for resigning from the company rather than exploring how he might change. Next, he said, he was fired three months into his new job. Only thereafter did he enter therapy and discover the degree to which he refused all well-meant attempts to influence him. Thus, the collaborative inquiry with which Sun Health Care's CEO and the consultant had engaged this vice president seems to have set the stage for an eventual significant change on his part.

The Next Challenge

A year later, the president invented a new **Collaborative Inquiry** procedure that was not merely a tactic for dealing with problems such as those involving the two vice presidents, but also a strategy for teamwide learning and change. He proposed that the entire senior management group create an executive development process for itself. The senior management team agreed, deciding to define together: (1) standards for the ideal senior management team member, (2) developmental issues that the team as a whole faced, and (3) a first-year set of developmental objectives for each member.

Table 11-1 shows how the team came to define its ideal member. Table 11-2 describes the senior team's ideal meeting process, and Table 11-3 shows the developmental objectives one of the vice presidents

Table 11-1   Standards for Ideal Sun Health Care
Senior Management Team Member

1. **Leadership**
   - Desire and ability to become strong leader, taking executive responsibility for entire company as it grows
   - Seen as a leader of the company (not just own department) both inside and outside the company
   - Seen as effective manager of own area who keeps it working harmoniously with corporate-wide objectives
   - Wants to teach others knowledge, skills, orientation, and judges own success by the ability to develop one's managers
   - Demonstrates creative problem solving under pressure
   - Gets things done well
2. **Vision/mission**
   - Dedicated to Sun and the health care industry
   - Exemplifies in daily practice who we are (mission) and who we want to become (vision)
   - Able to motivate staff to share in our vision, philosophy
3. **Creative work ethic**
   - Strong commitment to
     - working hard • honesty • conveying energy, enthusiasm • quality improvement • customer orientation
   - Acts with highest integrity as well as sensitivity to the culture of the company
   - Prioritizing skills guided by mission and strategic objectives
   - Manages time not just efficiently, effectively, but also creatively
4. **Knowledge of what's really going on**
   - Broad understanding of industry
   - Understanding of all areas of Sun Health Care
   - Knowledge of technical issues affecting our business
   - Expertise in matters concerning own department
   - Keeps finger on pulse, knows what's really going on
5. **Implementation-focused strategic approach**
   - Able to weigh business options objectively
     - uses effective problem-solving tools
     - acts on behalf of the corporation, even if not popular in own area
   - Demonstrates leadership in the development and execution of strategies and business plans
     - contributes innovative ideas
     - strong-willed, persuasive
     - seeks out disconfirming data

- Contributes to development and implementation of corporate priorities involving other departments
  - understands issues in other departments
- Oriented toward cross-functional problem solving and sharing of information

6. **Artful performance in meetings**
   - Assumes leadership accountability in all meetings in which he or she participates without usurping others' leadership
     - gives full attention to meeting
     - prompt at start of meeting and after breaks
     - carries out all assignments in a timely manner
     - willing to ask "dumb" questions to assure understanding
     - respects the contributions of others
     - willing to clarify/elaborate on ideas
     - willing to compromise, or craft a better third alternative
     - eases tension in the group without diverting attention from significant differences

7. **Transformational interpersonal skills**
   - Develops interpersonal skills consistent with Sun Health Care, such as
     - caring
     - down-to-earth
     - teamwork
     - ability to change
   - Excellent communication skills—listening, speaking, writing
   - Effective team player
     - actions help achieve consensus
     - supports achievement of agreed-upon goals
   - Negotiation skills
   - Recognizes, manages, and transforms conflicts into energizing new modes of cooperation

8. **A gravity-defying learning orientation**
   - Continual development of technical, business, managerial skills
   - Sees difficult challenges and stretch goals as a reason for being here
   - Thrives on notion that we defy gravity and will keep doing things people believe we can't achieve
   - Develops assessment processes for measuring own knowledge and leadership within own department
   - Physician executives learn business skills and business executives learn about medical thinking and the unique abilities needed to affect physician behaviour
   - Seeks new ways of understanding what customers want
   - Able to ask questions that keep you from being fooled for long

Table 11-2 Sun Senior Management Team Development Agenda

As agreed by the team members, the principal team development issue for this year is:

Developing a focused, overall agenda

The team has further agreed to rotate the agenda development and meeting leadership function to a different team member every three months. In addition, the team has defined six agenda categories, each of which requires creative and disciplined management:

1. Updates
2. Open Items
3. Visioning
4. Strategizing
5. Implementing
6. Assessing

The meeting leader manages the first two agenda categories, while four other team members serve as the "Advocates" for the remaining four categories. Each advocate is responsible for determining what items in his or her category deserve team attention and for coaching whoever is responsible for each agenda item. In addition, as particular agenda items are considered by the team, each advocate has a special responsibility for raising issues related to his or her advocacy area as appropriate.

In general, it is understood that there is a natural flow for particular agenda items from Visioning to Strategizing to Implementing to Assessing and from there to the Update or Open Item categories, if further senior management attention is warranted.

defined for the next year. It may be of interest to you to think of the senior managers in your own organization as you read through the standards for an ideal manager shown in Table 11-1.

How many of your managers meet the first five standards, which can be termed the "ordinary" ideals we have for people in executive leadership roles? And how many do you see as examples of the final three, which are more extraordinary ideals? Would we even recognize such subtle forms of leadership as "assuming leadership accountability for a meeting without usurping others' leadership"? How does one "ease ten-

Table 11-3   Sample of an Individual Senior Manager's
Developmental Goals

1. Consensus Building

To accomplish this goal, I will be implementing the senior management recommendations outlined during our discussion of my presentation. Specifically, if I experience opposition to a recommendation which I believe should be adopted, I will explore with individual senior management members the source of their resistance and address those concerns directly. In addition, I will try to identify those individuals who concur with my proposal and enlist their support in building consensus. Concomitantly, I will reassess my recommendations in the context of the questions raised and restructure my position to reflect my reassessment. Finally, I will solicit individual "evaluations" of whether I have demonstrated a more effective ability to build consensus.

2. Supporting and Managing Subordinate Development

To improve my skills in this area, I attended a management self-assessment program in which you are evaluated by your subordinates. I am currently reviewing these evaluations and I will meet with the evaluator, discuss the issues raised, and request reevaluations. Concomitantly, I plan to review relevant literature and possibly attend a program on managing professionals. Finally, I will be working with Human Resources on ways to foster employee development and to assess the effectiveness of my efforts.

3. Communication at External Meetings with Potential Strategic Allies

In response to the observation that I speak infrequently at external meetings, I will make a conscious effort to increase my input into these meetings, both to impart information and also to make known to an outside group the thinking of my department. If effectiveness at communicating appears to be a problem when I solicit team members' feedback after each such meeting, I will seek out remedial courses.

sion in [a] group without diverting attention from significant differences"? Certainly, if such performances occur at all, they must be the manifestation of the sort of simultaneous awareness of multiple territories of experience at multiple scales—self, group, task, and purpose—that we begin to cultivate as we move toward the **Strategist** stage and later.

As interesting as it may be to consider the eight ideal standards that the senior managers at Sun Health developed, perhaps it is even more important to emphasize that we are in no way suggesting that other senior managers pin these in front of themselves at their desks. What we are suggesting is that other senior management teams can gain clarity and inspiration by engaging in similar exercises. This one began by having each senior team member develop his or her own list of standards.

These individual lists of standards were then integrated and put into similar-sounding categories, but without assigning names to the categories. The subsequent discussion turned out to be both fun and touching, as members jokingly and truthfully vied to caricature how badly one another had failed to keep their fingers on the organization's pulse.

A number of the members also expressed their excitement at the idea of "defying gravity and doing things people believe we can't achieve." The president was delighted that this phrase had evoked such a spontaneous, positive response from others, admitting that he'd been the one to contribute it. These are the "moments of truth" that generate shared vision and commitment within a team.

Conclusion—Simultaneous Executive and Organizational Learning

In the sequence of events described, we see how the president of Sun Health Care generates organizational learning processes. The president is clearly getting more of a feel for creating *Collaborative Inquiry*-type opportunities for simultaneous managerial and organizational learning.

And the president himself has learned a great deal. He can feel confident in his discovery that one vice president was prepared to participate actively in transformational learning and one was not. He has also learned that there is a way of making difficult personnel decisions that is not unilateral and judgmental, but mutual and inquiring. Moreover, he now knows that he can use a difficult dilemma like this one to leverage a great deal of organizational learning.

Now the president no longer has any formal leadership role within the senior management meetings. Instead, he is available as an information source and as a coach to the formal leaders. He feels both liberated and empowered by this change, since he is now freer to represent himself as strongly as he wishes on either substantive, or procedural, or developmental issues. In other words, he wants to be as free as possible to move his attention back and forth among the four organizational territories of experience—visioning, strategizing, performing, and assessing. At the same time, he is pleased by the new level of leadership initiative on the part of the vice presidents because both he and they are increasingly involved in outside the company negotiation of strategic alliances—brief meetings with virtual strangers who are often competitors—where every possible skill in agenda management, clear communication, and inquiry is at a premium.

What are the organizational learnings in this case? The president, and the senior management team as a whole, along with the consultant, developed a number of organizational learning processes for the senior managers: (1) the set of ideal standards for a senior manager, (2) the new meeting leadership process, and (3) a new senior manager development process. Moreover, several of the vice presidents proceeded to craft shared leadership structures for their management teams.

In short, we see the senior management of Sun Health Care actively experimenting with *Collaborative Inquiry*-types of management of its own day-to-day and strategic affairs. Two years later Sun Health negotiated a 50/50 merger with an HMO twice its size.

PART FOUR

The Ultimate Spiritual and Societal Intent of Action Inquiry

TWELVE

The Fresh Action Awareness
of *Alchemists*

One day while we were still consulting to Sun Health Care, the organization described in Chapters 10 and 11, Sun's manager of employee development was describing his unusual contract with Sun. He had recently recontracted with the company, with the quick approval of his vice president and the CEO, to work one day a week as a consultant outside the health care industry. He felt that he needed a practical strategy like this to help him maintain his perspective on his work. Then he said, as a kind of logical conclusion, "You know, you need to keep your self fresh and your ideas fresh."

It sounds like an attractive idea, doesn't it? Especially to those of us who feel as though we are run a bit ragged by the demands of our work and our life! Keeping our selves and our ideas fresh? A simple idea—an obvious idea—and an enjoyable experience: Keeping fresh. Wouldn't we all rather feel fresh than stale? Isn't it obvious that improving the quality of our actions depends on fresh awareness of what's at stake, fresh ideas about how to operate more effectively, and fresh energies for actually doing so? Don't we want to find the right pace and keep changing pace as is freshly appropriate?

But if keeping ourselves fresh is such an intuitively appealing idea, why is it so rare to find anyone amidst the power brokers of organizational life who seems genuinely fresh, authentic, unassuming, good humored, and timely, and acting to align personal, organizational, societal, and global goods?

Why do we usually have to resort to the names of a few historical personages as examples of freshness—Socrates or the Buddha, Eleanor of Aquitaine or Hildegaard of Bingen, Gandhi or Pope John XXIII, Nelson Mandela or Vaclav Havel? Or perhaps when we think of freshness and spontaneity, we think of comedians like Robin Williams or Bill Cosby or actress-dancer-writer Shirley MacLaine. Why is this eternal freshness at the heart of the *Alchemist* action-logic so rare?

Why is continuing personal transformation to the *Alchemist* action-logic so rare that six different studies by different researchers in different industries found no managers or leaders whatsoever who scored at this developmental action logic on our Leadership Development Profile (see Table 5-1)? Why is it so rare that when we speak about this action-logic in public, managers ask us whether anyone approaching this action-logic could even work in an organization? Why is it so rare that even when we set out to search for innovative leaders who we imagined might well measure at this action-logic, we found that fewer than half of the extraordinary people who took the measure scored at the *Alchemist* action-logic?

To answer these questions, we begin by examining the half-dozen executives who did score at the *Alchemist* action-logic when we went looking for a few of those "rare birds" in the study just mentioned.

A Study of Six Alchemists

We can explore the daily, mundane activities of these six *Alchemist* executives because some agreed to tape their predictions and reflections for a week on their drives to and from work. Some agreed to let one of us shadow them for whole days at a time. And all participated in two or more hours of interviewing. Moreover, one or another of the authors knew four of these people over many years in one or more of the following roles: consultant, member of a board of directors, teacher, friend, or fellow participant in a spiritual community.

For our present purposes, we wish to see these people in action, to convey the sense of moment-to-moment attention, unpredictability, uniqueness, and cross-level analogizing that characterizes much of their work and play. We illustrate four particular themes we found in common within the sample of six. Then we offer a longer illustration of Vaclav Havel's evolution through earlier action-logics toward a continual play between opposites by the time he became president of Czechoslovakia.

The first thing that struck us forcibly as we became more intimately connected with our subjects' workdays was that they were key players not in one organization, but in *many*. Their days were unpredictably divided into initiatives and responses across a number of organizations. Perhaps the most extreme example of this diversity was the woman who interacted with between five and seven organizations each day of the week that she documented. Her primary organizational affiliation was as a member of a global consulting firm, and she acknowledged that when she was visiting a particular client, she would occasionally have brief contact by phone with no more than one or two other organizations in the course of a day.

But this week she was at her own firm's offices throughout. There, she (1) trained junior consultants, (2) served on a performance evaluation committee, (3) developed an affidavit for a suit against a board of which she was a member, (4) billed 37 hours to three different direct client firms as well as five other engagements that she more indirectly supervised, and (5) initiated 42 telephone calls and received 19 on behalf of a newly organizing industry trade association (she called this effort "market development"). In addition, she offered two different, ongoing workshops from 8–10 PM on two of the evenings. The participants in these workshops included former and current organizational clients who wished to engage in their own personal and professional development at a deeper level.

Although this illustration is offered from the outside in, giving no direct taste of this woman's inner experience, it suggests one way that people who measure at the late action-logics of development tend to live at once "symphonically" and "chaotically." One might mistakenly conclude that she and the other people we are profiling are in a constant rush. Quite the contrary. We found in all of them a sense of leisure, playfulness, or meditativeness at times; a sense of urgency, fierce efficiency, or craftlike concentration at others. (Indeed, a telling characteristic of their work and play is that they cannot really be distinguished; "work/play" is a conjugation that comes closer to describing the actual interweaving of business, art, and leisure in these peoples' lives). Our next illustration emphasizes this point by looking at the issue of pace as experienced by another one of our *Alchemist* executives from the inside-out.

This second illustration highlights another thing that struck us as we observed these executives directly: within a given day, their pace varied enormously. Indeed, in this particular case, the work/play behaviors co-existed simultaneously. This CEO intentionally works and lives in a different city from his corporation's headquarters. His office takes up parts of two floors in a large Victorian house, the rest of which is his home. The first floor office consists of an impressive, but more or less normal, outer office for the secretary and visitors. His inner office includes an informal seating area, a working table for meetings of up to 8 or 10, and a private bathroom. Within the bathroom a spiral staircase leads to the second floor.

The second floor room is dominated by a large exercise mat, a wall of books, and comfortable seating. A speakerphone makes it possible for this man to be exercising or lounging with total relaxation, yet project his voice over the phone in a rapid, staccato fashion. This technique, he explains, encourages callers to come to the point more quickly and seems to increase their cooperativeness when he slows down, momentarily, to give them what they can appreciate as "quality attention." Even in his busiest times in the office downstairs, this executive escapes upstairs for two or three minutes each hour to do sit-ups, pushups, aikido, or yoga postures. The point, he says, is to do both work and play at one's own pace, in a leisurely manner.

At the same time, we noted that this executive seems to begin by meeting each situation at the pace and in the action-logic of the person or group with whom he is interacting. Then at one or more moments in the meeting, he, in effect, digs up the conversation by the roots, names its pattern, often humorously, and proposes reconsidering the topic in terms of a different action-logic. Twice, we overheard him change pace on the phone from fast to slow and from current business to an emotional personal situation or historical analogy, his own voice catching and deepening, in such a way that the person on the other end evidently began weeping (as he later confirmed). In other words, these were by no means merely instrumental business negotiations; significant personal relationships were simultaneously being forged. Thus, this man's pace is not merely his own idiosyncratic pace, but one that includes others' paces as well, and he has the ability to transform the pace and focus of the current conversation or meeting.

One of us saw a touching example of this kind of subtly transforming leadership in another of our six executives—this one an artist, entrepreneur, and civic leader—as he fed supper to his three-year-old twins. Largely through the medium of baby talk and odd sounds, he conducted a meandering lesson in arithmetic and lifetime development, generated by the children's initiatives. The fact that this illustration does not occur at work shows that the *Alchemist's* interest in this fresh quality of awareness is not as a means to something else, but as an end in itself.

But how to learn what our own pace is and how it interplays with others rhythms, as we meet the world in all its various guises and in all our various relationships? Finding our own pace is not just a personal issue, but, rather, also a political and spiritual one. The CEO who exercises while working acknowledged to us that he belongs to a form of spiritual practice that offers meditative exercises to be tried in the midst of the business day—exercises that, in the language of this book, continuously freshen contact with the four territories of experiencing and encourage triple-loop learning. But he refused to describe the exercises or give the name of the spiritual tradition on the ground that the exercises are to be shared only with persons who commit to practicing them.

Another one of the six executives we followed in the late 1980s, a Swedish World Bank regional vice president, illustrates how sinuously the **Alchemist** action-logic analogizes among apparently distinct issues at different scales—in this case, intraorganizational personnel assessment issues at the World Bank and its extraorganizational issues of how to support political-economic development in poor countries. As part of a larger reorganization at the World Bank in which everyone's position was put at risk, this executive's subordinates were competing with others to regain or change their ongoing positions (and it was known that at least 10 percent would not be rehired because there were fewer openings in the new structure). The Swedish executive had only the week before rewon her own position. Likening the bank's own issues of personnel development and organizational transformation to the problems that most frequently inhibited success in third-world development programs, she asked her subordinates, as well as the several other candidates for their jobs from outside the team, to propose methods and other colleagues whom they saw as most qualified to resolve this type of dilemma. She proposed to choose those best at doing so to work in the future group.

Initially, most of the applicants did not recommend any other candidates for the positions, evidently regarding it as contrary to their own career interest to do so. The one who did was immediately hired with feedback to the rest of the applicants about the basis for the decision. Then the Swedish executive went through a rather painful developmental process with the remaining applicants (e.g., two very talented individuals who did not work well together were asked to take over what had previously been the other's department, with the aim of improving interdepartment cooperation). Three years later the new group had one of the two best performing loan portfolios among all the regional groups.

This example illustrates particularly well two *Alchemist* characteristics: (1) active attention to analogies across the individual, group, organizational, and international political scales of development and (2) the use of one's personal "charism"—one's personal spiritual energy—not to charm one's associates and generate worshipful subservience, but, rather, to challenge them to engage in collaborative action inquiry.

Thus the distinctive quality of the politics and spirituality of the *Alchemist* is not whatever conventional or unconventional package of beliefs the person may espouse (e.g., Protestant Republican, Jewish Democrat, Pagan Anarchist, etc.), but rather the moment-to-moment inquiry into the source of the life and love that he or she practices. Table 12-1 summarizes the characteristics of the *Alchemist*.

To highlight the challenging political and spiritual engagement of the *Alchemist,* we next offer a portrait of Czech playwright, dissident, leading "velvet revolutionary," and then president, Vaclav Havel. Through Havel's life, you will encounter the *Alchemist* themes of reframing spirit and of vulnerable power. But perhaps most of all, as a dissident artist who becomes a political founding father, Havel illustrates voluntarily standing in the tension of opposites. In him, we find a master of absurdity and of common sense, riding his child scooter around the presidential palace in between sessions of writing the country's constitution. We offer a rather long story and analysis in order to evoke Havel's entire lifetime to the present and in order to evoke the unpromising social order within which Havel discovered, honed, and exercised his transforming power.

Table 12-1   Managerial Style Characteristics Associated with the *Alchemist* Developmental Action-Logic

Alchemist	Continually exercises own attention, seeking single-, double-, and triple-loop feedback on interplay of intuition, thought, action, and effects on outside world; anchors in inclusive present, appreciating light and dark, replication of eternal patterns and emergence of the previously implicit; stands in the tension of opposites, seeks to blend them; intentionally participates in the work of historical/spiritual transformation; co-creator of mythical events that reframe situations; near-death experience, disintegration of ego-identity; treats time and events as symbolic, analogical, metaphorical (not merely linear, digital, literal).

The Personal, Artistic, and Political
Development of Vaclav Havel

Havel was born in 1936 into a middle-class family with intellectual and artistic interests. He showed early enthusiasm for reading, writing, and the theatre. But after the Nazi takeover of Czechoslovakia in the late 1930s, followed by the Communist takeover in the 1940s, he was expelled from some schools and refused entry to others because of his bourgeois background.

By the time he was 16, he formed his own group of friends who were interested in literature and philosophy. Although he wrote that the group was based on voluntary discipline, concord, and serious discussions, it was, in fact, he who rather forcefully suggested what books to read, what films to see, and which low-participating members should tactfully not be invited back. Because of his bourgeois background, his employment opportunities were severely limited. First, he worked as a chemist's assistant, while also publishing his first critical essays. These aspects of Havel's earliest recorded "managerial" style, along with his essays, suggest a young *Expert* at work, with a forceful and critical yet also sociable and inviting craft-logic. Perhaps this early ability to interweave the inviting, the critical, and the forceful foreshadows his later leadership proclivity for seeking to work in the midst of the tension of opposites.

Between 1957 and 1959, Havel entered the army as was required. In the army, he produced his first play, *You've Got Your Whole Life Ahead of You*, together with his friend Karel Brynda, and organized a troop theater where he staged it. The play is about a soldier who chooses the truth and morality and refuses the temptation of an easy undeserved promotion. Here we see strong meritocratic *Achiever* themes, both in the plot of the play and in the collaborative project of writing and producing it.

Only after the play was close to winning a top prize at a military theater competition did officials investigate Havel's background and suspect a hidden message in the play's sly humor about the predominant norms in the Communist army. After the performance, the play was condemned as anti-army and the theater company had to return all the awards it had won. In retrospect it is hard not to read premonitions of the *Strategist* and *Alchemist* action-logics into the theme of the play itself and the creative deviance of the whole event.

In addition to experiencing and reflecting on the conflict between himself and the army, Havel for the first time met with people outside his relatively intellectual circle, learned about their values and lives, and realized that inquiring friendships can cross the boundaries of background, of talent, and even of taste. In these ways, we can see signs of the *Individualist* action-logic beginning to emerge through this military period in Havel's life. (Although we did not systematically seek data on our subjects' biographies in our study of six *Alchemists,* we realized later that three of the six had spontaneously spoken of intense teenage friendships across differences of race, nationality, social class, and gender preference.)

When Havel was mustered out of the army, he became a known playwright by writing *An Evening with the Family.* Ineligible for "management" because of his bourgeois background, he joined the Theater on the Balustrade as a stagehand, but with the promise of being able to participate creatively in the work of the theater. Here he would spend eight years, would write some of his best plays, and would rescue the theater from a crisis of bad management by building stage sets, organizing all theater paperwork and trips, helping the director make decisions about contracts, and becoming the social heart of the enterprise as well. Largely because of Havel's presence and what over his whole lifetime can be seen as his genius for developing "working friendships," the divisions among roles at the theater—director, actors, stage crew, etc.— were not enacted hierarchically, but with mutual respect and with much humor. Here we can clearly see a *Strategist* action-logic at work and at play, uniting performers and staff in a shared vision through the exercise of mutual, vulnerable power.

In 1967, Havel was invited to become an editor of *Tvar,* a magazine for young writers that was established by the Writers' Union. The editorial board of *Tvar* chose not to espouse a particular ideology but simply published selected diverse works they considered good. This open-mindedness gained the support of reformist intellectuals who ousted most of the Stalinist hard-liners in January 1968, and elected Alexander Dubcek during the brief Prague Spring that followed. In less than a year, the Communist hard-liners requested so-called fraternal assistance from the Soviet Union, and censorship and political repression were immediately reimplemented. Many talented artists and writers were silenced, imprisoned, or forced into exile.

Havel made a choice to stay in Czechoslovakia, contrary to many intellectuals, and despite the fact that he was now branded as a political dissident because he believed that by standing in the tension of opposites, the powerless can generate a power that can change society. From this time forward, we begin to see many illustrations of the **Alchemist** "marriage of opposites" in Havel's public writings and other public actions. He stayed in Czechoslovakia's oppressing political/artistic climate because, he wrote, "The outlines of genuine meaning can only be perceived from the bottom of absurdity." And "It is difficult to explain, but without the laughter, we would simply be unable to do serious things," he reflects in his book *Disturbing the Peace* (1990, 113).

One of many examples of how Havel enacted the **Alchemist's** marriage of opposites between the seriousness and absurdity of life on a daily and hourly basis occurred during the writing of the manifesto of the Central Committees of the creative unions in 1969. This manifesto was supposed to be a testament to the nation that more and more citizens would sign and promise to adhere to no matter what happened. The day when the manifesto was supposed to be crafted, Havel promised to attend the opening of a painting show of one of his friends. During the writing of the serious manifesto, he excused himself to go to the bathroom and quietly left the building and attended his friend's opening, where he "sang patriotic songs out of tune and gave impassioned recitations" from the national literary classics (Havel 1990, 112). After the opening, Vaclav returned to finish the final paragraphs of the manifesto. "I would even claim," he said later in reflecting back on this event, "that, in the seventeen years that separate me from that manifesto, I have not really betrayed it to any great extent. And this was not despite the fact that during writing of it I took time off to play the clown: on the contrary, it may have been precisely because of that! And because I'm continually 'taking time off'" (Havel 1990, 113).

In the 1970s, Havel was a banned author. He lived with his wife Olga in their sparse country home, and only occasional visits by his friends prevented him from falling into complete melancholy. In 1977 he came to Prague to plan a defense of the Plastic People Band whom the government accused of spreading immoral behavior. The movement to defend the Plastic People resulted in a petition that was signed by over 70 people. The government did not expect such a unified response and slowly started to back off, releasing some of the arrested young people.

However, when Havel took a lead role in drafting a declaration called Charter 77, the Communist Party responded with massive arrests and interrogations. Havel spent four months in prison, from January to May 1977. This first imprisonment was a very difficult time for him. He was not only interrogated every day, but also manipulated in various ways.

At this time, Havel was preoccupied with the subject of how one can best resist a totalitarian society. His reflections on that subject led to the essay "The Power of the Powerless" (1978, republished in Havel 1985), which reframes the conventional notion that power belongs to those who control governmental institutions and is something that can be grasped or abolished. On the contrary, he viewed power as relational rather than as a substance that can be possessed. Every member of society is entrapped in a dense social network of the country's governing institutions and is a part of power relations that determine the society. Thus everyone has a choice to be either a supporter or an opponent. If one decides to be an opponent or to "live in truth," as Havel calls it, he has to isolate himself from the power of society by being completely different. We can see just how postconventional and inaccessible to the **Opportunist, Diplomat, Expert,** or **Achiever** action-logics these ideas are. And we can imagine just how hard these words were for him to live out during this period when his voice was silenced within his own country.

Havel returned to his position as a spokesman for Charter 77, but in 1979 was arrested again and sentenced to four and a half years in prison. This time he was calm and reconciled to what would follow, committed to "breathe some positive significance" into the experience (Havel 1990, 153). He found this positive significance in writing weekly letters to his wife Olga, letters which she shared widely. They were not really personal letters, but rather a way for him to express himself and communicate with the world outside the prison. In prison, Havel came close to dying. Because he was well known in the West by that time as a Czech dissident and his death in prison might have embarrassed the regime, he was released in 1984. (Note in Table 12-1 that a near-death experience is typical for **Alchemists** [e.g., Nelson Mandela's 27-year imprisonment and Gandhi's fasts], and public death scenes are also common [e.g., Socrates, Jesus, Martin Luther King].)

After his recovery, Havel returned to his country cottage in Hradecek. In the years between 1984 and 1989, many foreign delegations that visited Czechoslovakia also requested to meet with the opposition, so Havel met many of leaders of the West. He also wrote two of his most personal plays, *Largo Desolato* and *Temptation,* where he explored the feelings and challenges facing a person in prison, continuing the dialogue between his art and his politics, once again displaying vulnerable power in sharing his own inner struggles publicly.

When a peaceful vigil turned into a clash between students and police on November 17, 1989, Havel immediately traveled from his cottage to Prague. The following day, students continued the demonstration, called for a public show of support, and met with actors in the Realistic Theater in Prague, where all performances were cancelled. The theaters were converted into public discussion centers. On November 19, Havel announced the formation of the Civic Forum, which united all opposition groups. He spoke to over 200,000 students gathered on Wenceslas Square and threatened a general strike on November 27 if their demands for investigation of November 17, the release of political prisoners, and freedom of the press were not met. Thus had the inviting, critical, forceful teenager now grown into a 53-year-old interweaving the same three forces (positive-negative-reconciling) on behalf of a nation's transformation.

During the next several weeks Havel spoke at demonstrations, organized strikes, discussed the tactics of the movement with compatriots, and negotiated the peaceful resignation of the government and the Communist Party. He also oversaw the formation of a new Federal Assembly, allowing the election of new members who represented the opposition.

The newly formed Federal Assembly elected as its chairman, Alexander Dubcek, the leader during Prague Spring twenty years earlier. The following day, the Federal Assembly unanimously elected Vaclav Havel as president of Czechoslovakia. The powerless man and his friends had indeed generated a power that the powerful and their even more powerful allies did not know.

Although Czech society was feeling rage and hatred toward the old rulers, Havel emphasized that it was not necessary to come together "against." The state of their society was not only the responsibility of the Communist Party members, but of all Czech citizens. "In other words, we are all—though naturally to different extents—responsible for the operation of totalitarian machinery. None of us is just a victim: we are all also its co-creator" (Havel 1997, 4).

Vaclav Havel saw the biggest problem for Czechoslovakia to be not its ruined outer trappings, its dead economy, its poor educational system, and its peat-smoke polluted environment that shortened the average life to less than sixty. Revealing triple-loop learning, he told his compatriots during his New Year's Address to the Nation in 1990, "The worst thing is that we live in a contaminated moral environment. We fell morally ill because we got used to saying something different from what we thought. We learned not to believe in anything, to ignore each other, to care only for ourselves" (Havel 1990, 4). As is true of postconventional leaders generally, Havel focused on incongruities within himself or his own group, rather than on demonizing some out-group. While he saw economic reforms in Czechoslovakia as an absolute necessity, he rejected accepting the rules of the free market system as a dogma to be followed precisely. "The cult of 'systematically pure' market economics can be as dangerous as Marxist ideology, because it comes from the same mental position: that is, from the certainty that operating from theory is essentially smarter than operating from knowledge of life . . . ," he wrote in *Summer Meditations* (1992, 66).

His positions on foreign politics also reframed the role of Czechoslovakia on the world scene. He saw his country, located in the heart of Europe, as an equal member of the European and world society. He refused to hold prejudice against other countries based on previous historic misfortunes. His first foreign visit as president of Czechoslovakia was to Germany, where instead of attacking the Nazi takeover of Czechoslovakia, he publicly apologized to the Germans who were expelled from Czechoslovakia after the fall of the Nazi regime. His position was highly controversial and sparked debates in Czechoslovakia, but it clearly showed the world that Czechoslovakia had new leadership that was interested in restoring old relations more than in opening old wounds. The popularity of his ideas facilitated the return of Czechoslovakia to European society, and the country received an invitation to join NATO and the European Union.

The *Alchemists* in our small research sample and Vaclav Havel all seem dedicated to increasing their own and others' alertness, learning, sense of mutuality, and participation in transformation at multiple social levels. To this end, they exercise a capacity for intelligent analogy and an evident relish for an unpredictability that welcomes creative inspiration. For the *Alchemist,* the activity that we are naming action inquiry is no longer merely an occasional tactic to be tried when our usual approaches are failing, nor merely a strategic theory to be tried as frequently as we can remember to help enlarge our choices as leaders, but, rather, the very stuff of moment-to-moment living.

Why We Can Only Get Glimpses of the *Alchemist*

The previous illustrations offer only glimpses of people operating at the *Achemist* action-logic level. Why are "glimpses" the very best we can hope to achieve in this regard? Think about it this way: once an answer to all the questions we asked at the outset of this chapter becomes a settled intellectual truth—a mind-set—it is no longer fresh. It is no longer in contact with the color and the shock and the feeling of a fresh perception. The very essence of the *Alchemist* action-logic is that it cannot be stated as a settled truth in words or numbers, but is open instead to new revelation, new shadows, and new wonderment on a continuing basis.

The transformation from the *Strategist* action-logic toward this most elusive and flexible of action-logics is, like all other developmental transformations to a later action-logic, a movement from being *controlled by* something to having a peer *relationship with* it. The *Alchemist* ceases to be subject to the *Strategist* action-logic and comes to have a relationship with that and all the earlier action-logics as moment-to-moment options. This time we can say the transformation is from being in the right *frame of mind* (e.g., having the "right" theory of timing, the "right" names for the four territories of experience, etc.) to having a *reframing spirit*.

"The appearance in us of what is really true, our nature, is not a comfortable experience," John Pentland (1988) tells us (*Exchanges Within*, 251). A reframing spirit continually overcomes itself, awakening to its own presuppositions. A reframing mind continually listens into the dark of preverbal experience. It adjusts itself to the frames of reference held by other actors in a situation, to underlying organizational and historical developmental rhythms, and to the as yet unorganized chaos beyond. (As we now theoretically know, unorganized chaos represents by far the larger part of reality at any moment, yet is largely inaccessible to the language and assumption-bound mind.)

This listening into the dark within, between, and among the four territories of experience allows us to appreciate simultaneously both the absurdity and the common sense of a situation. Such listening is unique in seeking to discover and articulate a motivating challenge in the present situation in a language accessible to all participants. Discovering and articulating this motivating challenge can create a social jiu-jitsu effect: just as total disintegration is threatening, the person or organization or nation suddenly becomes fluid and acts with surprising vigor and resolve. For this reason, this vulnerable power is often experienced as alchemist-like, magician-like, or clownlike. After all, four weeks before he became president of Czechoslovakia, Vaclav Havel had no official position whatsoever.

This kind of creative dissolving and reconstituting of boundaries also occurred at the end of apartheid in South Africa, when, against all probability, Nelson Mandela and the Truth and Reconciliation Commission generated a surprisingly nonviolent transformation toward an interracial society. Astonishing gestures, such as Mandela appearing at a championship game in a white Afrikaner rugby jersey, repeatedly refreshed and renewed people's common sense of how far reconciliation can go.

The transformation to this managerial style requires no mere turning toward enlightenment, but also a turning to face all that is dark in the human condition as it manifests itself in ourselves and our surroundings. Unlike the *Opportunist,* the *Expert,* or the *Strategist,* who may believe that he or she is on the side of good and can rid the world of evil, the *Alchemist* recognizes that the polarization between good and evil—between victory and defeat, between the sacred and the profane, between classes, races, and sexes, between us and them, I and Thou—is recreated at each moment by our relatively fixed and one-sided perspectives of the world. Evil emanates from our own forgetfulness of presencing triple-loop awareness, from our own fallen, passive attention. It cannot be permanently defeated. Indeed, to fight against it as though it were only outside ourselves is to reinforce it. For the *Alchemist,* unlike the *Strategist,* developmental action inquiry becomes, not so much a stable theory for managing others as an ongoing jousting with our own attention and the outside world simultaneously.

Such a person requires no official role. His or her power and authority derive from listening to developmental rhythms and a-rhythm-ias. By virtue of this four-territory listening, he or she takes the executive role, a sense of responsibility for the whole that is open to anyone, regardless of official role. Listening in this way, with a sense of wonder repeatedly reawakening in body, heart, and mind, the *Alchemist* experiences the rhythms, the lives, and the setting of a particular conversation. He or she also listens to the wider historical circumstances radiating from the past and the future into the only time when awareness and action are possible: this inclusive present. Appolonius of Tyana, a contemporary of

Jesus of Nazareth, is said to have observed a five-year vow of silence in order to learn to listen in this way.

We have repeatedly advocated "listening into the dark," and in the chapters on organizational transformations (Chapters 8 through 11), we have documented the kinds of developmental rhythms one begins to hear when listening so. But we have not illustrated the listening process itself, except in Chapter 9 in the instant when the consultant to the software company takes 10 minutes before his meeting with the two partners to listen into the developmental rhythms his interviews suggest. In one sense, true listening is an active silence—an emptiness—that is in principle impossible to illustrate in a painting or a piece of writing (although Chinese "empty" landscape paintings and Japanese seventeen-syllable haiku poems are attempts at evoking such listening). In order to learn what true listening is, you must be in the presence of someone doing so and seek to enact it yourself. Nevertheless, here is one more attempt at an illustration, taken, with her permission, from the journal of a woman describing her participation in a Quaker meeting, where everyone is invited to listen into (and thereby create) a silence toward the implicit origin of being, knowing, doing, and effectuating.

> With heart beating [she writes], I stand up.
>
> During our first twenty minutes of silence together at the Friends meeting this morning, a silence broken only by occasional sniffles and coughs, I have in no way expected that I will be bringing any message. Indeed, it's been years since I last did so. Today, I have been attending to my breathing and to the circulation of sensation in my seated body.
>
> As the listening deepens, seeming to come from my heart, different flares of feeling/thought arc out as well, tracing the mutually-interrupting-or-reinforcing trajectories of the many relationships and institutional rhythms in which I have participated during my lifetime. It is as though the shape of my life as a whole in time is declaring itself to me, with occasional brief flashes of particular past events. This quality of thinking/feeling seems possible only if I continue my intentional listening, noticing the thoughts without being drawn into them.
>
> As the silence continues to concentrate itself, two simple lines announce themselves and then, no matter how often I let them go for the pleasure of pure listening, keep returning to ask me to speak them.
>
> Standing, I take a few more moments of silence to find my new balance. Then, seeking not to cease my active listening even as I speak, I slowly release:

"THE SILENCE . . . THAT PASSETH . . . ALL UNDERSTANDING . . .
I am wondering what it is in us
that wishes to listen to, and from, this silence . . ."

During the meeting's silence, this woman seems to be engaged in a "presencing" listening throughout, with an initial focus on patterns and specific memories from the past, but later on with the question of whether two phrases that are occurring and reoccurring to her may contribute to the meeting if spoken. The woman's thought process is not linear, but chaotic and transformational, and the person is not identified with any of it. This is indicated by the fact that she chooses not to communicate any of the content when she speaks or when she writes. She chooses instead to highlight the nonverbal, triple-loop attentional process of continual listening into the ground of all that becomes explicit.

If there is a chief fault in common among the *Opportunist, Expert,* and *Strategist* action-logics, it is their overconfidence in their right to speak with certitude at key moments when listening and self-reflective inquiry would better serve them and their world. If there is a chief fault in common among the *Diplomat,* the *Achiever,* and the *Individualist* action-logics, it is their reluctance to speak confrontationally when clear dissonance would serve them and the larger situation better than the appearance of harmony. When and how and why to blend passion, dispassion, and compassion in a listening that goes on even when we ourselves are speaking is a question that increasingly confronts the *Alchemist.*

To live at one's leisure, performing work of value to others, listening into the dark, exercising presencing attention, and loving even what turns from the light in ourselves and others: this is one good way to express what it is in a lifetime of action inquiry that can be named "the secret of timely and transforming leadership."

Conclusion

From the outside-in and considered as an abstraction, developmental theory may appear linear, rigid, and hierarchical. But in practice, experienced from the inside-out, as we transform to later action-logics where our attention becomes actively engaged in action inquiry on a more and more continual basis, the drama of development is seen to be occurring at many intersecting and interrupting levels, on a moment-to-moment basis—not just broadly across a whole lifetime.

People, projects, organizations, and nations spend time at different action-logics, learning from single-, double-, or triple-loop feedback. They also spend time in the chaotic transitions between action-logics, consciously or unconsciously.

We began this chapter with the question, why is the freshness characteristic of the **Alchemist** so difficult to rediscover in the ongoing struggles and tensions, habits, and comforts of our lives? One answer is that the effort to listen into the four territories of experience reveals many distances, gaps, incongruities, and disharmonies. To experience such incongruities is not just an intellectual exercise, but generates an existential, emotional shock.

Who among us would voluntarily take on the continual suffering of witnessing the gaps among intentions, espoused values, actual practices, and outcomes in ourselves, in others, in organizations, and in larger social processes? Who struggles to transform such suffering, not into imprisoning neuroses or social victories at others' cost, but, rather, into emancipating consciousness that graces each meeting afresh?

Our response is: everyone who is moving to the postconventional action-logics implicitly begins to prefer his or her own intentional suffering over blindly causing suffering to others. And a person moving toward the **Alchemist** action-logic is explicitly trying to co-create a setting—be it a business or a family setting, a professional, a cultural, or a spiritual setting—where inquiry about the most difficult issues is valued and practiced and where suffering is shared and transformed. We call such a setting a **Foundational Community of Inquiry** and will be exploring what that means in Chapter 13, our next, and final, chapter.

THIRTEEN

Creating *Foundational* *Communities of Inquiry*

In this chapter, we offer brief glimpses of what personal, communal, and institutional cultures of inquiry may come to look like, as we discuss the *Foundational Community of Inquiry* action-logic of organizing that parallels the *Alchemist* action-logic in personal development. We are hampered because we have only shadowy and fragmentary illustrations from the past to help stimulate our imagination. We believe that no fully embodied, public, society-wide example of this organizing action-logic has ever existed yet.

But because this is truly an action-logic of the future, we will call, before this chapter is complete, not just on shadowy memories from the past, and not just on some of the particular challenges and opportunities of the present, but also on a kind of social-science/fiction to help us begin to imagine more actively how each of us personally and all of us globally can envision and enact the future.

Table 13-1 shows the theoretical characteristics of the *Foundational Community of Inquiry* action-logic. The very name for this action-logic of organizing suggests two apparently opposite qualities—foundational stability and the transformational disequilibrium introduced by single-, double-, and triple-loop inquiry. It is the union of these opposites—the edge of chaos, as it is today sometimes named—that we are seeking in a *Foundational Community of Inquiry*.

If this sounds mystical, let's make it sound mundane. For example, boards of directors function, by intent and at their best, as foundational communities of inquiry for their organization, testing the clarity of, and the congruity among, mission, strategy, operations, and outcomes and creating a learning community for the CEO. In 2001 and 2002, the U.S.

194

Table 13-1   Characteristics of a *Foundational Community of Inquiry*

- Appreciation of continuing interplay of opposites: action/research, sex/politics, past/future, symbolic/diabolic, etc.
- Ongoing, experiential and empirical research on relations among spiritual/intuitive *visioning*, theoretical/practical *strategizing*, timely *performing*, and assessing *outcomes* in the visible, external world.
- All fundamentalist, universal ideologies are challenged by the community's emphasis on peerlike mutuality among people of diverse backgrounds and on the humble, vulnerable practice of timely action inquiry.
- Political friction among different paradigms/frames/action-logics within the organization and between the organization and the wider environment.
- *Collaborative Inquiry* structure fails because it does not meet the alchemical challenge of timely transformational, emancipatory, collective action.
- If timely transformational collective action is taken, shared purpose is revealed as sustaining and as generating multiple choices for action (and feedback on the consequences of such choices) from all participants.
- New experiences of time: his-story becomes my-story; interplay of time-bound needs, timeless archetypes, and timely creative inquiry.

economy reeled under the impact of companies, like Enron and Global Crossing, whose boards failed to function as foundational communities of inquiry. On the one hand, a board of directors is less likely to realize its potential if the chairman of the board is the CEO and if the majority of the board is employed by the organization. In such cases, the power asymmetry in favor of the CEO is likely to dampen both the sense of mutuality and the sense of inquiry on the board. On the other hand, outside board members are faced with a daunting task of getting to know just how the internal chemistry of the company works. In any event, our experiences of working both on and with boards of directors, as well as our developmental theory of organizing action-logics, suggests that building *Collaborative Inquiry* and *Foundational Community of Inquiry* processes into board activities will be at least as significant to their proper functioning as the roles their individual members play.

Having used an ideal version of boards of directors to help us get a first impression of a *Foundational Community of Inquiry*, can we now identify an actual institution that embodies the *Foundational Community of Inquiry* characteristics (Table 13-1) in its actual practice? Let us examine the organization called the Society of Friends, commonly known as the Quakers. The Quakers are a peerlike Protestant sect with no official or professional ministry. As illustrated at the end of Chapter

12, their meetings for worship (and their business meetings, too) are characterized by a silent, inquiring listening by each for an inner voice or Inner Light that may correspond to what we are calling in this book intuitive, multiterritory awareness. The occasional messages that participants offer to the gathered group gain dignity and resonance within this culture of intentional listening. Many people know of the Quakers primarily because of their pacifism. They refuse to engage in war, seeking to become conscientious objectors and peace mediators instead, thus placing themselves in powerful political tension with their own countries in times of war.

Another spiritually oriented organization that is partial example of a *Foundational Community of Inquiry* is an organization conceived at a picnic one day in the 1500s. Six University of Paris students who did not all know one another before the picnic were brought together that day by a former Spanish soldier, Ignatius of Loyola. Together, they dedicated themselves to founding the Society of Jesus, the Jesuit Order. Within a decade, Jesuits were traveling, often alone, to the far corners of the world, in order to immerse themselves in the cultures of India, China, the Paraguayan natives, and others. Rather than seeking to impose the European structure of Catholicism, they sought to understand how the Christian spirit could be communicated in each distinctive culture. So influential and so controversial did the Jesuit Order become in global exploration, politics, education, and science, as well as within the Catholic Church itself, in theology and in its Ignatian spiritual exercises, that it has twice during its history been proscribed and later resurrected. These experiences reflect the degree to which the Order has generated political friction with dominant paradigms of faith and truth.

During the late 1960s, the Beatles, the British music group, also partially represented a *Foundational Community of Inquiry*. Exploring the meaning of life, both individually and corporately, the Beatles inspired a more far-reaching—certainly a more artistic and more comic—cultural revolution than Mao. For a time, each new album seemed to introduce a new musical/consciousness paradigm. Or was that the Rolling Stones who were the shadow community? Or is the Grateful Dead really the example that we are looking for? In any event, all of these groups are peer organizations with global impact in both economic and cultural terms.

Joan Bavaria, Trillium Asset Management, and Socially Responsible Investing—An Evolving *Foundational Community of Inquiry?*

Just in case our offbeat spiritual and musical examples of male-only institutions (the Jesuits, the Beatles, etc.) are making you a little queasy about the economic practicality and the generalizability of this organizational action logic, we now offer a for-profit, majority-woman organization as a contemporary example of a *Foundational Community of Inquiry*. This organization is the relatively small investment advisory firm named Trillium Asset Management, the first company dedicated to focusing entirely on socially responsible investing. It was founded by its continuing CEO, Joan Bavaria, in 1982, and our knowledge of Trillium comes not only from public documents and a doctoral dissertation on the company, but also from an insider's view of Trillium's development that one of the authors has enjoyed while serving on its board of directors since 1989. We have already described in Chapter 3 how socially responsible investing represents a way of conducting single-loop, double-loop, and triple-loop action inquiry in stock markets, in order to optimize three bottom lines that their clients value: profitability, social equity, and environmental sustainability. In this way, Trillium Asset Management engaged in the second characteristic of a *Foundational Community of Inquiry*—experiential and empirical research on all four territories of experience (see Table 13-1). Trillium's clients receive not only financial returns comparable to the S&P 500, they also receive the satisfaction of knowing that their funds are predominantly supporting leadership companies in operationalizing the triple bottom-line concept.

Joan Bavaria has played a central coinitiating role since the early 1980s in creating the Social Investing Forum and the CERES Environmental Principles (serving as board chair for each), as well as the Global Reporting Initiative. Through these vehicles, socially responsible investing has grown despite being in continual friction with the dominant economic paradigm, the first characteristic of a *Foundational Community of Inquiry* listed in Table 13-1.

Bavaria initially conceived of Trillium Asset Management as a worker-owned company. She invited each employee who so wished—whether secretary, computer programmer, or president—to buy (at a nominal price) one share of stock and thereby gain an equal vote with the president at shareholder meetings. These annual shareholder meetings, in turn, elect the board of directors, including two employee members, and either confirm, disconfirm, or direct other board actions.

Trillium's history has not all been sweetness and light, however. As developmental theory predicts, starting with a late action-logic vision did not immediately springboard the company into late action-logic functioning. In its earliest years, many of its worker-owners tended to want to exercise the rights of owners, including the right to complain, while holding the president responsible for exercising all executive and ownership responsibilities (any parents of 17-year-olds recognize this archetype?). Then, during the early 1990s, the company experienced something like a prolonged "near-death" when it was harassed for several years by a lawsuit from one of its early investor-members. The silver lining in this cloud became the deep sense of unity that this challenge generated throughout the company and the board of directors. Only in the middle and late 1990s did the company attract significant new talent at the senior and board level and open new sites, thereby establishing multiple executive functions and a much truer parity in voice between Bavaria and her colleagues on a day-to-day basis (a parity that Bavaria had long been trying to cultivate).

Today, the one-employee–one-share structure has been modified to vest a larger proportion of ownership to those with longevity and with higher levels of decision-making responsibility. Also, about 30 percent of the stock has been sold to another company to create a friendly strategic alliance and to give the shares redeemable market value. In these ways, the original *Collaborative Inquiry* structure of the company died (as per the fifth characteristic listed in Table 13-1), and newer, more flexible collaborative structures have been generated. This collective ownership structure, along with the actual mutuality of day-to-day business relationships within the company has resulted in extraordinarily low turnover since the company's founding. Meanwhile, the company has grown to four branches and leads its sector in developing social research, measurement, and advocacy functions.

The commitment to mutual peer relations that we believe will characterize *Foundational Communities of Inquiry* is evident at Trillium in more ways than just its collective ownership structure. Historically, the company has been unusually diverse: not only have women always been in the majority, but there is a higher percentage of African-Americans and other ethnic minorities among employees and on the board of directors than the typical U.S. investment advisor. This composition is one way in which company members are challenged to attain "peerlike mutuality among people of diverse backgrounds" (the third characteristic of **Foundational Community of Inquiry** in Table 13-1).

The company is also unusually mutual in its customer relationships and in its methods of analyzing whether companies represent good investment opportunities. Because its investment strategy directly contradicts the conventional financial wisdom that an investment portfolio ought to be determined solely on criteria of financial return, Trillium works to identify companies that take responsibility for their ethical impact on their employees and the environment while operating profitably. Trillium also engages in shareholder initiatives and dialogue with companies if their policies seem problematic from social equity or environmental sustainability standpoints. Thus, Trillium seeks a peerlike mutuality both with its clients (inquiring into their investment criteria rather than taking them for granted) and in companies' relationships to their employees, communities, and environments. Trillium's corporate vision is expressed in its motto: INVESTING FOR A BETTER WORLD.

Bavaria's ability to lead through these various difficulties and transformations, while maintaining an almost uncanny calm and good cheer, as well as ongoing tactical light-footedness and strategic creativity over more than twenty years, suggests, as developmental theory would predict, that she is likely operating at the *Strategist* or *Alchemist* action-logic. What her action-logic is today we are not sure, but when she completed the Leadership Development Profile in the late 1980s, she measured as operating at the *Strategist* action-logic. Before she became a banker and then a social entrepreneur, Bavaria was an artist. Today, Trillium Asset Management and socially responsible investing as a whole are the fruits of her artistic exercise of her own personal brand of action inquiry and collaborative leadership.

The United Nations as a Foundational Community of Inquiry?

On a still larger scale, can organizational and national leaders meet the unexpected emergencies of the international economic, political, and spiritual scene with action inquiry? Since the terrorist attack on the United States on September 11, 2001, and during the debate on whether to wage a "preventive" war on Iraq in late 2002 and early 2003, the question of whether the United Nations (UN) can come to play a stronger role as a global foundational community of inquiry, or whether it will become weaker instead, became a more and more critical real-time concern. Given Saddam Hussein's performance as an *Opportunist*-like, unilateral bully within his country and region, and given the UN's history as a primarily *Diplomat*-like institution with little independent power, could the United States and the UN respond in a way that built a global community of inquiry and mutuality, rather than in a way that reinforced unilateral bullying?

A year after the attacks and just prior to declaring war on Iraq, how would President Bush address the UN on September 12, 2002? And then again, how would the UN Security Council respond to Bush's speech in the days that followed? Would a way of proceeding be framed or reframed that would deter and end the reign of unilateral bullies while simultaneously enhancing a sense of positive mutuality and inter-dependence among a wider and wider group of nations? As we have seen in this book, transformational leaders like Vaclav Havel and Joan Bavaria engaged their compatriots in dialogue to allow the emergencies of the moment to generate positive new visions for the future, grounded in action that marries principled firmness and joint openness.

Not too surprisingly, President Bush did *not* focus as strongly in his September 12, 2002, UN speech on the issue of constituting new degrees and kinds of global mutuality as the Franco-German Chirac Plan of that same time advocated. Indeed, Bush seemed to threaten U.S. action no matter what conclusion the Security Council reached. Nevertheless, the door was left open for a short time for the U.S. Congress and the UN Security Council to generate more mutual strategic initiatives. We all know today that neither Bush, nor Congress, nor France, nor Germany, nor anyone else on the world scene created new qualities of more mutual global authority in the year that followed.

Imagine, however, that in the two months following Bush's speech, the Security Council had voted a resolution that prioritized the five top political/military/peace-keeping goals of the UN for the next year as follows:

1. Terminating the efficacy of Al Qaeda.
2. Creating peace and freedom for both Israel and a Palestinian state.
3. Enforcing UN resolutions in Iraq by military force if necessary.
4. Continuing the nation-building process in Afghanistan.

5. Developing an ongoing process for gradually reconstituting the UN as an increasingly empowered, increasingly democratic, governing body with some taxing authority.

Imagine further that this Security Council resolution had specified that several nations take the leadership on each of the top priority goals:

1. That the United States, Egypt, and Pakistan coordinate the Al Qaeda initiative under U.S. leadership.
2. That France, Brazil, Syria, and Jordan coordinate a world peace conference on the Israel-Palestine initiative, chaired by UN Secretary-General Annan.
3. That Britain, Germany, and India coordinate the Iraq initiative, with possible U.S. troop support.
4. That China, Italy, and Canada coordinate the support for Afghanistan.
5. That Russia, Norway, and Mexico lead the process of visioning and strategizing a seven-year timetable for reconstituting the UN that includes one major operational change each year, along with an ongoing public assessment process for each operational change.

The point of this scenario is not to propose this specific solution—the time for that is now past. Rather, the point of this scenario is to highlight how a guiding concern for generating a global *Foundational Community of Inquiry* could have influenced real current affairs.

The question of how to gradually reframe the UN so that it can come to function more as a *Foundational Community of Inquiry* remains. There are many possible ways to accomplish this. For example, if the UN gains a modest initial taxing authority, it could create an Intercultural Inquiry and Investment Corps to do two things: (1) identify businesses and community projects in the poorest countries of the world that deserve microdevelopment investments and (2) provide consulting and training in leadership and assessment that would help those organizations develop later-action-logic cultures of inquiry and accountability.

The Inquiry and Investment Corps could be composed of six-person teams from six different countries assigned to a seventh country. Thus, the Inquiry Corps teams themselves would need to become cross-cultural, cross-paradigmatic *Foundational Communities of Inquiry*, basing their work in the host country on the vulnerable, mutual, transforming power of timely inquiry and action. The degree to which nations contribute to, and invite the presence of such teams would provide an immediate measure of their openness to inquiry and self-transformation. Veterans of the Inquiry and Investment Corps would represent a growing, global leadership cadre with transnational loyalties.

Future Possibilities

It may take our global system hundreds of years of experimenting with new kinds of business, political, and spiritual institutions before we develop a consistent public mastery of the later action-logics that welcome not just single-loop learning, but also double- and triple-loop learning now.

The pre-modern period was preeminently characterized by *Opportunist* action-logic warrior cultures interspersed with class or caste hierarchies that represented the *Diplomat* action-logic. The modern period has been preeminently characterized by scientific progress emanating from the *Expert* action-logic and by market growth exemplifying the *Achiever* action-logic. In the past quarter century, we have seen a growth in individualism in the West that points toward postmodern relativism and the *Individualist* action-logic, along with a fundamentalist backlash in both the United States and Middle East.

In the so-called developed world, we have learned a good deal about how to lead our own lives and our companies on the basis of single-loop feedback during the modern period. Moreover, a small minority of particular individuals and organizations have transformed to later action-logics, as illustrated in this book. But throughout the world, in every culture, people and organizations still tend—personally, politically, and technologically—to defend against potential double- and triple-loop learning by using power unilaterally.

A New Organizational Form—The Not-for-Prophet

What if, over the next four generations of the 21st century, millions of institutional leaders, families, and scholars around the world begin to seek support for their own development toward the *Strategist* action-logic and beyond? What if they increasingly address themselves to the challenge of helping whole organizations develop toward *Collaborative*

Inquiry and beyond? And what if they come increasingly to value integrity, mutuality, and sustainability in the transformational ways this book begins to illustrate?

We may, of course, project infinite possibilities, and the aim of the following social-science/fiction scenario is not to predict which particular future will occur. Whether you are inspired or repelled by the following unlikely scenario, its aim is to encourage each of you to go a step or two further in envisioning a qualitatively different future that you wish to co-create with others. (A number of contemporary consulting firms, like Generon and the Global Business Network, develop such future scenarios for companies and whole countries.)

The following future scenario offers a social vision of not-for-profit organizations in health care and in other institutional fields at the *Foundational Community of Inquiry* stage. This scenario is a slightly adapted version of one of a number of different scenarios constructed in the late 1990s as part of a year-long visioning and strategizing process of a leading U.S. health management organization, in order to provoke board members and senior management to reconsider the existing paradigm of medicine. The scenarios responded in different ways to the question: Where might a fundamental transformation in health care organizing lead, and how best might the organization play a leadership role in such a transformation?

Here is the scenario. Remember, the point of the scenario is not to make you believe it, but, rather, to get you inquiring. How will you feel in 2025 if this scenario plays out? What do you like about it and what don't you like? Why do you feel that way? What future do *you* want to participate in creating?

Philadelphia Quaker Health in 2025

By 2025, Philadelphia Quaker Health (PQH) becomes the most trusted and respected name in health care. It is one of the Nine Majors—the nine largest Not-for-Prophets (NFPs) in the world.

Philadelphia Quaker Health has close to one billion members globally, and, of these, more than nearly 100 million are fully vested. (Once fully vested, NFP members' income and life care through death is guaranteed and at least half of their economic assets become fully integrated into the NFP's Intergenerational Trust. However, even more important than this financial security is the deep friendships that the NFP develops among its members, so that they are held in community till death "doeth" them part.)

In 2025, NFPs already account for approximately one-fifth of global annual revenues, having grown very rapidly in the previous 15 years. Unlike for-profit corporations and government agencies, Not-for-Prophets, like Arborway Investing and the Inner Chapters Driving School, have become global, multisector organizations by accepting the challenge of cultivating, not just the negative freedoms so well managed by the U.S. and European Community Constitutions (under which most of the top 500 NFPs are incorporated), but also and in particular, as Philadelphia Quaker Health's mission statement puts it:

> *The balanced eco-spiritual, social, physical, and*
> *financial development of members and clients*

Philadelphia Quaker offers personal budgetary options in regard to elective care for members who successfully maintain their health (and more than 80 percent of the membership in every age group of the octave does). Currently, the Mass-age Mess-age unit, which conducts the Active Health Triangles, receives the largest proportion of the elective budget. Active Health Triangles meet at least once every three weeks for exercise and conversation, to address each member's spiritual, organizational, and physical health dilemmas. In these Triangles members typically discuss their most perplexing and troubling issues and share suggestions, via the Web and the Intranet, about alternative resources they can access from other PQH services, or about how to deal with a dilemma at work or with a loved one. They also exercise together, sharing meditational, conversational, martial arts, and sexual disciplines. Of course, to be successful, these triangles must develop trust across all four of their internal relationships (the three "couples" and the "triangle"). This requires a more and more continual and refined attention to the currents of passion, dispassion, and compassion among the threesome.

The opportunity to join a different Triangle every other year is what initially attracts most clients to become members of PQH. As everyone is well aware, the Triangles shift membership based on the stated partner preferences of each member. "Free love," new PQH members fondly imagine. But, as they learn, and as another of the Nine Majors advertises: "Dreams do come true . . . Dis-illusion-ingly . . . Trans-form-ingly . . . ." In other words, these Triangles support members' developmental transformations toward greater integrity, mutuality, and sustainability in their intimate relationships.

Like the others of the Nine Majors in relation to their original sectors, PQH is far and away the largest and most respected player in the health care industry globally. It is also a Liberating Discipline that generates enormous trust and longevity among its doctors, business associates, member beneficiaries, and clients. Health statistics show that adults whose action-logics transform are healthier. Also, late-action-logic adults play more effective executive roles within PQH. Therefore, aspirants seeking full vesting must at a minimum accomplish two adult transformations prior to vesting. As a result of this requirement, the organization is more likely to choose to discontinue its relationship with members prior to their final, full vesting (after as many as 21 years) than the members are to discontinue their relationship with PQH.

In the wider global market and in the U.S. political process, there is great controversy about the adult development orientation that all chartered Not-for-Prophets share. Spiritual, scientific, political, and economic fundamentalists—those who wish without question to preserve traditional forms of religious authority, empirical validity, individual rights, and property rights—tend to regard the Nine Majors as emanations of the Great Satan (the more so, when members of their own families join an NFP and their family inheritance is threatened).

Why do the Not-for-Prophets generate such contestation and consternation? Because the NFPs' 21-year vesting process for adults tests whether members will voluntarily undergo more than one developmental transformation, and these transformations challenge a person's inherited, fundamental, taken-for-granted beliefs and practices. For example, most of the Nine Majors put primary emphasis on Triangles and Quartets rather than Couples. Also, they divert wealth by inheritance from the blood family to the NFP community. Moreover, they encourage "Fast Forwarding" (a fasting and communal celebration process through which Senior Peers choose their time of death).

Religious and individual rights fundamentalists decry such transformational initiatives, arguing they are often cult-inspired or cult-manipulated (which neatly mirrors NFP members' views of fundamentalists!). During the past fifteen years, the Nine Majors and the next 491 of the "Good Life 500" have continued to gain market share by comparison to the Fortune 500, the global governmental sector, and the traditional religious and educational not-for-profits.

So ends this social-science/fiction scenario. As of 2003, the gap between the world-leading excellence of U.S. medical education and technology and the world-leading dysfunction of U.S. national health care organizing and financing yawns ever wider. The percentage of uninsured and underserved citizens grows annually, as does the percentage of dissatisfied doctors and nurses. And people increasingly die unconscious and unattended within days of having used more medical resources than ever before in their lives. As they age, the baby-boom generation is increasingly asking what kind of personal disciplines, communal arrangements, and health institutions will support dying calmly and in conversation with good friends. Will new kinds of global institutions evolve during the 21st century, as different from modern nuclear families, corporations, and democratic governments as they, in turn, have been from pre-modern extended families, war lord clans, and kingdoms or empires?

Communities of Practice and Communities of Inquiry

As early intermediate steps between the small Active Health Triangles and the huge Not-for-Prophets envisioned in the previous future scenario, so-called communities of practice—voluntary and usually temporary networks of co-professionals who share know-how and invent leading edge practices, sometimes face-to-face but more often Internet-based—have received much attention in the business community during the past decade as vehicles for change and innovation. In the context of the developmental perspective introduced in this book, we wonder what action-logics such communities of practice may represent. An obvious candidate as the developmental action-logic both fueling and setting the limits for such professional, playful, yet resolutely work-oriented communities of practice is the *Expert/Experiments* action-logic.

When we begin to look at such voluntary communities of practice and business networks in a developmental light, we can see the more action-oriented CEO breakfast and luncheon clubs, where confessions are heard and deals are made, as representing the *Achiever/Systematic Productivity* action-logic.

Exercise, dance, psychodrama, and therapy groups, as well as the interpersonal self-study groups introduced in Chapter 2, and at least some of the Lifecare Communities for elders that now dot the landscape in the United States can be understood as communities of practice that represent the self-reflective *Individualist/Social Network* action-logic.

Voluntary groups that combine leading-edge invention, production of economic goods or services, and self-study—like the group of interdisciplinary faculty members and business partners at Boston College who invented its Leadership for Change executive program and have delivered it as an ongoing collaborative for 10 years, with monthly meetings that combine dinner, celebration, business, and reflection—can be understood as representing the *Strategist/Collaborative Inquiry* action-logic.

The eleven associates who are co-producing this book may be taken as an illustration of a virtual group that is at once a community of practice and a community of inquiry for its members. Although we have never once met as an entire group, all eleven of us have engaged in many self-study disciplines over the past 20 to 40 years. Two of the associates have only been engaged with a few others of us for a couple of years, but personal and professional relationships among the other nine of us go back as long as 43 years and average 17 years. In addition, there are three different, but overlapping, subgroups among us who have worked and inquired together for 23 years, 9 years, and 6 years, respectively. Like a good soccer team or dance troop, we know each other's strengths, foibles, and vulnerabilities very well indeed and delight in confronting and supporting one another in our common and individual enterprises.

Indeed, four of our associates belong to what one of us calls his "Constellation of Lifetime Friends," a truly invisible, mythical organization that may count as an actual *Foundational Community of Inquiry.* This associate counts 24 persons (14 men and 10 women) among his Lifetime Friends, in relationships that average 29 years in length. At various points in his life, he has lived in the same home with 11 of these friends, and he anticipates a future sharing of homes with many of them as they age together, losing one partner or the other in the 11 ongoing first marriages within the constellation. As in the case of the associates in writing this book, not all the members of this constellation of friends know all the others well, but most have known most for many years. Perhaps such Constellations of Lifetime Friends will become more common in the future, will provide a similar kind of security, activity, and friendship among elders that Lifetime Care communities do for those who can afford them today, while continuing to perform as *Foundational Communities of Inquiry* for their members until their chosen moment of death.

Conclusion

How will these various examples of incipient *Foundational Communities of Inquiry*—past, present, and future—spiritual, political, and financial—affect you? How will this book as a whole, about the multiple personal and organizational transformations that you invite if you commit yourself to the path of developmental action inquiry, affect your life?

We hope that the way this book is organized will help any of you who so wish to begin your own process of action inquiry little by little in your own work and personal life. If you do begin to try an occasional action inquiry experiment, you will soon want to get some help for continuing. We hope that Chapters 1 through 3 provide a number of clues about the sorts of small groups you may start or join to support one another's action inquiry practice. Chapters 4 through 7 raise the action inquiry ante, from particular actions that may improve your effectiveness within your current action-logic, to longer-term transformations of action-logic—from the more common *Opportunist, Diplomat, Expert,* and *Achiever* action-logics to the postconventional *Individualist* and *Strategist* action-logics that are more closely aligned at their heart with action inquiry's moment-to-moment concern with timing, mutuality, and transforming leadership.

As, through your practice, you increasingly come to feel an internally motivated wish to move through such action-logic transformations, you will want to seek out mentors, teachers, schools, work organizations, forms of exercise and therapy, friends, and spiritual disciplines that can help you. Chapters 8 through 11 help to define the later-action-logic organizations that can help you transform. Those chapters also help you visualize how you can accelerate your leadership development by beginning to help meetings, projects, teams, and whole organizations to transform from one action-logic to the next.

The two final chapters, Chapters 12 and 13, that you are just now completing may repel you, or make you feel dizzy or queasy, because they project a degree of ongoing transformation that is endurable only to the degree that we are passionately, dispassionately, and compassionately anchored in four-territory experiencing now.

We imagine that creating an in-person or cyber reading and discussion group to engage in a slow second reading and in deliberate exercises and mutual coaching may be a useful next step for you. But, whatever you choose to do next, we thank you for your attention and wish you good questions, good friends, and good work for the future.

APPENDIX

Concluding Scientific Postscript on Methods of Inquiry

> *Suppose someone wished to communicate that the truth is not the truth, since it is the way which is the truth— that the truth exists only as a process . . . Well, his statement would of course turn into a result . . .*
> Kierkegaard
> *Concluding Unscientific Postscript*

This appendix is organized into three distinct sections. The first section covers the Leadership Development Profile (LDP). It describes how you can access and use the Profile to assess your own leadership action-logic. It then proceeds to offer a scholarly account of the development and validity-testing of the LDP measuring instrument itself.

The second section describes the current scientific status of the measure of an organization's developmental action-logic that we used in the study of 10 organizations to test which did and which did not transform.

The third section describes how developmental action inquiry as a whole has developed over the past 40 years, and how this approach to social science relates to empirical positivism.

Overall, whereas the 13 chapters of this book are addressed primarily to adult professionals and secondarily to all adults in our day-to-day efforts to generate a good life, this "Concluding Scientific Postscript" is addressed primarily to our social science colleagues. Consequently, unlike the body of the book, this appendix assiduously discusses and references related scholarly work. Moreover, the language of this appendix is more technical and scholarly. Thus, we invite our readers to skip on to the beginning of the next section in this appendix whenever the material becomes more technical than is currently useful to you.

The Leadership Development Profile

How to Access and Use the LDP to Assess Your Own Leadership Action-Logic

To explore taking and receiving feedback on the LDP, go to www.harthillusa.com or www.harthill.co.uk. The Profile consists of 36 sentence stems (e.g., "When a person steps out of line at work . . .") that you complete as you wish, giving yourself an hour free to do so (which is usually more than enough time).

You can submit your responses online, and there are directions for sending the appropriate fee. You then receive a feedback package that shows your results as compared to a number of other samples of managers or citizens, with accompanying explanatory literature. Both of the Web sites also provide related literature.

Many executive coaches and consultants invite their clients to take the LDP and combine feedback of the results with development planning. Indeed, consultants will find notice at the Web sites of regular three-day workshops to become certified to give feedback on the LDP.

The Scientific Evolution of the LDP

The theory and empirical basis for discriminating among the personal action-logics we describe in this book in Chapters 4 through 7 and 12 (*Opportunist, Diplomat, Expert, Achiever, Individualist, Strategist, Alchemist*) has a rich history. The individual developmental action-logics measured by our Leadership Development Profile correspond closely to the developmental stages identified by developmental psychologists Skip Alexander (Alexander and Langer 1990), Bob Kegan (1982, 1994), Larry Kohlberg (1984), Jane Loevinger (Loevinger and Wessler 1970), and Ken Wilber (2000). Indeed, as is described in the following, the LDP has emerged from our coauthor Cook-Greuter's theoretical and empirical modifications of Loevinger's work.

The overall distribution of developmental action-logic scores in numerous studies of professional adults in the United States using the Profile (total $n = 497$) is virtually identical with the overall distribution of developmental scores in numerous studies of professional adults in the United States using Kegan's more intensive Subject-Object Interview (total n = 342), based on his version of developmental theory (Kegan 1994; Torbert 1991). This fact suggests just how synchronous this family of developmental theories and measures is. Both sets of studies found that 58 percent of the subjects scored at action-logic IV (*Expert*) or below, and both found that 35–36 percent scored at action-logic V (*Achiever*), with the 6–7 percent remainder scoring at later action-logics (as per Table 5-1 in text).

The LDP has emerged through 20 years of modifications of Jane Loevinger's Washington University Sentence Completion Test (WUSCT), during the long-term and ongoing collaboration among four of the associate authors: Susanne Cook-Greuter, Dal Fisher, David Rooke, and Bill Torbert. Cook-Greuter (1990) is a senior WUSCT scorer who has become a leading developmental theorist and methodologist herself. The Loevinger WUSCT is itself one of the most widely used and thoroughly validity-tested instruments in psychometrics (Loevinger 1985; Loevinger and Wessler 1970). The WUSCT contains 36 sentence stems (e.g., "I just can't stand people who . . ."). When completed, these reflect a subject's reasoning and thinking processes and ways of relating to others. Embedded in the content and form of the sentence completions is the subject's overall way of mapping the world as conceptualized by his or her developmental action-logic. The scoring manual is extremely thorough, containing virtually every possible early action-logic response to each of the sentence stems. Loevinger has shown less theoretical and empirical interest in the rarer, later action-logics, and Cook-Greuter (1999) has taken the lead in redefining and measuring these, as is described later in this section.

An unusual virtue of this scoring procedure is the internal reliability test that can be performed on each protocol. First, a single item on many protocols (say, 10 or 20) is scored separately (to avoid a halo effect of early scores on a given protocol predisposing a scorer to more of the same), then the second item, and so on. These scores will eventually be added together to create an overall statistical score for the protocol, and the scores within a certain range are categorized as indicating the dominance of a particular action-logic (a protocol characterized as *Expert* may, for example, include the following distribution of responses: 2 *Opportunist*, 8 *Diplomat*, 20 *Expert*, 5 *Achiever*, and 1 *Individualist*). Before looking at the aggregate scores or computing the foregoing result, however, the scorer can review each entire protocol, with special attention to outlying scores, and assign an intuitive score based on the whole gestalt. Any difference between the two scores leads to still further discernment, or an invitation to another trained scorer to score the protocol, as a further reliability test. For postconventional ratings, explicit and complex additional scoring rules are used to determine to what degree the quality of the overall protocol reflects the statistically derived score (Cook-Greuter 1999). For advanced scores, the two scores are identical well over .8 of the time and within a single action-logic of one another well over .9 of the time. Inter-rater reliability of above .8 is considered strong.

Loevinger and Wessler (1970) report high inter-rater reliability and internal consistency on the WUSCT. Other studies report generally high levels of inter-rater reliability (e.g., Cox 1974; Hoppe 1972), internal consistency (Redmore and Waldman 1975), and split-half reliability (Novy and Francis 1992; Redmore and Waldman 1975). It is virtually impossible to contrive a result on the WUSCT. Experiments have shown that persons almost never succeed in producing a protocol at a later action-logic from their own, even after the theory underlying the scoring procedure has been explained to them (Redmore 1976).

The validity of the WUSCT has been criticized on two counts: (1) it is simply a matter of verbal fluency, since later action-logic respondents write significantly longer protocols and (2) ego development's status as a "master trait," as proposed by Loevinger, has not been proven psychometrically. On the issue of verbal fluency, it may be countered that the correlation is inevitable, since the expression of greater conceptual complexity and creativity characteristic of the later stages requires longer responses (Loevinger and Wessler 1970; Vaillant and McCullough 1987). At the same time, it is clear from numerous studies that ego development, as measured by the WUSCT, entails many more facets than verbal fluency. Personality characteristics found appropriately associated with predicted developmental action-logics include rule-boundedness (in this case, a curvilinear relationship, lower in pre- and postconventional action-logics, higher at conventional action-logics), nurturance, conscientiousness, trust, tolerance, interpersonal sensitivity, psychological mindedness, creativity, moral development, and a variety of measures related to mental health (Kohlberg 1963, 1964; Lorr and Manning 1978; Vaillant 1977; Vaillant and McCullough 1987).

A more recent study by Novy et al. (1994) tested the structural validity of Loevinger's model, using structural equation modeling to examine whether ego development serves hierarchically as the source of covariation for specific personality constructs. While not proven to be a "master trait" by this analytic model, ego development was positively and significantly related to each of the four constructs posited by Loevinger: impulse control, interpersonal style, conscious preoccupations, and cognitive style. Those wishing to review the scholarly literatures on the WUSCT can also refer to the 1993 special issue of *Psychological Inquiry* devoted to Loevinger's work, as well as the 1998 Westenberg et al. book in honor of her 80th birthday, *Personality Development: Theoretical, Empirical, and Clinical Investigations of Loevinger's Conception of Ego Development.*

The Leadership Development Profile used in the studies underlying this book amends, supplements, and transforms the validity testing on the WUSCT in five ways. First, the LDP adds independently validated work-related items (e.g., "A good boss . . .") (Molloy 1978) to increase the measure's face validity for people in work settings.

Second, the LDP uses the Cook-Greuter definitions and scoring manuals for the later action-logics (Cook-Greuter 1999). Loevinger conceives of her highest stage as a search for integrated identity, but she does not imagine or theorize the possibility, central to this book's argument, that integrity may be the fruit of developing the postcognitive observing and listening attention that registers ongoing transformation across all four territories of experience. Thus, for example, she offers neither theory nor method for scoring the "I am . . ." sentence stem when it is completed as follows: "I am—finally, in the long run, mostly unfathomable, but I enjoy the process of trying to fathom." Cook-Greuter (1999, 31) cites this response, commenting that it can reasonably be interpreted as meaning that the person "is abdicating the search for identity in favor of being a witness to the ongoing process of self-becoming."

Third, the LDP changes evaluative terminology into less-evaluative terminology (e.g., from "lower and higher stages" to "earlier and later action-logics," from "Conformist" to "Diplomat," etc.). This change makes it feasible and effectual to use the instrument and to offer feedback on people's performance on it in executive coaching and organizational consulting situations.

Fourth, offering feedback to people who take the measure has permitted additional validity tests on the measure. For example, developmental theory suggests that people at earlier action-logics are more likely to avoid feedback, especially of a double-loop nature that questions their current action-logic, whereas people at later action-logics will

increasingly seek out such feedback opportunities. This theoretical prediction was confirmed when we offered the opportunity for feedback on
their measured action-logic to 281 people who had taken the measure:
we found that an increasing proportion of each later action-logic, in
fact, chose to receive such feedback.

Fifth, as the foregoing finding begins to suggest, our laboratory and
field action inquiry studies have augmented the validity testing of the
LDP by concentrating, not on its internal validity as correlated with
other paper and pencil psychological tests, but, rather, on its external validity in predicting significant differences in the real-world performance
of people. Early on, Hauser (1976) showed statistically significant relationships between the WUSCT and interpersonal behavior. We have
summarized other findings in Chapter 7 on (1) the statistically significant difference in managerial performance on in-basket tests and in an
interview study between conventional and postconventional action-logics (Merron, Fisher, and Torbert 1987; Fisher and Torbert 1991) and (2)
the statistically significant difference in success between conventional
and postconventional CEOs in achieving organizational transformation
(Rooke and Torbert 1998).

In another third-person study (Torbert and Fisher 1992), we showed
that voluntary participation in groups that encouraged first- and second-
person action inquiry over a two- to four-year period (formed and guided
by a postconventional action-logic practitioner) generated transformation to postconventional action-logics among 22 of the 24 participants.
By contrast, only 3 of 165 persons in a control group (who started the
same MBA program at the same time as the participants) showed positive developmental transformation over the same period when retested.

In addition, first-person research/practitioners of the meditative
practice called Transcendental Meditation have conducted many third-
person studies (using the WUSCT) that document the positive effects of
the first-person research/practice of meditating for generating transformation to postconventional action-logics (Alexander and Langer 1990;
Chandler 1991; Torbert 2000).

In general, what one sees in the transformation of the WUSCT into
the Leadership Development Profile is typical of developmental transformations from conventional action-logics to postconventional action-logics. First, the third-person, "Expert" scientific base of the WUSCT is
preserved. Second, new, postconventional action-logics are conceived, defined, and operationalized through Cook-Greuter's work. Third, the third-
person measure is reoriented so that it can play a role in a wider field

where the effort is to integrate it with practitioners' first- and second-person research/practices in the field, as illustrated throughout this book.

Assessing an Organization's Developmental Action-Logic

The theoretical and empirical basis for the organizational action-logics we describe in Chapters 8 through 11 and 13 (**Conception, Investments, Incorporation, Experiments, Systematic Productivity, Social Network, Collaborative Inquiry,** and **Foundational Community of Inquiry**) is much more modest. These stages of organizational development were originally defined by Torbert (1974) by comparing nine different stage theories of interpersonal, group, or organizational development (e.g., Bennis 1964; Dunphy 1968; Erikson 1959; Greiner 1972; Lippitt and Schmidt 1967; Mills 1964) to a close analysis of five organizing cycles in one organization. This new multistage theory of organization development offered richer descriptions of both early and later stages than other organizational development theories at that time (Greiner 1972; Lippitt and Schmidt 1967) and than later organizational life cycle theories (Cameron and Whetten 1983; Quinn and Cameron 1983).

Later (Torbert 1987, 1989), these developmental action-logic descriptions of organizations were amplified into whole chapters on each stage, with case studies of a variety of other organizations, including the 100-year history of IBM. Thereafter, the theory was used clinically and heuristically in consulting interventions, such as those described in Chapters 9 through 11, in order to test its transformational efficacy when deployed by seasoned action inquiry practitioners. This usage represents a second-person, real-time validity testing process unperformed and undocumented in most third-person empirical positivism. As each case indicates, there are significant assessment data that indicate efficacy; at the same time, the cases of inefficacy reported in Chapter 10 show that we have not ignored disconfirming data. In addition, since the early 1980s, thousands of managers, consultants, and MBA students have worked with this organizational development theory diagnostically and heuristically in determining the stage of development of their own work groups and organizations, as well as in designing and implementing strategic projects to help their teams or organizations to transform. Guiding and learning from their studies further enriched the authors' clinical sense of the theory in application.

Two explicitly quantitative, empirical studies have now successfully quantified this developmental theory of organizing in different ways. The first is the study of 10 organizations and their CEOs reported in Chapter 10 (Rooke and Torbert 1998). In this study, three of the consultants, each of whom had participated in some, but not all, of the interventions, worked independently to score what organizational transformations (if any) had occurred during each extended relationship. Each scorer had direct experience of some of the cases, case write-ups of all the cases, and the chapters on each stage of development from *Managing the Corporate Dream* (Torbert 1987). The three scorers achieved perfect 1.0 reliability on whether each of the 10 organizations transformed and in what direction. They achieved .9 reliability on specifying the exact transformations that occurred (one scorer disagreed with the other two in one case, and the discrepancy was resolved after conversation among the three scorers). Methodologically, this study shows that scholar-practitioners who interact as consultants and second-person action researchers with relatively small companies (10–1,000 employees) and who use the theory to guide their diagnoses, their strategic designs, and the timing of their actions can agree, with very high reliability, on an organization's stage of development and on whether and how much it transforms over time.

The second study (Leigh 2002) examined much larger companies from a much greater distance. Using company Web sites and annual reports, two researchers achieved a .85 level of reliability in coding five different variables derived from this theory of organization development on three-point scales that distinguished among early, middle, and late stages of development. Restricting the sample to companies across several industries whose financial performance was in the top quartile of that industry, and whose social responsibility rating (according to the KLD Social Investing Index) was either in the top or the bottom quartile, the study found a strong correlation between those companies rated as combining financial and social responsibility and those rated as operating at later developmental action-logics. Theoretically, this finding confirms the developmental prediction that later action-logic organizations are more likely to attend to and balance multiple modes of assessing effectiveness. Methodologically, the study shows that a meaningful approximation of developmental action-logic can be computed for large companies to which researchers do not have direct access.

So far, attempts to create a questionnaire by which organizational members can assess their own organization's current stage of development have foundered. For one thing, organization members tend to experience their organization on a day-to-day basis primarily through the variable conditions of their local work site and group, and to rate their direct experience rather than the overall organizational system. For another thing, organization members tend to interpret their organizational experience through their own individual developmental action-logic, further confounding their ratings of the overall organization.

Thus, how to generate reliable third-person ratings of an organization's specific developmental stage? From the first quantitative study previously described, it currently appears that action researchers and consultants are the most likely sources of such ratings, if they have extensive access to and interaction with a number of organizational layers and sites, and if they operate at postconventional individual action-logics, where one is less likely to project one's own frame onto other systems. Put more simply, persons engaged in ongoing first- and second-person research/practice in the midst of their ongoing practice are the most likely to produce good third-person research in this realm.

Participatory Action Research, Action Science, and Developmental Action Inquiry

Bill Torbert started his career in his early twenties by seeking federal funding for and then directing the Yale Upward Bound program, a seven-week multiracial summer school for high school students from backgrounds of poverty who were very likely to drop out of school during the coming year. Despite the racial riots in New Haven and throughout the country that year, and the assassinations of Martin Luther King and Robert Kennedy, only 2 of 60 students dropped out the following year, and New Haven's dropout rate was cut in half.

Bill was concurrently enrolled as a PhD student at Yale and was studying his effort to lead Upward Bound (including his errors, misconceptions, and infelicities) as his doctoral dissertation, a study eventually published as the book *Creating a Community of Inquiry: Conflict, Collaboration, Transformation* (Torbert 1976). This book was the first to formulate the notion of engaging in social science research and social action simultaneously, calling this approach "action science."

Four related streams of work on action research method and on action learning theory have been initiated during the past four decades, and we acknowledge and take pride in our close relationship to all four through their initiators:

1. Chris Argyris, who was Torbert's dissertation advisor at Yale, later a colleague at Harvard, and still later borrowed the phrase "action science" to characterize his own work (Alderfer 1988, 1989; Argyris, Putnam, and Smith 1985; Argyris and Schon 1974).

2. Peter Senge, who hails from the MIT "systems dynamics" group and who is a founding partner with Torbert and others of the Society for Organizational Learning, a triune partnership among major organizations, consultants, and researchers (Senge 1990; Senge et al. 1994).

3. Peter Reason, who is Torbert's closest academic colleague of the past quarter century and who has played a lead role in sponsoring and legitimizing participatory action research that conjoins first-, second-, and third-person research and practice through founding the University of Bath Center for Action Research in Professional Practice and through publishing the *Handbook of Action Research* (Reason and Bradbury 2001).

4. Ken Wilber, who invited Torbert to be a founding member of the Integral Institute where Wilber continues his lifetime work on developmental theory with new efforts to influence people's practice.

Others of the associate authors have had close associations with one or more of these four scholar/practitioners as well.

Along with the significant influence of these related approaches, there are three unique aspects about developmental action inquiry as an approach. First, developmental action inquiry integrates action and inquiry not just sequentially, but *simultaneously.* Second, action inquiry seeks to generate *timely* leadership and inquiry by citizens and professionals in the field and by each of us in our personal lives. Third, developmental action inquiry treats not just individual persons, but all social systems from brief conversations to intergenerational institutions as capable of developmental transformation. In contrast, the other four approaches (1) tend to emphasize inquiry more than action; (2) tend to create distinct settings for inquiry and reflection *about* action, the lessons from which may be applied in *subsequent* action; (3) do not make the timeliness of action an explicit focus; and (4) do not integrate third-person quantitative, empirical measures of personal and organizational development with first- and second-person action inquiries, as particularly illustrated in the Chapter 7 study of attempting to transform 10 organizations.

Readers may wonder, how does this new kind of action inquiry that interweaves first-, second-, and third-person research in the midst of our practice relate to modernist empirical social science and to postmodernist critical social science? We address this question next. (For additional scholarly discussion of this question, see Reason and Torbert 2001; Sherman and Torbert 2000; and Torbert 2000.)

Interweaving First-, Second-, and Third-Person Action Inquiry

In contemporary social science, the idea of interweaving first-, second-, and third-person research and practice has only taken shape since the late 1990s (Torbert 1998; Wilber 1998; Varela and Shear 1999; Sherman and Torbert 2000; Velmans 2000; Malin 2001; Reason and Bradbury 2001; Reason and Torbert 2001). Let us briefly consider how interweaving first-person, subjective action inquiry, second-person, intersubjective action inquiry, and third-person objective action inquiry can be a transformative approach for scientific research itself. We begin by creating a kind of commonsense image of all the domains that the human sciences may touch on in one way or another. Then we examine which domains empirical positivist approaches tend to inhabit, which domains action inquires tend to inhabit, and to what degree there is or can be overlap.

Figure A.1 shows the 3 × 3 × 3 image that is generated by distinguishing three dimensions of difference and three qualitative differences on each dimension, for a total of 27 kinds of social science (see Chandler and Torbert [2003], for a more detailed discussion and illustration of these 27 types). The three dimensions of difference are the "temporal" dimension, the "practice" dimension, and the "voice" dimension. The temporal dimension is divided into the past, the present, and the future. The practice dimension is differentiated according to whether the research focuses on the researcher's own practice (first-person practice), the practice of a group of which she or he is a member (second-person practice), or the practice of some broader population of which the researcher may or may not be a member (third-person practice). And, finally, the voice dimension is differentiated according to whether the inquiry is conducted in (1) the frankly subjective first-person voice of the action inquirer (such as we repeatedly heard in the early

Figure A.1   Twenty-Seven Flavors of Action Research
and the Proportion of the Research Spectrum Studied Through
Empirical Positivist Methods

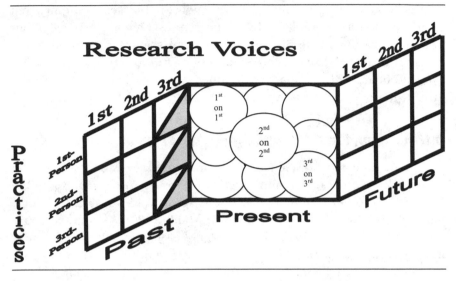

chapters of this book in the excerpts from managers learning action inquiry); (2) the multiple, intersubjective second-person voices of multiple action inquirers (such as we heard in Chapters 10 and 11 where the two vice presidents of Sun Health worked with the feedback they were receiving from their peers); or (3) an anonymous, generalized, intendedly neutral third-person voice (e.g., this paragraph).

Within these 27 domains of inquiry, *empirical positivism* is a form of science that researches events that occurred in the past. (The events may already have been in the past when the data are collected, but they are definitely in the past once the data have been analyzed, validity tested through statistical and peer review procedures, and publicly reported.) Moreover, empirical positivism strives always to achieve a truly neutral, generalizable third-person voice (the first- and second-person pronouns and voices are rigorously abjured [except when properly framed and introduced as additional data]). Finally, empirical positivist methods are typically used to study third-person practices and social processes in which the researcher is not a direct participant.

But these same third-person methods can, in fact, also be used to study the researcher's own first-person practice, or to study a group's second-person practices. For example, we authors have filled out the

Leadership Development Profile and received feedback on the resulting findings about our first-person practice; so this fits in the "third-person research voice on first-person practice in the past" box of Figure A.1. Likewise, videotaping a football game, rigorously analyzing and counting various categories of actions (e.g., number of penalties against the team each quarter), and then doing a film debriefing session with the players is a form of third-person research voice on second-person practices in the past.

But even though empirical positivist methods can be applied to all three types of practice, they do not provide guidance for subsequent feedback and learning activities, and such learning activities rarely occur. Moreover, even when such researchers offer nominal feedback, they tend to do so "after the study" rather than including these interactive events in the study (see Hartwell and Torbert 1999, for an example of a study that *does* include the feedback as part of the data). Thus, as shown by the half-shaded areas in Figure A.1, empirical positivism studies "first-, second-, and third-person practices, in the past, in a third-person voice," but not the interactions between the researchers and those studied (so each box is only half shaded).

In short, empirical positivism studies about half of 3 of the 27 possible domains of inquiry. From the perspective of the image in Figure A.1, empirical positivism studies 3/54 or approximately 6 percent of all of the reality domains of everyday life. (Of course, this precision is spurious because it assumes all 27 boxes are of equivalent scope and significance, and that may not be the case.) If this percentage is even an approximation of the case, we should hardly be surprised that findings about the influence of an independent variable on a dependent variable based on this type of science, no matter how significant in terms of statistical probability, usually account for no more than 5–15 percent of the variance in the dependent variable (not enough, one would think, to make a rational action taker want to risk basing his or her action on the relationship, no matter how certain it is).

Contrast such relatively weak findings (weak from the point of view of identifying variables that account for a large proportion of the variance and thus have a significant practical influence on one another) with the findings from the Rooke and Torbert (1998) study of CEOs' and consultants' influence on organizational transformation, summarized in Chapter 7. In this study, if we treat the quality of leadership (as measured by the sum of the CEO's and the lead consultant's action-logic scores on the Leadership Development Profile) as the independent variable, it accounts for an unusually large 59 percent of the variance in the dependent variable (organizational transformation, as measured by three trained scorers working independently) and the result is statistically significant at the .01 level.

We suggest that this result is so much stronger than is usual for purely third-person science because the independent variable itself concerns the relative capacity of an individual to interweave first-, second-, and third-person action inquiry and to cultivate transformation in self or others through single-, double-, and triple-loop learning. Because the consulting interventions at the companies required this very interweaving of the types of action inquiry for success (if the theory as a whole is valid), the independent variable should, in fact, be significantly responsible for variance in the dependent variable (organizational transformations), as it turns out to be.

(Some researchers have objected that the small total number of cases in this research project reduces the confidence we can place in these results. Certainly, further testing of these results is warranted and will increase our confidence if it confirms the current findings. However, the belief that the small number of cases reduces the validity and significance of the finding from a statistical point of view is spurious. Because the number of cases is small, the association between the independent and dependent variable must be all the stronger if the result is to be considered true at the .01 level [meaning that the chance of its being false is less than 1 in 100]. Statistical significance at the .01 level means the same thing whether there are 10 cases or 1,000 cases.)

When we retrospectively examined how many of 27 types of action research members of the 10 companies actually engaged in during the consulting interventions, we found that it varied from 9 in the least successful cases to 15 in the most successful cases (see Figure A.2). For example, all 10 CEOs took the LDP and received feedback on their action-logic (third-person research on first-person practice in the past), and all 10 organizations participated in senior management strategic planning supported by the consultants (this involved a combination of third-person research on third-person practice in the past [e.g., competitive information on other major companies in the industry] and second-person research on third-person practice for the future [e.g., explicating and harmonizing senior managers' values about company strategic priorities over the next three years]).

In contrast, only the seven organizations that successfully transformed had earlier distributed, rotated, and received feedback on lead-

Figure A.2   Types of Action Inquiry Practiced in
Organizations That Successfully Transform

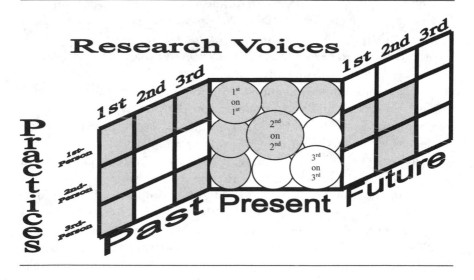

ership functions within their senior management team meetings (second-person research on second-person practice in the present). And there were several types of action inquiry that only the five CEOs measured as *Strategists* engaged in (e.g., offering developmental mentoring to senior management team members [first-person research on second-person practice for the future]).

Thus, the results suggest that later action-logic CEOs and consultants tend to engage in an increasing proportion of the 27 types of action research, and that this activity increases the likelihood of generating organizational transformation. (Of course, this is only a suggestion based on a retrospective inspection of this single study, so it is offered as a possible guide for future action inquiries, not as a predicted and statistically substantiated conclusion.)

From the empirical positivist point of view, however, the image in Figure A.1 seems misleading and the claim just made may seem almost desperately confused. In general, the positivist may say, the validity-testing procedures of third-person empirical science cannot be applied to research conducted in first-person and second-person voices. Therefore, first- and second-person action inquiries can't be counted as scientific research at all. Moreover, once researchers engage in feedback and learning activities with research subjects, the researchers lose their disinterested position and are actively influencing all further data. Furthermore, the validity-testing procedures of third-person empirical science cannot be applied to data generated and used in the present, and the very notion of "data" does not apply to the future. How can we collect data on something that hasn't yet happened? How can we know when it is formulated whether one strategic plan is better than another?

To these arguments we reply that different validity tests that can disconfirm hypotheses and assumptions are currently being developed for first-person and second-person research in the present and for the future (Argyris, Putnam, and Smith 1985; Torbert 2000), even though there is as yet no textbook about them. For example, each of us can potentially ask ourselves at any time whether "my" attention is fixated within one of the four territories of experience that we have mentioned so often in this book, or whether "my" attention is now touching all four. This is one first-person test of how validly "I" am inquiring into the full range of "my" own internal experiencing at any given present moment (and the test usually shows "me" that "my" experience has been entirely enfolded within but one of the territories just prior to the test). Similarly, a person who inquires carefully of other group members about her proposed framing for the next part of the meeting is conducting a second-person validity test of her future design. (One may also conduct third-person research on the relative efficacy "after the act" of different first- and second-person validity tests, but this is not a better form of validity testing, just a different kind.)

The argument that researchers sacrifice their disinterested position once they engage in consulting/learning activities with the research subjects is a spurious one as well. A researcher may bias research results whether or not he or she engages in consulting/learning activities. Moreover, if theoretically significant differences among the researchers and the quality of the consulting/learning activities are themselves measured as part of the "experimental treatment," then the researcher effect and the intervention effect become a part of the study. This result is precisely what occurred in the third-person study of attempted organizational transformation in 10 organizations. This study not only contributes to intergenerational third-person knowledge, but also provides us—the scholar/practitioners who engaged in the action study—a clearer perspective on our first- and second-person successes, failures, and learning challenges.

The main point is that interweaving first-, second-, and third-person action inquiry is an immense social scientific project that can help transform social science itself toward developmentally later action-logics over several generations (Torbert 2000), but only if more and more social science practitioners commit themselves to exploring this vast unknown experiential and empirical timescape.

Other Scholar/Practitioners Who Are Engaging in First-, Second-, and Third-Person Research and Practice

The best way for social scientists to gain a next impression of what this kind of social science will look like is to look at other scholars who are today interweaving first-, second-, and third-person action inquiry (in quite different ways). At the turn of the millenium, one of us asked colleagues (predominantly from the United States) to nominate scholar/practitioners associated with the field of management who are concerned with the question of timely action. Thirty-five scholar-practitioners (including, e.g., Chris Argyris, Ella Bell, Warren Bennis, Rosabeth Kanter, Margaret Wheatley, and Ken Wilber) were mentioned more than once. Of these, we have chosen nine who were among the most frequently mentioned and whom the primary author can personally confirm have engaged over long periods of time in first-, second-, and third-person action inquiry disciplines intended to (1) exercise their inner attentiveness; (2) help social systems in which they participate to inquire, offer mutual feedback, and transform the immediate system; and (3) establish an intergenerational legacy through third-person research and publication.

These nine scholar/practitioners are:

1. Charles Alexander (1994; Alexander and Langer 1990; Orme-Johnson, Alexander, et al. 1988)
2. Jean Bartunek (1984; Bartunek, Gordon, and Weathersby, 1983; Bartunek and Moch 1994; Bartunek and Necochea 2000)
3. David Cooperrider (Cooperrider and Whitney 1999; Shrivastva and Cooperrider 1990)
4. Robert Kegan (1982, 1994; Kegan and Lahey 1984)
5. Judi Marshall (1984, 2001)
6. Richard Nielsen (1993a, 1993b, 1996)
7. Robert Quinn (1988, 1996, 2000; Cameron and Quinn 1999)

8. Peter Reason (1994; Reason and Rowan 1981; Reason and Bradbury 2001)
9. Peter Senge (1990; Senge et al. 1994, 1998)

As indicated by (and in) the foregoing references for each of the
nine, their third-person research/practices have in all cases contributed
to peer-reviewed journal articles or books. The second-person re-
search/practices or action inquiries of the nine include the creation or
leadership of wide-reaching not-for-profit educational networks for
first-, second-, and third-person research/practice (e.g., Bartunek's presidency of the Academy of Management; Marshall and Reason's Center
for Action Research in Professional Practice; and Senge's Society for
Organizational Learning). Their second-person action inquiries also include board memberships, consulting for executive and organizational
transformation, the creation of new doctoral programs, and long-term
engagement in reform of corrupt social systems.

The first-person action inquiry vocations of these nine scholar/prac-
titioners derive from a wide variety of traditions of spiritual awareness-
practice, including a Catholic religious order, Hassidism, Hinduism,
Mormonism, the Native American Medicine Wheel, the Society of
Friends (Quakers), and Taoism. (Among the authors of this book an
equally wide range of spiritual awareness-practice is represented, including, in addition to those already mentioned, evangelical Christian-
ity, the Gurdjieff Work, and paganism.) This strong association between
first-person awareness-practice and spiritual traditions may at first surprise readers. But these research/practitioners are attempting to live, not
only into a theory, but through it to a postlinguistic awareness in more
and more moments, against which incongruities in the theory or in one's
way of performing show up; so they aspire to engage in first-person action inquiry that tests given theories in all moments of real time.

Taking the spirit of inquiry this seriously is as profound a spiritual
commitment as one can make, a faith in seeing our performances across
all four territories of experience (which we can call "presencing") as
contrasted to a blind, proclaimed faith. All spiritual traditions recognize
a so-called mystical path whereby some dedicate their lives to such inquiry ("mysticism" 1999); but few spiritual traditions elaborate how
such first-person action inquiry can interweave with second- and third-
person action inquiries. This interweaving can only occur as our personal awareness-practice seeks to enter more and more moments of our

daily lives with others and in institutional roles. This effort requires differentially experiencing and blending the different time horizons and time-experiencing of the different action-logics. But a deep concern with the mystery of timely action only begins to take shape as one enacts the *Strategist* action-logic. Thereafter, the concern for timely action may eventually be seen to entail the *Alchemist* action-logic of ongoing practice of presencing in all four territories of experience now.

Bibliography

Alderfer, C., 1988. Taking our selves seriously as researchers. In D. Berg and K. Smith, eds., *The Self in Social Inquiry.* Newbury Park, CA: Sage.

Alderfer, C., 1989. Theories reflecting my personal experience and life development, *Journal of Applied Behavioral Science* 25(4), 351–364.

Alexander, C., 1994. Transcendental meditation. In R. Corsini, ed., *Encyclopedia of Psychology.* New York: Wiley Interscience, pp. 5465–5466.

Alexander, C., and E. Langer, eds., 1990. *Higher Stages of Human Development.* New York: Oxford University Press.

Argyris, C., 1980. *Inner Contradictions of Rigorous Research.* New York: Academic Press.

Argyris, C., and D. Schon, 1974. *Theory in Practice: Increasing Professional Effectiveness.* San Francisco: Jossey-Bass.

Argyris, C., R. Putnam, and D. Smith, 1985. *Action Science: Concepts, Methods, and Skills for Research and Intervention.* San Francisco: Jossey-Bass.

Bartunek, J., 1984. Changing interpretive schemes and organizational restructuring: the example of a religious order, *Administrative Science Quarterly* 29, 355–372.

Bartunek, J., and M. Moch, 1994. Third-order organizational change and the Western mystical tradition, *Journal of Organizational Change and Management* 7, 24–41.

Bartunek, J., and R. Necochea, 2000. Old insights and new times: Kairos, Inca cosmology, and their contributions to contemporary management inquiry, *Journal of Management Inquiry* 9, 103–113.

Bartunek, J., J. Gordon, and R. Weathersby, 1983. Developing complicated understanding in administrators, *Academy of Management Review* 8, 272–284.

Bavaria, J., 2000. The Global Reporting Initiative, *Investing in a Better World* 15(2), 1.

Becker, E., 1999. Social funds track record lengthens, strengthens, *Investing in a Better World* 14(8), 1–6.

Bennis, W., 1964. Patterns and vicissitudes in training groups. In L. Bradford, K. Benne, and J. Gibb, eds., *T-Group Theory and Laboratory Methods.* New York: Wiley.

Cameron, K., and D. Whetten, 1983. Models of the organizational life cycle: Applications to higher education, *Review of Higher Education* 6(4), 269–299.

229

Cameron, K., and R. Quinn, 1999. *Diagnosing and Changing Organizational Culture: Based on the Competing Values Framework.* Reading, MA: Addison-Wesley.

Carlson, V., and P. Westenberg, 1998. Cross cultural application of the WUSCT. In J. Loevinger, ed., *Technical Foundations for Measuring Ego Development.* Mahwah, NJ: Lawrence Erlbaum, pp. 57–75.

Carse, J., 1986. *Finite and Infinite Games: A Vision of Life as Play and Possibility.* New York: Ballantine Books.

Chandler, D., and W. Torbert, 2003. Transforming inquiry and action: Interweaving 27 flavors of action research, *Journal of Action Research* 1(2), 133–152.

Chandler, H., 1990. "Transcendental Meditation and Awakening Wisdom: A 10-Year Longitudinal Study of Self-Development." Fairfield, Iowa, Maharishi International University, unpublished dissertation.

Collins, J., 2001. *Good to Great.* New York: HarperCollins.

Cook-Greuter, S., 1990. Maps for living: Ego-development stages from symbiosis to conscious universal embeddedness. In M. L. Commons, C. Armon, L. Kohlberg, F. A. Richards, T. A. Grotzer, and J. D. Sinnott, eds., *Adult Development*, vol. 2, *Models and Methods in the Study of Adolescent and Adult Thought.* New York: Praeger, pp. 79–104.

Cook-Greuter, S., 1999. "Postautonomous Ego Development: A Study of Its Nature and Measurement." Cambridge, MA, Harvard University Graduate School of Education, doctoral dissertation.

Cooperrider, D., and D. Whitney, 1999. *Collaborating for Change: Appreciative Inquiry.* San Francisco: Berrett-Koehler.

Cox, L., 1974. Prior help, ego development and helping behavior, *Child Development* 45, 594.

Deutsch, K., 1966. *The Nerves of Government.* New York: Free Press.

Drewes, M., and P. Westenberg, 2001. The impact of modified instructions on ego-level scores: A psychometric hazard or indication of optimum ego level? *Journal of Personaluity Assessment* 76(2), 229–249.

Dunphy, D., 1968. Phases, roles, and myths in self-analytic groups, *Journal of Applied Behavioral Science* 4, 195–225.

Entine, J., 2003. The myth of social investing: A critique of its practice and consequences for corporate social performance research, *Organization and Environment* 16(3), 349–368.

Erikson, E., 1959. Identity and the life cycle, *Psychological Issues,* Monograph 1.

Fisher, D., and W. Torbert, 1991. Transforming managerial practice: Beyond the Achiever stage. In R. W. Woodman and W. A. Pasmore, eds., *Research in Organization Change and Development,* vol. 5. Greenwich, CT: JAI Press, pp. 143–173.

Greiner, L., 1972. Evolution and revolution as organizations grow, *Harvard Business Review* 50(4), 37–46.

Hartwell, J., and W. Torbert, 1999. A group interview with Andy Wilson, founder and CEO of Boston Duck Tours and Massachusetts entrepreneur of the year; and

Analysis of the group interview with Andy Wilson: An illustration of interweaving first-, second-, and third-person research/practice, *Journal of Management Inquiry* 8(2), 183–204.

Hauser, S., 1976. Loevinger's model and measure of ego development: A critical review, *Psychological Bulletin* 83(5), 928–955.

Hauser, S., 1993. Loevinger's model and measure of ego development: A critical review, pt. II, *Psychological Inquiry* 4, 23–30.

Havel, V., 1985. *The Power of the Powerless.* London: Hutchinson.

Havel, V., 1990. *Disturbing the Peace: A Conversation with Karel Hvizdala.* New York: Alfred A. Knopf.

Havel, V., 1992. *Summer Meditations.* New York: Alfred A. Knopf.

Havel, V., 1997. *The Art of the Impossible: Politics as Morality in Practice.* New York: Alfred A. Knopf.

Hoppe, C., 1972. "Ego Development and Conformity Behavior." St. Louis, MO, Washington University, doctoral dissertation.

Jaques, E., 1982. *The Form of Time.* New York: Crane Russak.

Jaques, E., 1989. *Requisite Organization: The CEO's Guide to Creative Structure and Leadership.* Arlington, VA: Cason Hall & Co.

Kegan, R., 1982. *The Evolving Self.* Cambridge, MA: Harvard University Press.

Kegan, R., 1994. *In Over Our Heads: The Demands of Modern Life.* Cambridge, MA: Harvard University Press.

Kegan, R., and L. Lahey, 1984. Adult leadership and adult development. In B. Kellerman, ed., *Leadership.* Englewood Cliffs, NJ: Prentice Hall, pp. 199–230.

Kierkegaard, S. 1992. *Concluding Unscientific Postscript to Philosophical Fragments,* H. Hong and E. Hong, eds./trans., Princeton, NJ: Princeton University Press.

Klamer, A., 1989. A conversation with Amartya Sen, *Journal of Economic Perspectives* 3(1), 135–150.

Kohlberg, L., 1963. The development of children's orientations towards moral order: I. Sequence in the development of moral thought, *Vita Humana* 6, 11–33.

Kohlberg, L., 1964. Development of moral character and moral ideology. In M. Hoffman and L. Hoffman, eds., *Review of Child Development Research,* vol 1. New York: Russell Sage, pp. 383–431.

Kohlberg, L., 1984. *Essays on Moral Development,* vol. 2, *The Psychology of Moral Development.* San Francisco: Harper & Row.

Leigh, J., 2002. "Developing Corporate Citizens: Linking Organizational Developmental Theory and Corporate Responsibility." Paper presented at Denver Academy of Management Symposium, "New Roles for Organizational Citizenship," Denver, CO, August.

Lippitt, G., and W. Schmidt, 1967. Non-financial crises in organizational development, *Harvard Business Review* 47(6), 102–112.

Loevinger, J., 1982. *Ego Development.* San Francisco: Jossey-Bass.

Loevinger, J., 1985. Revision of the Sentence Completion Test for ego development, *Journal of Personality and Social Psychology* 48, 420–427.

Loevinger, J., ed., 1998. *Technical Foundations for Measuring Ego Development: The Washington University Sentence Completion Test*. Mahwah, NJ: Lawrence Erlbaum Associates.

Loevinger, J., and R. Wessler, 1970. *Measuring Ego Development*, vols. 1 and 2. San Francisco: Jossey-Bass.

Loevinger, J., and T. Hy, 1996. *Measuring Ego Development*, Second Edition. Mahwah, NJ: Lawrence Erlbaum Associates.

Lorr, M., and T. Manning, 1978. Measurement of ego development by sentence completion and personality test, *Journal of Clinical Psychology* 34, 354–360.

Malin, S., 2001. *Nature Loves to Hide: Quantum Physics and the Nature of Reality, a Western Perspective*. New York: Oxford University Press.

Marshall, J., 1984. *Women Managers: Travellers in a Male World*. Chichester, UK: Wiley.

Marshall, J., 2001. Self-reflective inquiry practices. In P. Reason, P. Bradbury, and H. Bradbury, eds., *Handbook of Action Research*, London: Sage, pp. 433–439.

Merron, K., D. Fisher, and W. Torbert, 1987. Meaning making and management action, *Group and Organizational Studies* 12(3), 274–286.

Mills, T., 1964. *Sociology of Small Groups*. Englewood Cliffs, NJ: Prentice-Hall.

Molloy, E., 1978. "Toward a New Paradigm for the Study of the Person at Work: An Empirical Extension of Loevinger's Theory of Ego Development." Dublin, Ireland, University of Dublin, doctoral dissertation.

"Mysticism," 1999. *Encyclopedia Britannica Online* at http://search.eb.com/bol/topic?eu=117397&sctn=22 (accessed Nov. 3, 1999).

Nielsen, R., 1993a. Woolman's "I am we" triple-loop, action-learning: Origin and application in organization ethics, *Journal of Applied Behavioral Science* 29, 117–138.

Nielsen, R., 1993b. Triple-loop action-learning as human resources management method. In *Research in International Human Resources Management*. Greenwich, CT: JAI Press, pp. 75–93.

Nielsen, R., 1996. *The Politics of Ethics*. New York: Oxford University Press.

Novy, D., and D. Francis, 1992. Psychometric properties of the Washington University Sentence Completion Test, *Educational and Psychological Measurement* 52, 1029–1039.

Novy, D., et al., 1994. An investigation of the structural validity of Loevinger's model and measure of ego development, *Journal of Personality* 62(1), 87–118.

Orme-Johnson, D., C. Alexander, J. Davies, H. Chandler, and W. Larimore, 1988. International peace project in the Middle East: The effect of Mahirishi Technology of the Unified Field, *Journal of Conflict Resolution* 32, 776–812.

Pentland, J., 1988. *Exchanges Within*. San Francisco: Far West Publishing.

Piaget, J., 1952/1937. *The Language and Thought of the Child*. London: Routledge & Kegan Paul.

Quinn, R., 1988. *Beyond Rational Management*. San Francisco: Jossey-Bass.

Quinn, R., 1996. *Deep Change*. San Francisco: Jossey-Bass.

Quinn, R., 2000. *Change the World: How Ordinary People Can Achieve Extraordinary Results.* San Francisco: Jossey-Bass.

Quinn, R., and K. Cameron, 1983. Organizational life cycles and shifting criteria of effectiveness, *Management Science* **29**, 33–51.

Reason, P., 1994a. *Participation in Human Inquiry.* London: Sage.

Reason, P., 1994b. Three approaches to participative inquiry. In N. Denzin and Y. Lincoln, eds., *Handbook of Qualitative Research.* Thousand Oaks, CA: Sage.

Reason, P., and H. Bradbury, 2001. *Handbook of Action Research.* London: Sage.

Reason, P., and J. Rowan, 1981. *Human Inquiry: A Sourcebook of New Paradigm Research.* Chichester, UK: Wiley.

Reason, P., and W. Torbert, 2001. The action turn toward a transformational social science: A further look at the scientific merits of action research, *Concepts and Transformation* **6**(1), 1–37.

Redmore, C., 1976. Susceptibility to faking of a sentence completion test of ego development, *Journal of Personality Assessment* **40**(6), 607–616.

Redmore, C., and K. Waldman, 1975. Reliability of a sentence completion measure of ego development, *Journal of Personality Assessment* **39**(3), 236–243.

Rooke, D., and W. Torbert, 1998. Organizational transformation as a function of CEOs' developmental stage, *Organization Development Journal* **16**(1), 11–28.

Rudolph, J., 2003. "Into the Big Muddy and Out Again: Error Persistence and Crisis Management in the Operating Room." Chestnut Hill, MA, Boston College School of Management, doctoral dissertation.

Rudolph, J., E. Foldy, and S. Taylor, 2001. Collaborative off-line reflection: A way to develop skill in action science and action inquiry. In P. Reason and H. Bradbury, eds., *Handbook of Action Research.* London: Sage, pp. 405–412.

Schein, E., 2003. *DEC Is Dead, Long Live DEC.* San Francisco: Berrett-Koehler.

Sen, A., 1982. *Choice, Welfare and Measurement.* Cambridge, MA: MIT Press.

Sen, A., 1987. *On Ethics and Economics.* London: Blackwell.

Senge, P., 1990. *The Fifth Discipline.* New York: Doubleday Currency.

Senge, P., A. Kleiner, C. Roberts, R. Ross, and B. Smith, 1994. *The Fifth Discipline Fieldbook.* New York: Doubleday Currency.

Senge, P., et al., 1998. *The Dance of Change.* New York: Doubleday Currency.

Sherman, F., and W. Torbert, eds., 2000. *Transforming Social Inquiry, Transforming Social Action.* Boston: Kluwer Academic Publishers.

Shrivastva, S., and D. Cooperrider, 1990. *Appreciative Leadership and Management: The Power of Positive Thought in Organizations.* San Francisco: Jossey-Bass.

Skolimowski, H., 1994. *The Participative Mind.* London: Arkana.

Social Investment Forum, 2001. *2001 Report on Responsible Investing Trends in the United States,* available at www.socialinvest.org.

Torbert, W., 1973. *Learning from Experience: Toward Consciousness.* New York: Columbia University Press.

Torbert, W., 1974. Pre-bureaucratic and post-bureaucratic stages of organizational development, *Interpersonal Development* **1**(5), 1–25.

Torbert, W., 1976. *Creating a Community of Inquiry: Conflict, Collaboration, Transformation*. London: Wiley.

Torbert, W., 1987. *Managing the Corporate Dream: Restructuring for Long-Term Success*. Homewood, IL: Dow Jones–Irwin.

Torbert, W., 1989. Leading organizational transformation. In R. Woodman and W. Pasmore, eds., *Research in Organizational Change and Developments*, vol. 3. Greenwich, CT: JAI Press.

Torbert, W., 1991. *The Power of Balance: Transforming Self, Society, and Scientific Inquiry*. Newbury Park, CA: Sage.

Torbert, W., 1994. Cultivating post-formal adult development: Higher stages and contrasting interventions. In M. Miller and S. Cook-Greuter, eds., *Transcendence and Mature Thought in Adulthood: The Further Reaches of Adult Development*. Lanham, MD: Rowman & Littlefield, pp. 181–203.

Torbert, W., 1998. Developing wisdom and courage in organizing and sciencing. In S. Srivastva and D. Cooperrider, eds., *Organizational Wisdom and Executive Courage*. San Francisco: New Lexington Press.

Torbert, W., 1999. The meaning of social investing, *Investing in a Better World* 14(10), 2.

Torbert, W., 2000. A developmental approach to social science: Integrating first-, second-, and third-person research/practice through single-, double-, and triple-loop feedback, *Journal of Adult Development* 7(4), 255–268.

Torbert, W., 2002. *Learning to Exercise Timely Action Now: In Leading, Loving, Inquiring, and Retiring*, available at www2.bc.edu/~torbert.

Torbert, W., and D. Fisher, 1992. Autobiographical awareness as a catalyst for managerial and organizational development, *Management Education and Development* 23(3), 184–198.

Torbert, W., and P. Reason, eds., 2001. Toward a participatory worldview: In physics, biology, economics, ecology, medicine, organizations, spirituality, and everyday living, *ReVision* 23(3–4), 2001.

Vaillant, G., 1977. *Adaptation to Life*. Boston: Little Brown.

Vaillant, G., and L. McCullough, 1987. The Washington University Sentence Completion Test compared with other measures of adult ego development, *American Journal of Psychiatry* 144(9), 1189–1194.

Varela, F., and J. Shear, eds., 1999. *The View from Within: First-Person Approaches to the Study of Consciousness*. Thorverton, UK: Imprint Academic.

Velmans, M., 2000. *Understanding Consciousness*. London: Routledge.

Waddock, S., 2001. *Leading Corporate Citizens*. New York: McGraw-Hill Irwin.

Waddock, S., 2003. Myths and realities of social investing, *Organization and Environment* 16(3), 369–380.

Westenberg, M., J. Jonckheer, P. Treffers, and M. Drewes, 1998. *Personality Development: Theoretical, Empirical and Clinical Investigations of Loevinger's Conception of Ego Development*. Mahwah, NJ: Lawrence Erlbaum.

Wilber, K., 1980. *The Atman Project: A Transpersonal View of Human Development*. Wheaton, IL: Quest.

Wilber, K., 1995/2000. *Sex, Ecology, Spirituality: The Spirit of Evolution*. Boston: Shambhala.

Wilber, K., 1998. *The Marriage of Sense and Soul: Integrating Science and Religion*. New York: Random House.

Wilber, K., 2000. *Integral Psychology: Consciousness, Spirit, Psychology, Therapy*. Boston: Shambhala.

Index

About the Author and Associates

Bill Torbert, now professor of management at the Carroll School of Management at Boston College, earlier served as the school's graduate dean and director of the PhD Program in Organizational Transformation. He is also one of the founding faculty of the Executive Program Leadership for Change at Boston College, as well as a founding research member of the international Society for Organizational Learning, and a board member of Trillium Asset Management (the first and largest independent socially responsible investing advisor).

Torbert has previously consulted widely in Europe, Latin America, and the United States, and served on numerous company and journal boards. With regard to scholarship, some of his recent books are his national Alpha Sigma Nu award-winning *Managing the Corporate Dream* (1987); his Terry Award Finalist book *The Power of Balance: Transforming Self, Society, and Scientific Inquiry* (1991); and *Transforming Social Inquiry, Transforming Social Action* (coedited with Francine Sherman [Sherman and Torbert 2000]).

Torbert received a BA in political science and economics and a PhD in administrative sciences from Yale University, holding a Danforth Graduate Fellowship during his graduate years, and directing the Yale Upward Bound War on Poverty Program. He taught at Yale, Southern Methodist University, and Harvard prior to joining the Boston College faculty in 1978. Most of all, though, he takes great pleasure and pride (not to mention occasional pain) in the ongoing development of collaborative inquiries among his lifetime friends and colleagues and with his three sons, Michael, Patrick, and Benjamin.

Susanne Cook-Greuter is a leading scholar in mature adult development. She is a founding member of Ken Wilber's Integral Institute and directs HarthillUSA. HarthillUSA helps mature professionals in using action inquiry and personal integral transformative practices to enhance their own and their clients' effectiveness. Harthill's Leadership Development Profile is an application of Cook-Greuter's 20-year research into assessing the worldviews of mature adults. She has a doctorate from Harvard University in psychology and human development. Her 1994 book, *Transcendence and Mature Thought in Adulthood,* coedited with Mel Miller, has become a classic in the field of positive psychology (Cooke-Greuter and Miller 1994). She teaches seminars and workshops in the United States and Europe, consults to research projects, and dedicates time to her writing as an independent scholar. Personally, she is committed to the spiritual path of Kriya yoga and to serve others in exploring life and work with openness, joy and compassion. Nature study, weeding, song and dance, travel, meditation, and Swiss chocolate, as well as dear friends and family sustain, restore, and delight her on her journey.

Dalmar Fisher teaches organizational communication, interpersonal effectiveness, and teambuilding at Boston College. His research and writing is aimed at improving managers' interpersonal skills. Books he has authored and coauthored include *Communication in Organizations, Autonomy in Organizational Life,* and *Personal and Organizational Transformations through Action Inquiry.* He has long enjoyed running, from the 400-meter race at Northwestern to marathons with the 60+ age group to more leisurely jogging in recent years. After both running at and graduating from Northwestern, he received an MBA from Boston College and a DBA from Harvard Business School. His wife of 33 years is Laura; children are Deirdre, Nathaniel, and Naomi; and grandchildren are Sarah, Caitlin, and Ocean.

Erica Foldy is an assistant professor of public and nonprofit management at the Wagner School of Public Service at New York University. She is also affiliated as a researcher with the Center for Gender in Organizations at the Simmons School of Management. Her research interests include identity and diversity in organizations, organizational learning and reflective practice, and the interaction of individual, organizational, and social change. Foldy has published articles in several journals and edited volumes. She also coedited, with Robin Ely and Maureen Scully, the *Reader in Gender, Work and Organization.* Currently, she is a research team member of the Leadership for a Changing World program of the Ford Foundation. Prior to her PhD program, Foldy worked for 15 years with nonprofit organizations working in the areas of foreign policy, women's rights, and occupational health and safety. She holds a BA from Harvard College, a PhD from Boston College, and was a Post Doctoral Fellow at Harvard Business School in 2002–2003.

Alain Gauthier is an international consultant, facilitator, and educator who focuses on developing new collaborative leadership capabilities within partnerships across the public, private, and civil society sectors. Over the last 38 years, he has served a wide range of clients, from large European and American corporations to a number of not-for-profit organizations and global foundations. A graduate from HEC (Paris) and a Stanford University MBA, Gauthier is currently executive director of Core Leadership Development in Oakland, California. He has adapted and prefaced in French three of Peter Senge's *Fifth Discipline* books, and is a coauthor of *Learning Organizations: Developing Cultures for Tomorrow's Workplace*. Gauthier is an active member of the Society for Organizational Learning in the United States and Europe, and a visiting professor for the International MBA Program at the ENPC in Paris. He enjoys being in the mountains, as well as with his circles of friends and family members on both continents.

Jackie Keeley and **David Rooke** are the founding partners of the Harthill Group consulting firm in England. Their dozens of clients have included Norwich Insurance Union, Volvo, and Hewlett-Packard. They are also the parents of two lovely and energetic daughters, epic world travelers, and hosts to unique workshops and celebrations among friends at their country home, conference center, and place of business at Harthill Grange.

Sara Ross is an action researcher-practitioner, spiritual director, former CPA, and is currently working on her doctorate in international political development. For 25 years, she has been a developer of organizational change and transformative group processes. Contexts for that work, in which she has also been a curriculum designer, teacher, and supervisor, have included management advisory services, personal and spiritual development of adolescents and adults, community leadership training programs, ministerial training programs, analyses of complex public issues, public politics training programs, and action research in public settings.

Catherine Royce, a writer, speaker, consultant, and former dancer, earned a BA from Wesleyan University in dance and humanities and an MBA from Simmons College School of Management. For the past 20 years, Royce has been working with entrepreneurs, writers, policy makers, and others to ensure that their work accurately reflects their true vision. Since she began her own practice 1989, her clients have included individuals and small groups, one-on-one and in corporate settings, in philanthropy, health care, business communications, government, and nonprofits. The clarity of her understanding is especially sought by authors of nonfiction work, several of whom have books currently in production under her guidance.

Jenny Rudolph is an assistant professor at the Boston University School of Public Health, having received a PhD in management from Boston College and a BA from Harvard College. She is an organizational scholar, educator, and consultant who has published in such places as *Administrative Science Quarterly* and the *Handbook of Action Research*. Rudolph's research and consulting focuses on situations such as operating room crises, nuclear power plant accidents, or difficult conversations, and on how people can learn to think, act, and communicate effectively even when social or physical stakes are high.

Steve Taylor is an assistant professor of management at Worcester Polytechnic Institute in Worcester, Massachusetts, where he teaches courses in leadership, organizational behavior, and creativity. He received a BS in humanities from the Massachusetts Institute of Technology, an MA in performing arts from Emerson College, and a PhD in management from Boston College. Steve's research focuses on the aesthetics of organizational action, with particular interest in reflective practice and organizational interventions using artistic forms. His work has been published in journals such as *Human Relations, Action Research, Organization Studies, Management Communication Quarterly, Tamara, Journal of Management Inquiry,* and *Management Learning.*

Mariana Tran was born in a small, secluded town in Bulgaria. She remembers springtime when the snowcaps on the mountain peaks melted and roses started to bloom. School was cancelled and students helped collect roses for the production of rose oil, one of the few products that communist Bulgaria exported to the world market. Beholding the sunrise in the rose fields made her wonder about other beautiful places and people in the world. Her desire to explore new places and cultures guided her decision to move to Russia and study biophysics at Leningrad State Technical University, then to move to Boston College for a PhD in biology and an MBA, and then to move to California. She has published numerous book chapters and articles in such journals as *Epilepsia* and the *Journal of Neurochemistry.*

Berrett–Koehler
Publishers

Berrett-Koehler is an independent publisher dedicated to an ambitious mission: Connecting people and ideas to create a world that works for all.

We believe that the solutions to the world's problems will come from all of us, working at all levels: in our organizations, in our society, and in our own lives. Our BK Business books help people make their organizations more humane, democratic, diverse, and effective (we don't think there's any contradiction there). Our BK Currents books offer pathways to creating a more just, equitable, and sustainable society. Our BK Life books help people create positive change in their lives and align their personal practices with their aspirations for a better world.

All of our books are designed to bring people seeking positive change together around the ideas that empower them to see and shape the world in a new way.

And we strive to practice what we preach. At the core of our approach is Stewardship, a deep sense of responsibility to administer the company for the benefit of all of our stakeholder groups including authors, customers, employees, investors, service providers, and the communities and environment around us. Everything we do is built around this and our other key values of quality, partnership, inclusion, and sustainability.

This is why we are both a B-Corporation and a California Benefit Corporation—a certification and a for-profit legal status that require us to adhere to the highest standards for corporate, social, and environmental performance.

We are grateful to our readers, authors, and other friends of the company who consider themselves to be part of the BK Community. We hope that you, too, will join us in our mission.

A BK Business Book

We hope you enjoy this BK Business book. BK Business books pioneer new leadership and management practices and socially responsible approaches to business. They are designed to provide you with groundbreaking and practical tools to transform your work and organizations while upholding the triple bottom line of people, planet, and profits. High-five!

To find out more, visit **www.bkconnection.com.**

Berrett–Koehler
Publishers

Connecting people and ideas
to create a world that works for all

Dear Reader,

Thank you for picking up this book and joining our worldwide community
of Berrett-Koehler readers. We share ideas that bring positive change into
people's lives, organizations, and society.

To welcome you, we'd like to offer you a free e-book. You can pick from
among twelve of our bestselling books by entering the promotional code
BKP92E here: http://www.bkconnection.com/welcome.

When you claim your free e-book, we'll also send you a copy of our e-news-
letter, the *BK Communiqué*. Although you're free to unsubscribe, there are
many benefits to sticking around. In every issue of our newsletter you'll find

- A free e-book
- Tips from famous authors
- Discounts on spotlight titles
- Hilarious insider publishing news
- A chance to win a prize for answering a riddle

Best of all, our readers tell us, "Your newsletter is the only one I actually
read." So claim your gift today, and please stay in touch!

Sincerely,

Charlotte Ashlock
Steward of the BK Website

Questions? Comments? Contact me at bkcommunity@bkpub.com.

MIX
Paper from
responsible sources
FSC® C008955

Certified

Corporation
bcorporation.net